BUILDING EVALUATION CAPACITY

Building Evaluation Capacity

72 Activities for Teaching and Training

HALLIE PRESKILL
University of New Mexico

DARLENE RUSS-EFT
Oregon State University

SAGE Publications
Thousand Oaks ▪ London

For information:

Sage Publications, Inc.
2455 Teller Road
Thousand Oaks, California 91320
E-mail: order@sagepub.com

Sage Publications Ltd.
1 Oliver's Yard
55 City Road
London EC1Y 1SP
United Kingdom

Sage Publications India Pvt. Ltd.
B-42, Panchsheel Enclave
Post Box 4109
New Delhi 110 017 India

Printed in the United States of America

Library of Congress Cataloging-in-Publication Data

Preskill, Hallie S.
Building evaluation capacity: 72 activities for teaching and training / Hallie Preskill, Darlene Russ-Eft.
p. cm.
Includes bibliographical references.
ISBN 0-7619-2810-3 (pbk.)
1. Evaluation. 2. Evaluation—Methodology. 3. Performance standards. I. Russ-Eft, Darlene F. II. Title.
AZ191.P73 2005
001.4—dc22 2005007117

04 05 06 07 10 9 8 7 6 5 4 3 2 1

Acquisitions Editor:	Lisa Cuevas Shaw
Editorial Assistant:	Margo Beth Crouppen
Production Editor:	Melanie Birdsall
Copy Editor:	Cheryl Duksta
Typesetter:	C&M Digitals (P) Ltd.
Proofreader:	Teresa Herlinger
Cover Designer:	Janet Foulger

Contents

Acknowledgments

A book such as this could not have been written without the generosity and support of many individuals. We would first like to thank the students and trainees we have had in our courses and workshops over the last 20 years. They have been our guinea pigs for nearly all of the activities presented in this book. In their role they have provided us feedback about what worked, what didn't work, and how to improve the activities' effectiveness. Their honesty and candor are greatly appreciated. There is little doubt that our students and trainees have significantly influenced our desire to be better teachers, trainers, mentors, and evaluation practitioners.

We also wish to thank (*in alphabetical order*) Bob Covert, Marguerite Foxon, Donna Mertens, Joan Slick, Bob Stake, Andy Tibble, Rosalie T. Torres, Nicole Vicinanza, and Barbra Zuckerman for sharing their activities. While we didn't set out to elicit activities from many people, we came across their ideas through word of mouth and from our professional experiences with them. We believe their activities are valuable additions to this book. We are also grateful to Laura Boehme, Glenis Chapin, and Phil Krolick for allowing us to use portions of their evaluation plans. Five additional individuals were reviewers of this book's proposal; we would like to thank Carol Hansen, Sharon Korth, Michael Newman, Roger A. Rennekamp, and one anonymous reviewer for their insightful and helpful comments and suggestions.

Our heartfelt thanks also go to C. Deborah Laughton (former editor with Sage) for her unceasing energy and encouragement of our work over the years. As with this book, she has worked tirelessly to ensure that our visions and dreams became a reality. Lisa Cuevas Shaw, who became our editor in the middle of writing this book, never skipped a beat. We have greatly appreciated Lisa's excitement for the book and her responsiveness to our many questions and requests.

Finally, Hallie wishes to thank her husband, Stephen, and son, Benjamin, for their wonderful support and good humor throughout this process. Darlene wants to thank her husband, Jack, and her daughter, Natalie, for their ongoing encouragement, understanding, and support, all of which made this work possible.

Preface

It could be said that this book has been in the making for more than 20 years. During the last two decades, each of us has provided numerous workshops on evaluation in a variety of corporate, education, nonprofit, health care, government, and professional organizations for new and experienced evaluators. In addition, we have taught introductory and advanced courses on evaluation at several universities. Adding to our education and experiences with evaluation, we each have a background in the areas of adult learning, training design and delivery, and consulting. This background makes us acutely aware of the need to design instruction using sound adult-learning principles. Thus, when we develop and teach our workshops and courses, we seek ways to make them accessible, relevant, and interactive so that participants increase their capacity and capability for doing evaluation work. This often means finding ways to enliven a lecture or, more often, creating activities that actively engage participants with the knowledge and skills being taught.

In 2001, we published an evaluation textbook titled *Evaluation in Organizations: A Systematic Approach to Enhancing Learning, Performance, and Change,* which is a comprehensive approach to understanding evaluation practice within a variety of organizational settings. After receiving positive feedback on the book, we decided that the next step was to develop and share some of the activities we use in our evaluation courses and workshops that convey the concepts and skills discussed in the textbook.

HOW TO USE THIS BOOK

The 72 activities in this book cover most aspects of common evaluation practice. That is, they address various definitions and types of evaluation; the politics and ethics of evaluation; multicultural aspects of evaluation; evaluation models, approaches, and designs; data collection and analysis methods; validity and sampling issues; communication about and reporting on an evaluation's progress and findings; evaluation management; and evaluation building and support. As such, the activities can be used in undergraduate or graduate evaluation courses at colleges and universities, by trainers who provide professional development workshops, by students and participants in evaluation courses and workshops, by organization consultants who want to coach their clients about evaluation, and by managers who wish to help their employees more fully understand evaluation practice.

The 72 activities are organized into 12 sections that generally follow the conceptualization, design, and implementation of an evaluation. Each section includes a brief background of the content covered in the activities; it is not intended to be a full treatment of the subject. Where it is necessary for participants to have some background information prior to implementing an activity, this is noted in the time estimate for each activity. Each section overview also includes a list of resources for those who wish to learn more about the topics covered.

Each of the 72 activities follows a standard format that includes the following:

- Overview (of the activity)
- Instructional objectives (what participants will learn or do)
- Number of participants (minimum and maximum)
- Time estimate (range of time required)
- Materials needed (including handouts)
- Primary instructional method (most activities use two or more instructional methods)
- Procedures (for the facilitator)

Most of the activities include handouts that may be duplicated as long as the copyright information is provided on the handout.

Depending on the topic you are covering, you may choose one or more of the activities that fit your purpose and your participants' learning styles and level of evaluation knowledge and experience. To help you choose a particular activity, we have included an activity matrix that lists each activity by section (topic), primary instructional method, time estimate, and needed background information. We have also provided a glossary of instructional methods, which briefly describes each method, and a list of strategies for forming small groups, which can be used to assign participants to groups of two to five people.

HOW TO LEARN MORE ABOUT EVALUATION

Thanks to some wonderful evaluation writers, there are many books available on a wide range of evaluation topics. There are also a number of professional development opportunities available to help build evaluation capacity and expertise. These include the following resources:

- American Evaluation Association (AEA) (www.eval.org)
- American Evaluation Association annual conference (see AEA Web site)
- American Evaluation Association local affiliates (see list on AEA Web site)

- Other national evaluation associations, societies, and networks (see AEA Web site)
- The Evaluators' Institute (www.evaluatorsinstitute.com) (endorsed by the AEA)
- The teaching section of the *American Journal of Evaluation* (an AEA publication)
- University graduate education programs that emphasize evaluation (see list on AEA Web site)

OUR HOPES

It is an exciting time for those new and experienced with evaluation. The evaluation profession is growing throughout the world, as evidenced by the many national evaluation associations forming and the increasing membership of the American Evaluation Association. As more individuals are being asked to conduct evaluations, it is critical that they develop the knowledge and skills required for doing high-quality work. We hope that the activities provided in this book not only help facilitate others' learning about evaluation but also inspire a commitment to making evaluation an effective, meaningful, and useful enterprise.

As we continue to teach and train others about evaluation, we will also search for additional learning activities. If you would like to share any evaluation teaching and training activities you have used or suggest any additional topics for possible inclusion in a later book, please feel free to contact either of us. We also invite you to provide any feedback you have about the activities in this book by e-mailing us at hallie@flash.net and zmresearch@aol.com. We wish you much enjoyment and success in your teaching and training endeavors.

Matrix of Activities

Activities	*Primary Instructional Method*	*Time Estimate (minutes)*	*Background Info Needed*
1. Overview of Evaluation			
Background and Resources			
1. Images and Purposes of Evaluation	Visual representation	75–120	No
2. Applications of Developmental, Formative, and Summative Evaluations	Case scenario	30–45	Yes
3. Evaluating Chocolate Chip Cookies Using Evaluation Logic	Small-group work	45–90	No
4. Tracing Evaluation's History	Visual representation	45–60	Yes
5. Evaluation Versus Research	Case scenario	45–60	Yes
2. The Politics and Ethics of Evaluation Practice			
Background and Resources			
6. The World of Evaluation and Politics	Case scenario	45–60	No
7. The Political Nature of Evaluation	Individual work/ large-group discussion	45–60	Yes
8. Ethical Dilemmas for Evaluators	Case scenario	45–60	Yes
9. Debating an Ethical Dilemma	Debate	60–75	Yes

(Continued)

Activities	*Primary Instructional Method*	*Time Estimate (minutes)*	*Background Info Needed*
3. Multicultural and Cross-Cultural Aspects of Evaluation			
Background and Resources			
10. Understanding the Influence of Culture in Evaluation Practice	Storytelling	40–75	No
11. Defining Evaluation Within a Cultural Context	Small-group work	45–60	No
12. Cultural Sensitivity in Evaluation	Small-group work	60–90	Yes
13. Defining Cultural Competence: Evaluation in Multicultural Settings	Small-group work	60–75	Yes
14. Exploring the Role of Assumptions in Evaluation Practice	Round robin	30–45	No
4. Focusing the Evaluation			
Background and Resources			
15. Using a Logic Model to Focus an Evaluation	Small-group work	60–90	Yes
16. Creating a Flowchart Logic Model	Small-group work	45–60	Yes
17. Developing an Evaluation's Purpose Statement	Small-group work/individual work	45–60	Yes
18. Identifying Stakeholders and Developing Key Evaluation Questions	Case scenario	45–60	Yes
19. Developing Evaluation Questions	Small-group work	45–60	Yes
5. Evaluation Models, Approaches, and Designs			
Background and Resources			
20. Determining When to Use Various Evaluation Models and Approaches	Small-group work	45–60	Yes
21. Recommending an Evaluation Approach	Case scenario	45–90	Yes
22. Applying Kirkpatrick's Four-Level Approach to Evaluation Training	Case scenario	45–60	Yes

(Continued)

Activities	*Primary Instructional Method*	*Time Estimate (minutes)*	*Background Info Needed*
23. Debating the Usefulness of the Kirkpatrick Four-Level Approach to Evaluating Training and Development Programs	Debate	45–60	Yes
24. Paradigms Exposed!	Questionnaire	30–60	No
25. Comparing and Contrasting Different Evaluation Designs	Small-group work	45–60	Yes
26. Identifying Evaluation Designs	Case scenario	30–60	Yes
27. Using Evaluation Questions to Guide an Evaluation's Design and Data Collection Methods	Small-group work	30–60	Yes
28. Debating the Usefulness of Return on Investment	Debate	45–60	Yes
29. Is It Really a Return on Investment Evaluation?	Case scenario	30–45	Yes
30. Calculating the Return on Investment	Small-group work	45–60	No
6. Issues of Validity and Sampling			
Background and Resources			
31. Reliability and Validity 101	Large-group discussion	30–45	No
32. Understanding Validity	Visual representation	45–60	Yes
33. Detecting Threats to Validity	Case scenario	45–60	Yes
34. Ensuring the Quality of Qualitative Data	Small-group work	60–75	Yes
35. Sampling Matters	Case scenario	30–45	Yes
36. Making the Case for Using a Random Sample	Large-group discussion	30–45	Yes
37. Choosing an Appropriate Sample	Case scenario	45–90	Yes
38. Sampling With Bias	Case scenario	30–60	Yes
7. Collecting Evaluation Data			
Background and Resources			
39. Choosing Data Collection Methods	Small-group work/case scenario	45–90	Yes

(Continued)

Activities	*Primary Instructional Method*	*Time Estimate (minutes)*	*Background Info Needed*
Surveys and Questionnaires			
40. Comparing and Contrasting Open-Ended and Closed-Ended Survey Formats	Small-group work/fieldwork	90–120 over two sessions	No
41. Critiquing a Survey's Content and Format	Small-group work	30–45	Yes
42. Using Incentives to Increase Survey Response Rates	Small-group work	30–60	Yes
43. Following Up on Survey Nonrespondents	Round robin	30–60	No
44. Developing a Concept Map for the Use of Online Surveys	Visual representation	60–75	Yes
Individual and Focus Group Interviews			
45. Tips for Conducting Effective Interviews	Round robin	30–60	Yes
46. Role-Playing Individual Interviews	Role play	75–105	Yes
47. Individual Interviewing Challenges	Case scenario	30–45	Yes
48. Mock Focus Group Interviews	Role play	60–90	Yes
Observation and Archival Data			
49. Conducting Observations	Fieldwork/ large-group discussion	45–60	No
50. Collecting Unobtrusive Measures Data	Case scenario	30–60	Yes
51. Collecting Documents and Records (Archival Data)	Brainstorming/ individual work	20–40	No
8. Analyzing Evaluation Data			
Background and Resources			
52. Planning for Data Analysis	Small-group work	45–60	Yes
Qualitative Data Analysis			
53. Developing Qualitative Data Analysis Categories and Themes	Small-group work	15–30	No
54. Using Comics to Understand Qualitative Data Analysis Processes	Small-group work	45–60	No
55. Analyzing and Interpreting Qualitative Data	Small-group work	45–60	No

(Continued)

Activities	*Primary Instructional Method*	*Time Estimate (minutes)*	*Background Info Needed*
Quantitative Data Analysis			
56. Understanding Descriptive Statistics	Small-group work	30–45	No
57. Understanding Quantitative Data Analysis	Small-group work	60–90	Yes
58. Analyzing and Interpreting Quantitative Data	Small-group work	45–60	Yes
9. Communicating and Reporting Evaluation Processes and Findings			
Background and Resources			
59. Communicating and Reporting Evaluation Formats	Small-group work	45–90	No
60. Challenges in Communicating and Reporting	Case scenario	30–45	No
61. Developing a Communicating and Reporting Plan	Individual work	45–60	Yes
10. Managing the Evaluation			
Background and Resources			
62. Developing Evaluation Management Plans	Small-group work	45–60	No
63. Creating an Evaluation Budget	Small-group work	45–60	Yes
64. Anticipating Evaluation Challenges	Small-group work	30–45	No
11. Building and Sustaining Support for Evaluation			
Background and Resources			
65. Reflecting on Evaluation Successes	Small-group work	45–75	No
66. Overcoming Resistance to Evaluation	Small-group work	20–45	No
67. Building a Supportive Evaluation Environment	Small-group work	45–75	No
68. Evaluating the Evaluation (Metaevaluation)	Small-group work	45–60	Yes

(Continued)

Activities	*Primary Instructional Method*	*Time Estimate (minutes)*	*Background Info Needed*
12. Reflections on Learning			
Background and Resources			
69. Headlining Learning	Visual representation	30–45	No
70. Creating a Model of Learning	Visual representation	40–60	No
71. Critical Incidents of Learning	Small-group work	40–60	No
72. The Elevator Speech	Small-group work	30–45	No

Glossary of Instructional Methods

For each activity, the primary teaching and learning method is noted. However, most activities involve two or more types of participant-facilitator interaction. The following paragraphs detail the instructional methods used for the activities in this book.

Small-Group Work

Participants work in pairs or in small groups of two to five people. The activity is structured so that each member contributes to its completion; success is based on the performance of the group rather than on the individual.

Case Scenario

Participants are presented with a brief scenario that represents an evaluation situation, dilemma, or opportunity. In small groups, participants analyze the case and respond to a series of discussion questions.

Large-Group Discussion

The facilitator engages all participants in a discussion concerning a particular evaluation topic.

Brainstorming

Participants generate ideas related to an evaluation issue or problem.

Debate

Teams of participants argue the pros and cons of a particular evaluation issue. The purpose of the activity is to help participants work together to understand common issues.

Role Play

Participants engage in a real or hypothetical evaluation situation and observe each other's actions and comments. The role plays enable participants to gain insights into their own values, attitudes, and skills, in addition to the challenges evaluators face in the course of their work.

Storytelling

Participants engage in telling personal stories to illustrate various evaluation concepts and issues.

Visual Representation

Participants draw or create an artistic interpretation of something they have learned.

Round Robin

Participants contribute ideas and information to a series of flipchart pages that are posted around the room.

Fieldwork

Participants are asked to collect data outside of the classroom or workshop.

Individual Work

Participants work independently on an evaluation task relevant to their own practice.

Questionnaire

Participants complete a self-assessment questionnaire concerning issues related to evaluation.

Strategies for Forming Small Groups

There are several activities in this book that require participants to get into small groups to accomplish a task. Although the facilitator could ask participants to self-organize into groups, there may be times when it is more effective or desirable to assign participants to groups. The following are several strategies that could be used to accomplish this goal.

For Forming Groups of Three to Five Participants

• For the number of groups you want, buy different kinds of bite-sized candy. Distribute candy randomly and ask people to get into groups with people who have the same kind of candy. For example, if you want four groups, distribute four different kinds of candy.

• For developing groups of four people, use a deck of playing cards. Take out four cards of the same number. For example, if there are 24 participants, take out six full sets of numbers—four aces, four kings, four queens, and so on. Distribute the cards and have participants find those with the same card.

• Count off participants in another language. Take the number of participants, divide it by the number of groups you want, and then number each person accordingly. For example, if you have 24 participants, and you want 4 people in each group, then count aloud, *"Number uno, dos, tres, cuatro, cinco, seis."* Ask participants to get into groups with those who have the same number.

• Pieces of children's toys, such as Legos, blocks, and Tinker Toys, that have several colors or sizes can be used. Without looking into the bag or box, participants select a toy. Those with the same shape, color, or size form a group.

• Cut up as many postcards as groups to be formed, with one piece for each member of the group. Jumble these up. Participants each take one part and then try to find their counterparts to make the picture.

• Students stand in a straight line. Have students count off by twos. The facilitator says, "All twos take two giant steps forward." Those participants become a group. All the ones remaining on the line also become a team. This also works well for forming three or four groups. Just have the students count off by threes or fours. This method can also be used if you want to form groups with different levels of experience. In this case, you ask people to line up according to their years of experience, education, or training in a particular area.

• Make a pack of playing-size cards with the names of the participants. Shuffle the cards and call the participants' names as the cards are pulled from the pack. This method can be used to develop any size of small group.

• Have participants line up according to a particular attribute, such as birth month, or state, country, or city where they are currently living. Then, form groups according to those attributes.

For Forming Pairs of Participants

• Obtain a deck of cards for the children's game of Old Maid. Take out the pairs until you have as many cards as participants. For example, if there are 24 participants, take out 12 pairs. Mix them up and have participants select a card. Ask participants to find the person who matches their card.

• Ask participants to find someone who has a birthday in their same month. If more than two people come together, ask participants to pair with the person whose birthday is the nearest in date or time.

• On 3 in. × 5 in. index cards, write the names of famous historical couples (e.g., Napoleon and Josephine, cartoon characters, Batman and Robin). Give each participant a card. Participants form pairs by finding their partner.

• Ask participants to find someone who works in a similar work environment (e.g., school, corporation, nonprofit organization, government agency) and with whom they have not worked before.

• Ask participants to line up according to height. Then, ask the line of participants to fold that line in half so that the tallest person meets the shortest person to form a pair and so forth.

• Purchase a deck of children's rhyming cards and have participants pair up with the person who has a card that rhymes with theirs (e.g., *dog, log; chair, care*).

1

Overview of Evaluation

BACKGROUND

This section includes activities that address

- Defining evaluation
- Using evaluation logic
- Understanding different types of evaluation
- Exploring the history of evaluation
- Understanding the differences between evaluation and research

The following information is provided as a brief introduction to the topics covered in these activities.

DEFINITION OF EVALUATION

Various definitions of evaluation have been offered over the years. While each definition takes a slightly different view of evaluation, they all share important commonalities. First, evaluation is viewed as a systematic process. It should not be conducted as an afterthought; rather, it is a planned and purposeful activity. Second, evaluation involves collecting data regarding questions or issues about society in general and organizations and programs in particular. Third, evaluation is a process for enhancing knowledge and decision making, whether the decisions are for improving or refining a program, process, product, system, or organization or for determining whether

SOURCE: Adapted from Russ-Eft and Preskill (2001).

or not to continue or expand a program. And, in each of these decisions, there is some aspect of judgment about the merit, worth, or value of the evaluand (that which is being evaluated). Finally, the notion of evaluation use is either implicit or explicit in most definitions. Ultimately, evaluation is concerned with asking questions about issues that arise out of everyday practice. It is a means for gaining better understanding of what we do and the effects of our actions in the context of society and the work environment. A distinguishing characteristic of evaluation is that, unlike traditional forms of academic research, evaluation is grounded in the everyday realities of organizations. Evaluations can be conducted of programs, processes, products, systems, organizations, personnel, and policies.

EVALUATION LOGIC

One distinguishing feature of evaluation is that it has a particular logic that supports evaluation practice. This logic refers to specific reasoning principles to support decisions regarding how one determines the processes and impact of a program (or that which is being evaluated). The logic of evaluation generally involves the following actions:

- *Establishing Criteria.* On what dimensions must it do well?
- *Constructing Standards.* How well should it perform on each dimension?
- *Measuring Performance and Comparing With Standards.* How well did it perform on each dimension?
- *Synthesizing and Integrating Evidence Into a Judgment of Worth.* What is its merit, worth, or value?
- *Making Recommendations.* What recommendations should be made?

Following the logic of evaluation helps evaluators and program staff understand the steps one undertakes to come to an evaluative judgment about the merit, worth, or value of the evaluand.

TYPES OF EVALUATION

Evaluation is often conducted to gain information before a program's development, as in a needs analysis; to improve and refine a program; or to make judgments about a program's future. The following are descriptions of the different types of evaluation.

- *Developmental evaluation* positions the evaluator as a part of a program's design and development process. The evaluator collects information and provides informal feedback to members of the design team and possibly organization members to help them perfect the program being designed before it is ready for beta or pilot testing.

- *Formative evaluation* is typically conducted for the purpose of improvement.
- *Summative evaluation* is implemented for the purpose of determining the merit, worth, or value of the evaluand in a way that leads to making a final evaluative judgment. It is usually conducted after a program's completion.

HISTORY OF EVALUATION

The development of the evaluation profession is described in the following highlights.

- Until the late 1950s and early 1960s, evaluation mainly focused on educational assessment and was conducted by social science researchers in a small number of universities and organizations.

- President Lyndon Johnson's War on Poverty and the Great Society programs of the 1960s spurred a large investment of resources in social and educational programs. Senator Robert Kennedy, concerned that the federal money would be misspent and not used to help disadvantaged children, delayed passage of the Elementary and Secondary Education Act (ESEA) until an evaluation clause was included. The resulting bill required the local education agency to submit an evaluation plan, and the state agency, a summary report. Consequently, evaluation requirements became part of every federal grant. Early expectations of evaluation were that it would illuminate the causes of social problems and the clear and specific means with which to fix such problems.

- Two U.S.-based professional evaluation associations emerged in 1976: the Evaluation Network, which mostly consisted of university professors and school-based evaluators, and the Evaluation Research Society, which attracted primarily government-based and university evaluators. In 1985, these two organizations merged to form the American Evaluation Association (AEA; www.eval.org), whose membership includes approximately 3,700 individuals from across the globe.

- Throughout the 1970s and 1980s, growing concerns were voiced about the utility of evaluation findings and the use of experimental and quasi-experimental designs.

- In the 1980s, huge cuts in social programs resulted from President Ronald Reagan's emphasis on less government involvement. The requirement to evaluate was removed or lessened from many federal grants.

- During the 1980s, many school districts, universities, private companies, state departments of education, the Federal Bureau of Investigation (FBI), the Food and Drug Administration, and the General Accounting Office (GAO) developed internal evaluation units.

- In the 1990s, there was an increased emphasis on government program accountability and organizations' efforts to be lean, efficient, global, and more competitive. Evaluation was conducted not only to meet government mandates but also to improve programs' effectiveness, to enhance organizational learning, and to make resource allocation decisions in a wide variety of both public and private organizations. In addition, an increasing number of foundations created internal evaluation units, provided support for evaluation activities, or both.

- The reauthorization of ESEA that resulted in the No Child Left Behind (NCLB) Act of 2001 (signed into law on January 8, 2002, by President George W. Bush) is considered the most sweeping reform of elementary and secondary education since 1965. It has redefined the federal role in K–12 education by focusing on closing the achievement gap between disadvantaged and minority students and their peers. Its four basic principles include (1) stronger accountability for results, (2) increased flexibility and local control, (3) expanded options for parents, and (4) an emphasis on proven teaching methods. This legislation has had a profound influence on educational evaluation designs and methods by emphasizing the use of randomized control group experiments. Concern over this situation led to the development of a response to the U.S. Department of Education by the AEA in 2003. The AEA's response expressed concern that the legislation "manifests fundamental misunderstandings about (1) the types of studies capable of determining causality, (2) the methods capable of achieving scientific rigor, and (3) the types of studies that support policy and program decisions" (American Evaluation Association, 2003).

- At present, there is increasing interest in participatory, collaborative, and learning-oriented formative evaluations in lieu of summative evaluations conducted by the lone evaluator. Evaluators readily accept that few evaluations are value-free, and, indeed, most are politically charged.

- National evaluation associations are becoming established througout the world. These include, but are not limited to, the Australasian Evaluation Society, the African Evaluation Association, the Canadian Evaluation Society, the European Evaluation Society, the United Kingdom Evaluation Society, the Malaysian Evaluation Society, the Central American Evaluation Association, and the Japan Evaluation Society.

EVALUATION VERSUS RESEARCH

The terms *evaluation* and *research* are sometimes used interchangeably. Although the two forms of inquiry use the same data collection and analysis methods, they differ significantly in several ways.

- They have different purposes.
- They respond to different audiences' information needs.
- They pose different kinds of questions.
- They communicate and report their findings in different ways and to different groups.
- They have different expectations regarding the use of the results.

Although it is important to understand the difference between these two forms of inquiry, some may view this difference as merely technical and not particularly practical. What is important is the inquiry itself—the collection of quality information that will inform and guide decision making, learning, and action.

RESOURCES

American Evaluation Association. (2003). *Scientifically based evaluation methods.* Fairhaven, MA: Author. Retrieved April 1, 2004, from http://www. eval.org/doestatement.htm

Cronbach, L. J., Ambron, S. R., Dornbusch, S. M., Hess, R. D., Hornik, R. C., Phillips, D. C., et al. (1980). *Toward reform of program evaluation.* San Francisco: Jossey-Bass.

House, E. R. (1993). *Professional evaluation: Social impact and political consequences.* Thousand Oaks, CA: Sage.

Patton, M. Q. (1997). *Utilization-focused evaluation: The new century text* (3rd ed.). Thousand Oaks, CA: Sage.

Preskill, H., & Torres, R. T. (1999). *Evaluative inquiry for learning in organizations.* Thousand Oaks, CA: Sage.

Rog, D. J., & Fournier, D. (Eds.). (1997). *Progress and future directions in evaluation: Perspectives on theory, practice, and methods* (New Directions for Evaluation, Vol. 76). San Francisco: Jossey-Bass.

Rossi, P. H., Freeman, H. E., & Lipsey, M. W. (2004). *Evaluation: A systematic approach* (7th ed.). Thousand Oaks, CA: Sage.

Russ-Eft, D., & Preskill, H. (2001). *Evaluation in organizations: A systematic approach to enhancing learning, performance, and change.* Boston: Perseus.

Scriven, M. (1967). The methodology of evaluation. In R. W. Tyler, R. M. Gagne, & M. Scriven (Eds.), *Perspectives of curriculum evaluation* (pp. 39-83). Chicago: Rand-McNally.

Scriven, M. (1991). *Evaluation thesaurus* (4th ed.). Thousand Oaks, CA: Sage.

Witkin, B. R., & Altschuld, J. W. (1999). *From needs assessment to action: Transforming needs into solution strategies.* Thousand Oaks, CA: Sage.

Worthen, B., Sanders, J. R., & Fitzpatrick, J. L. (1997). *Program evaluation: Alternative approaches and practical guidelines.* New York: Longman.

Activity 1

Images and Purposes of Evaluation

Overview

This activity helps participants articulate their current perceptions of evaluation: what it is, why it is done, and how it is performed. It also provides an overview of the different types of evaluation.

Instructional Objectives

Participants will

- Reflect on their assumptions and experiences regarding evaluation
- Learn how different people perceive the value of evaluation
- Understand the various definitions, purposes, and types of evaluation

Number of Participants

- Minimum number of participants: 3
- Maximum number of participants: unlimited

Time Estimate: 75 to 120 minutes

There are three components to this activity. The first one, which asks participants to draw a picture of evaluation, requires approximately 30 to 45 minutes. The second component, which involves a discussion of evaluation definitions, requires approximately 15 to 30 minutes. The third component, which involves a discussion of purposes and types of evaluation, can be accomplished in 30 to 45 minutes.

Materials Needed

- Pens/pencils
- Paper for drawing
- Flipchart, markers, tape

- Handout "Definitions of Evaluation"
- Handout "Types of Evaluation"

Instructional Method

Visual representation

Procedures

Part 1 (30 to 45 minutes)

Facilitator's tasks:

- Distribute blank pieces of paper and markers or other writing utensils.
- Ask participants to draw the first image that comes to mind when they hear or see the word *evaluation.* Ask participants to label their drawings with one or two words that describe or represent the image. Tell participants they have 3 to 4 minutes to do this.
- Ask participants to get into groups of three to five people and share their images, identify common themes in their images, and write their group's themes on a piece of flipchart paper.
- Invite participants to share their group's themes.
- Refer to the themes and images while leading a discussion about individuals' common perceptions of evaluation and the implications these perceptions may have on evaluation practice. Ask participants the following questions:
  - Why do you think you drew that particular image? What experiences have you had that influenced what you drew?
  - When individuals perceive evaluation as a negative endeavor, what consequences might this have for conducting evaluation within organizations? Conversely, what implications do positive images have for conducting evaluations within organizations?

Part 2 (15 to 30 minutes)

Facilitator's tasks:

- Distribute the handout "Definitions of Evaluation" and ask the following questions to the entire group:
  - What are some commonalities among these definitions?
  - How do these definitions differ?
  - Which of these definitions resonate with your own evaluation experiences?
  - Are any of these definitions reflected in your images of evaluation?
  - How important do you think it is to define evaluation?

Part 3 (30 to 45 minutes)

Facilitator's tasks:

- Distribute the handout "Types of Evaluation."
- Ask participants to get into pairs to complete the worksheet.
- Invite participants to share some of the questions they developed for each type of evaluation. Write their questions on the flipchart.
- Debrief the activity with the following questions:
  - What new insights did you gain from these activities?
  - How would you now describe evaluation to someone?
  - How is your current understanding of evaluation different from your understanding before this activity?

Definitions of Evaluation

Handout for Activity 1

Several definitions of evaluation have been offered over the years. Michael Scriven (1967, 1991) developed one of the earliest definitions that is still commonly used today:

> Evaluation refers to the process of determining the merit, worth, or value of something, or the product of that process. Terms used to refer to this process or part of it include: appraise, analyze, assess, critique, examine, grade, inspect, judge, rate, rank review, study, test. . . . The evaluation process normally involves some identification of relevant standards of merit, worth, or value; some investigation of the performance of evaluands on these standards; and some integration or synthesis of the results to achieve an overall evaluation or set of associated evaluations. (Scriven, 1991, p. 139)

Another definition, which stems from evaluation's long history with social programs and takes on a social science research perspective, comes from Rossi, Lipsey, and Freeman (2004):

> Program evaluation is the use of social research methods to systematically investigate the effectiveness of social intervention programs. It draws on the techniques and concepts of social science disciplines and is intended to be useful for improving programs and informing social action aimed at ameliorating social problems. (p. 28)

A definition used by many evaluation practitioners is from Patton (1997), who emphasizes the use of evaluation findings:

> Program evaluation is the systematic collection of information about the activities, characteristics, and outcomes of programs to make judgments about the program, improve program effectiveness, and/or inform decisions about future programming. (p. 23)

Preskill and Torres (1999) offer a definition that focuses on evaluative activities specifically conducted within organizations for the purpose of organizational learning and change:

> We envision evaluative inquiry as an ongoing process for investigating and understanding critical organization issues. It is an approach to learning that is fully integrated with an organization's work practices, and as such, it engenders (a) organization members' interest and ability in exploring critical issues using evaluation logic, (b) organization members' involvement in evaluative processes, and (c) the personal and professional growth of individuals within the organization. (pp. 1–2)

References

Patton, M. Q. (1997). *Utilization-focused evaluation: The new century text* (3rd ed.). Thousand Oaks, CA: Sage.

Preskill, H., & Torres, R. T. (1999). *Evaluative inquiry for learning in organizations.* Thousand Oaks, CA: Sage.

Rossi, P. H., Lipsey, M. W., & Freeman, H. E. (2004). *Evaluation: A systematic approach* (7th ed.). Thousand Oaks, CA: Sage.

Scriven, M. (1967). The methodology of evaluation. In R. W. Tyler, R. M. Gagne, & M. Scriven (Eds.), *Perspectives of curriculum evaluation* (pp. 39-83). Chicago: Rand-McNally.

Scriven, M. (1991). *Evaluation thesaurus* (4th ed.). Thousand Oaks, CA: Sage.

Types of Evaluation

Handout for Activity 1

Types of Evaluation	*Questions an Evaluation Would Address*
Developmental evaluation positions the evaluator as a part of a program's design and development process.	
Formative evaluation is typically conducted for the purpose of refining or improving a program and is often conducted by internal evaluators.	
Summative evaluation is implemented for the purpose of determining the merit, worth, or value of the evaluand in a way that leads to a final evaluative judgment. It is usually conducted after completion of the program (for ongoing programs) and for the benefit of some external audience or decision makers. External evaluators often conduct summative evaluations.	

Monitoring and auditing are often associated with the need to determine if a program is being administered in ethical or legal ways; it is a means for checking the program's implementation. A monitoring type of evaluation would focus on the extent to which program administrators are wasting funds, inappropriately using staff resources, or ineffectively tracking participants' involvement in the program.	
Outcome evaluation seeks to understand intended changes in knowledge, attitudes, and practices that result from a program or project's intervention.	
Impact evaluation focuses on what happens to participants because of the intervention or program.	
Performance management is typically undertaken within governments and the nonprofit sector to meet a demand for documentation of results. It focuses on program activities (process), direct products and services delivered by a program (outputs), and the results of those product and services (outcomes).	

Activity 2

Applications of Developmental, Formative, and Summative Evaluations

Overview

This activity helps participants understand the purposes and uses of developmental, formative, and summative approaches to evaluation.

Instructional Objectives

Participants will

- Consider when and how to frame an evaluation as developmental, formative, or summative
- Identify the purposes and associated questions for an evaluation that may have a developmental, formative, or summative focus
- Understand the implications and issues related to conducting developmental, formative, and summative evaluations

Number of Participants

- Minimum number of participants: 3
- Maximum number of participants: unlimited when participants are in groups of 3 to 5

Time Estimate: 30 to 45 minutes

In addition to providing the necessary background information on developmental, formative, and summative approaches to evaluation, this activity requires approximately 30 to 45 minutes, depending on the number of participants (or groups) and the time available for discussion.

Materials Needed

- Pens/pencils
- Flipchart, markers, tape
- Handout "Developmental, Formative, and Summative Evaluations: Purposes and Questions"

Instructional Method

Case scenario

Procedures

Facilitator's tasks:

- Ask participants to get into groups of three to five people.
- Distribute the handout "Developmental, Formative, and Summative Evaluations: Purposes and Questions."
- Instruct participants to discuss and complete the handout and to transfer their work to a piece of flipchart paper.
- Ask participants to attach their flipchart page to a wall.
- Invite participants to discuss the purposes and questions they developed.
- Debrief the activity with the following questions:
  - What issues did this activity raise for you?
  - How would an organization choose whether to do a developmental, formative, or summative evaluation (or all of these)?
  - What are the implications of implementing each of these approaches to evaluation?
  - Why might an organization conduct only a summative evaluation?
  - Some might say that conducting a developmental evaluation is not an appropriate role for an evaluator. What is your response to this?

Developmental, Formative, and Summative Evaluations: Purposes and Questions

Handout for Activity 2

A school district wants to provide leadership training and development opportunities to its administrators. They ask the Professional Staff Development Department (PSDD) to develop a leadership development program for the district's 90 principals, assistant principals, and department heads.

	What might be the purpose of the evaluation?	*What questions might the evaluation try to answer?*
Developmental Evaluation		
As the PSDD designs the program, what kinds of evaluative feedback should it seek?		
Formative Evaluation		
The program has been designed, and the first 30 administrators have now completed the program. What kinds of evaluative feedback should the PSDD seek?		
Summative Evaluation		
The program has been offered to all of the district's 90 administrators over the last three years. What kinds of evaluative feedback should the PSDD seek?		

Activity 3

Evaluating Chocolate Chip Cookies Using Evaluation Logic

Overview

In this activity, participants take a normal, everyday experience, such as evaluating chocolate chip cookies, and learn what it means to make evaluative criteria, standards, and judgments explicit.

Instructional Objectives

Participants will

- Understand the concept of evaluation logic and how it is the foundation for evaluation practice
- Use evaluation logic to evaluate chocolate chip cookies
- Describe how evaluation logic applies to evaluating programs, services, policies, procedures, systems, and organizations

Number of Participants

- Minimum number of participants: 3
- Maximum number of participants: unlimited when participants are in groups of 3 to 5

Time Estimate: 45 to 90 minutes

This activity requires approximately 45 to 90 minutes, depending on the number of participants (or groups) and the time available for discussion.

Materials Needed

- Pens/pencils
- Four different kinds of chocolate chip cookies. The cookies should be different brands yet of the same type. For example, all of the cookies should have either milk chocolate chips or semisweet chips, and all of them should be without nuts or coconut. If you wish to introduce the

notion of confounding variables, then you might include a cookie that has nuts, coconut, or another ingredient not represented in the other cookies.

- Plastic bags in which to put the cookies
- Plastic or paper plates
- Napkins
- Handout "Evaluating Chocolate Chip Cookies Using Evaluation Logic"

Instructional Method

Small-group work

Procedures

Prior to Class

Facilitator's tasks:

- Purchase four different brands of chocolate chip cookies and paper napkins and plates.
- Determine how many groups will participate and obtain four small plastic bags for each group.
- Break cookies into bite-size pieces and place each brand into separate plastic storage bags, one bag for each brand. Label the bags *A, B, C,* and *D.* Repeat this for each group. For example, if four groups are participating, you need four bags of cookie *A,* four bags of cookie *B,* four bags of cookie *C,* and four bags of cookie *D.*

During Class

Facilitator's tasks:

- Tell participants that they will be conducting an evaluation of chocolate chip cookies. Explain that this is an exercise in understanding the underlying logic of evaluation.
- Ask participants to get into groups of three to five people.
- Provide each group with four cookie bags (labeled *A, B, C,* and *D;* each group now has four bags with a different brand of cookie in each bag). Give each group napkins and paper plates on which to put their cookies when they are ready for the taste test.
- Ask participants to keep notes on their process, the decisions they made, and any challenges they experienced.
- Distribute the handout "Evaluating Chocolate Chip Cookies Using Evaluation Logic."

- Tell participants that if they do not wish to eat the cookies (due to health, diet, or other reasons), they do not have to do so. Ask them to be participant observers.
- Explain that they are to first discuss and complete the first two columns on the handout—the criteria for which chocolate chip cookies should be judged and the standards that should be used to judge a chocolate chip cookie.
- Tell participants to then taste each cookie and complete the third and fourth columns on the handout.
- Debrief the activity with the following questions:
  - How would describe your experience in establishing criteria for evaluating the cookies? Was it difficult? What were some of the things you discussed in your group?
  - How did you determine what standards to use? Were you all in agreement on these standards? How did you reconcile your differences?
  - How comfortable were you with your final judgment about which cookie was best and which you would recommend?
  - For those of you who did not taste the cookies, what role did you play in this evaluative process? What did you observe about your group's behavior? What impact did you have on your group's evaluative judgment and recommendation?

Evaluating Chocolate Chip Cookies Using Evaluation Logic

Handout for Activity 3

Establishing Criteria	*Constructing Standards*	*Measuring Performance and Comparing With Standards*	*Synthesizing and Integrating Evidence Into Judgment of Worth*
What are the dimensions or criteria on which a chocolate chip cookie should be judged (e.g., type of chocolate, texture, color, aroma)?	How well should the cookie perform on each of the dimensions (what are your standards)? Develop a rating system.	Based on your criteria for a good cookie, how well does each cookie measure up against the standards you set?	Which cookie is worth buying?

Which cookie would you recommend?

Activity 4

Tracing Evaluation's History

Overview

This activity helps participants understand the origins of modern-day evaluation practice and the various contexts in which it has evolved into a thriving profession.

Instructional Objectives

Participants will

- Discuss the origins of the evaluation profession beginning in the 1960s
- Develop a timeline that highlights key points in the profession's development
- Identify and discuss the various cultural, societal, economic, and political influences on evaluation practice since the 1960s

Number of Participants

- Minimum number of participants: 3
- Maximum number of participants: unlimited when participants are in groups of 3 to 5

Time Estimate: 45 to 60 minutes

In addition to providing the necessary background on the history of evaluation, this activity requires approximately 45 to 60 minutes, depending on the number of participants (or groups) and the time available for discussion.

Materials Needed

- Pens/pencils
- Flipchart, markers, tape
- Handout "Tracing Evaluation's History"

Instructional Method

Visual representation

Procedures

Facilitator's tasks:

- Ask participants to get into groups of three to five people.
- Distribute the handout "Tracing Evaluation's History."
- Instruct participants to develop a timeline that represents the development of the evaluation profession by including key cultural, societal, economic, and political milestones.
- Ask each group to attach their completed timeline to a wall.
- Invite participants to describe their timelines.
- Debrief the activity with the following questions:
  - What insights have you gained from this activity regarding the evaluation profession's development? What surprised you? What do you know now that you did not know before?
  - What do you think has had the greatest influence on the profession's development?
  - Based on where evaluation has been, where do you think the profession is heading? What might be new areas of development?
  - What do you think evaluation will look like in 10 years? What might influence the practice of evaluation in the next few years?

Tracing Evaluation's History

Handout for Activity 4

Directions:

1. Discuss what you believe are key dates in the evaluation profession's development.

2. Identify the cultural, societal, economic, and political influences that might have influenced the profession's development at these points in time.

3. Develop a timeline that depicts these dates and influences.

Activity 5

Evaluation Versus Research

Overview

This activity helps participants understand the similarities and differences between evaluation and research.

Instructional Objectives

Participants will

- Identify the similarities and differences between evaluation and research as forms of inquiry
- Understand why evaluation is often confused with research
- Be able to articulate the differences between evaluation and research

Number of Participants

- Minimum number of participants: 4
- Maximum number of participants: unlimited when participants are in groups of 3 to 5

Time Estimate: 45 to 60 minutes

In addition to providing the necessary background information on the differences between evaluation and research, this activity requires approximately 45 to 60 minutes, depending on the number of participants (or groups) and the time available for discussion.

Materials Needed

- Pens/pencils
- Flipchart, markers, tape
- Handout "Evaluating and Researching the Learning Pill"

Instructional Method

Case scenario

Procedures

Prior to Class

Facilitator's tasks:

- Purchase a large bag of M&M candies.
- Purchase enough small plastic bags or cups so that each participant has one.
- Place 10 M&Ms into each bag or cup.

During Class

Facilitator's tasks:

- Ask participants to get into groups of three to five people.
- Announce that one or more of the groups are "evaluators" and the other groups are "researchers."
- Hand out one bag or cup of M&Ms to each participant.
- Distribute the handout "Evaluating and Researching the Learning Pill."
- Provide the following directions:

  > You have just read of a new discovery that could potentially revolutionize learning and development. A group of pharmaceutical researchers has developed a learning pill. Coincidentally, soon after reading about this discovery, you receive a call from one of the pill's developers who asks you to help them study the effects of this learning pill. The person explains that her company would like you and your colleagues to conduct an evaluation of the pill and conduct research on the pill. Because of the high development costs associated with this learning pill, you each have been given only 10 pills to use in your studies, which you may use in any way you wish. Your task is to design each of these inquiries using the handout.

- Instruct participants to complete the handout.
- After the specified time for the small-group work, ask the evaluator group(s) to meet with the researcher group(s) to do the following:
  - Compare the results from their handouts.
  - Discuss similarities in their designs.
  - Discuss differences in their designs.

- Debrief the activity with the following questions:
  - What did you learn about the differences and similarities of these two forms of inquiry?
  - What surprised you? What hadn't you thought of before?
  - To what extent do you think that any distinction between evaluation and research is artificial?
  - How would you now describe the differences between research and evaluation to someone who used the terms interchangeably?

Evaluating and Researching the Learning Pill

Handout for Activity 5

Directions:

Circle whether your group represents evaluators or researchers in the first column. Write your answers to each of the questions in the second column.

Evaluation or Research Design Component	*Evaluation or Research Design Notes*
What is the purpose of the study?	
Who are the intended users of the study's findings?	
What is the focus of the study?	
What methods would you use to collect data (e.g., tests, interviews, surveys, observation)?	
How would you report the results of your study, and to whom?	
If your study found that the pill had no effect, would the findings still be reported? Explain your reasons.	

2

The Politics and Ethics of Evaluation Practice

BACKGROUND

This section includes activities that address

- Understanding how and why evaluation is always political
- Understanding the professional ethics of evaluation practice

The following information is provided as a brief introduction to the topics covered in these activities.

THE POLITICS OF EVALUATION PRACTICE

Evaluation is inherently a political act. Therefore, it is important that evaluators clearly understand that regardless of the evaluation's depth and scope, it deals with issues of power, position, and resources. In 1973, Carol Weiss urged evaluation researchers to publicly recognize the importance of politics and values within the evaluation and policy-making process. She identified three ways in which evaluation and politics are related: (1) The policies and programs with which evaluation deals are creatures of political decisions; (2) because evaluation is undertaken to feed into decision making, its reports enter the political arena; and (3) evaluation itself has a political stance. By its very nature, evaluation makes implicit political statements about such issues

SOURCE: Adapted from Russ-Eft and Preskill (2001).

as the problematic nature of some programs and the unchallengeability of others, the legitimacy of program goals and program strategies, the use of strategies of incremental reform, and even the appropriate role of the evaluator in policy and program development and implementation. Thus, even for programs that seem nonpolitical, there are political implications from the mere act of evaluation, not to mention the findings (Guba & Lincoln, 1985). While the political nature of any evaluation may vary considerably, it is never absent.

THE ETHICS OF EVALUATION PRACTICE

Newman and Brown (1996) define ethics as "principles of morality, particularly those dealing with the right or wrong of an action, as the rules of conduct for members of a particular profession" (p. 20). Such standards or rules help to guide individuals and, in this case, evaluators, when facing difficult situations.

The Joint Committee on Standards for Educational Evaluation (1994), which is accredited by the American National Standards Institute (ANSI), published *The Program Evaluation Standards* to help guide evaluators in their work. These standards are divided into four major categories:

- *Utility.* The utility standards are intended to ensure that an evaluation will serve the information needs of intended users. They include stakeholder identification, evaluator credibility, information scope and selection, values identification, report clarity, report timeliness and dissemination, and evaluation impact.

- *Feasibility.* The feasibility standards are intended to ensure that an evaluation will be realistic, prudent, diplomatic, and frugal. They include practical procedures, political viability, and cost effectiveness.

- *Propriety.* The propriety standards are intended to ensure that an evaluation will be conducted legally, ethically, and with due regard for the welfare of those involved in the evaluation, as well as those affected by its results. They include service orientation, formal agreements, rights of human subjects, human interactions, complete and fair assessment, disclosure of findings, conflict of interest, and fiscal responsibility.

- *Accuracy.* The accuracy standards are intended to ensure that an evaluation will reveal and convey technically adequate information about the features that determine worth or merit of the program being evaluated. They include program documentation, content analysis, described purposes and procedures, defensible information sources, valid information, reliable information, systematic information, analysis of quantitative information, analysis of qualitative information, justified conclusions, impartial reporting, and metaevaluation.

The American Evaluation Association (AEA; 1994) developed and published *Guiding Principles for Evaluators* to guide the practice of evaluation. The five major principles include the following:

- *Systematic Inquiry.* Evaluators conduct systematic, data-based inquiries about whatever is being evaluated.
- *Competency.* Evaluators provide competent performance to stakeholders.
- *Integrity/Honesty.* Evaluators ensure the honesty and integrity of the entire evaluation process.
- *Respect for People.* Evaluators respect the security, dignity, and self-worth of the respondents, program participants, clients, and other stakeholders with whom they interact.
- *Responsibilities for the General and Public Welfare.* Evaluators articulate and take into account the diversity of interests and values that may be related to the general and public welfare.

RESOURCES

American Evaluation Association. (1994). *Guiding principles for evaluators.* Retrieved March 8, 2004, from http://www.eval.org/EvaluationDocuments/aeaprin6.html

Chelimsky, E. (1997). The political environment of evaluation and what it means for the development of the field. In E. Chelimsky & W. R. Shadish (Eds.), *Evaluation for the 21st century* (pp. 53-68). Thousand Oaks, CA: Sage.

Fitzpatrick, J. L., & Morris, M. (Eds.). (1999). *Current and emerging ethical challenges in evaluation* (New Directions for Evaluation, Vol. 82). San Francisco: Jossey-Bass.

Gellerman, W., Frankel, M. S., & Ladenson, R. F. (1990). *Values and ethics in organization and human systems development: Responding to dilemmas in professional life.* San Francisco: Jossey-Bass.

Guba, E. G., & Lincoln, Y. S. (1985). *Effective evaluation.* San Francisco: Jossey-Bass.

House, E. R. (1993). *Professional evaluation.* Newbury Park, CA: Sage.

Joint Committee on Standards for Educational Evaluation. (1994). *The program evaluation standards* (2nd ed.). Thousand Oaks, CA: Sage.

Mathison, S. (1999). Rights, responsibilities, and duties: A comparison of ethics for internal and external evaluators. In J. L. Fitzpatrick & M. Morris (Eds.), *Current and emerging ethical challenges in evaluation*

(New Directions for Evaluation, Vol. 82, pp. 25-34). San Francisco: Jossey-Bass.

Morris, M. (1999). Research on evaluation ethics. In J. L. Fitzpatrick & M. Morris (Eds.), *Current and emerging ethical challenges in evaluation* (New Directions for Evaluation, Vol. 82, pp. 15-24). San Francisco: Jossey-Bass.

Morris, M. (1999–2004). Ethical challenges [editorial column]. *American Journal of Evaluation.*

Newman, D. L., & Brown, R. D. (1996). *Applied ethics for program evaluation.* Thousand Oaks, CA: Sage.

Owen, J. M., & Rogers, P. J. (1999). Program evaluation: Forms and approaches (2nd ed.). St. Leonards NSW, Australia: Allen & Unwin.

Patton, M. Q. (1997). *Utilization-focused evaluation: The new century text.* Thousand Oaks, CA: Sage.

Preskill, H., & Lackey, R. (1998, March). *The politics of program evaluation and the misuse of evaluation findings.* Paper presented at the Academy of Human Resource Development annual conference, Chicago.

Russ-Eft, D., & Preskill, H. (2001). *Evaluation in organizations: A systematic approach to enhancing learning, performance, and change.* Boston: Perseus.

Shadish, W. R., Newman, D. L., Sheirer, M. A., & Wye, C. (Eds.). (1995). *Guiding principles for evaluators* (New Directions for Evaluation, Vol. 66). San Francisco: Jossey-Bass.

Weiss, C. H. (1987). Where politics and evaluation research meet. In D. J. Palumbo (Ed.), *The politics of program evaluation* (pp. 47-70). Thousand Oaks, CA: Sage.

Activity 6

The World of Evaluation and Politics

Overview

This activity highlights the political nature of evaluation and asks participants to consider the ways in which an interviewee behaved politically.

Instructional Objectives

Participants will

- Understand that organizational politics is always a factor in the design and implementation of evaluation studies
- Recognize when and how an evaluation may become political
- Discuss various options evaluators have in responding to political situations during the course of an evaluation

Number of Participants

- Minimum number of participants: 3
- Maximum number of participants: unlimited when participants are in groups of 3 to 5

Time Estimate: 45 to 60 minutes

This activity requires approximately 45 to 60 minutes, depending on the number of participants (or groups) and the time available for discussion.

Materials Needed

- Pens/pencils
- Handout "An Interview With the Vice President of Product Development"

Instructional Method

Case scenario

Procedures

Facilitator's tasks:

- Distribute the handout "An Interview With the Vice President of Product Development."
- Ask participants to get into groups of three to five people.
- Ask participants to silently read the background section of the case scenario.
- Ask for two volunteers to role-play the interview, using the handout.
- After the role play, ask participants to discuss, in their groups, the questions posed on the handout.
- Ask each group to share its answers to the discussion questions.
- Debrief the activity with the following questions:
  - What is your reaction to the scenario presented in the case?
  - In what ways was the situation political?
  - What, if anything, should the evaluator have done differently?
  - What issues does this interview raise concerning how the data will be analyzed and used in the final report?

An Interview With the Vice President of Product Development

Handout for Activity 6

Background

The following interview was one of 50 interviews conducted both in person and over the phone with individuals involved in implementing a new product development process for a midsize manufacturing corporation that has a corporate office and 10 manufacturing plants. After meeting with the organization's director of product development, the evaluator learned the following about the organization:

- It reorganized into 10 manufacturing plants (reduced from 17 plants) 5 years ago.
- More than 50% of the employees have worked for the company more than 15 years.
- The relationship between the corporate office and the plants' employees has been strained in recent years—the plant employees don't believe the corporate office is in touch with the reality of their work environment.
- A large percentage of plant employees don't trust the corporate office employees' motives.
- Historically, plant employees have been autonomous, and the new organization's structure has decreased this level of autonomy.
- In an effort to standardize the new product development process and increase the quality of new product development, the organization developed a six-stage model and process based on extensive research and in consultation with two large national consulting firms. It was rolled out nearly 1 year ago. Various individuals were trained on the process, and written materials were provided to each of the organization's manufacturing offices/plants.

- To better understand how well the new product development process is working, an external evaluator has been hired to conduct a formative evaluation. The evaluation's purpose is to
  - Understand the ways in which the new product development process is viewed by various groups of individuals
  - Explore the extent to which employees are using the model and process in developing new products
  - Determine the extent to which organization members understand their roles and responsibilities regarding new product development

- Before this model's implementation, various individuals throughout the organization developed new products. There were few, if any, guidelines or standards, and they often took 2 to 7 years to be developed. Plus, new products were rarely pilot tested with target populations.
- The evaluator has been told by the director of product development that the new product development model and process have become very political. He explains that his boss, the vice president of product development, supports the idea of having a model and process to ensure higher quality and marketable products, but her actions say otherwise. The following is a transcript of the interview between the evaluator (E) and the vice president (VP).

The Interview

E: What are your thoughts about how well the new product development process is being implemented?

VP: The evidence I have seen is that the product development model is the right one. I feel good about that. I have always wanted to make sure we have the right model for the right outcomes and products.

At the same time, I think it's under fire more than anything else, at least from my supervisors. I think it has too much process; it's viewed as taking lots of hours—we can't develop anything quickly. We end up spending so much time asking questions about whether it's needed: Is it the right design? Are others companies doing it? And so on. It's becoming a very big problem. The plant offices complain about the time it takes to develop new products. At the same time, my supervisors don't understand why we can't get new products out there more quickly. I don't understand.

Now we have to do pilot evaluations of the new products, which takes much too long. What is the point? I am in favor of customer satisfaction, but why does it take so long to find out if the product's going to work? It's very important that

I think the process is good, well documented, the right thing to do. I might modify it a little.

E: How do you get people to buy in to using the new product development process?

VP: I don't think they need to know the process. There is no reason to continually tell people what the process is. All they care about is what comes out the other end.

The people doing the work have to understand the process. I don't see the need for everyone else to know. I don't tell them how we come up with the organization's strategic goals. Adults want to know things when they want to know them. You don't have to tell them every time. I am going to tell the whole product development department that I don't want them to talk about this new process. The bulk of people in the plants don't need to know about it. The plant directors want to know, but once we get them all trained, we don't have to talk about it anymore.

E: You don't want your staff to be talking about the new product development process?

VP: That's right. There's this whole language thing with this process, and it sometimes seems as though we're using it as an excuse. We say, "It has to go through the Advisory Committee,[1] so that's why it's not ready," instead of saying, "The product is not complete." Instead of saying, "We are almost finished," we say, "Oh it has to go through another committee review." This morning it was, "We're collecting some additional research." To the plant supervisors, this is nothing but a bunch of garbage. We think we should explain everything, and it's just not necessary. It's been part of our culture to think we have to explain everything.

E: How do you think employees can better understand their roles and responsibilities regarding the product development process?

VP: Generally, if they see the rationale, they will get it. I think the rationale is missing. I suspect that they know I think the process is right and that they have to do it, and therefore they don't know the rationale, they assume how it's implemented

1. The Advisory Committee consists of seven individuals, five of whom have been with the organization for several years. It also includes one vendor, a member of the executive team. This committee acts as a quality checkpoint for new product development. They review the development team's proposal and provide feedback in terms of the product's viability and readiness for development. The Committee may choose to reject a team's proposal if there is insufficient need for, or information about, the product being proposed.

is right. But they don't understand. I hear people say, "Please don't make me go through this."

E: What do you think about the expectation that new products should be developed and rolled out within a 12-month period?

VP: I can't believe, you can't convince me, that other companies go through all the questions we have to go through. My employees have taken a really great process, but when they went to implement it, it became more like implementing a research study—data, data, and more data! When will we just get the product out the door?

I'm tired of all of this, so I am circumventing the process. I am pulling my projects out of it. One of my new product groups doesn't even fit the model. It kept failing the Advisory Committee review process. They are holding certain kinds of new product ideas up to a standard that doesn't fit. It's great for guidance. It's as if they've forgotten that the point is to end up with a great product that we need now. It doesn't mean that it has to go on and on forever. I don't want the thing endlessly researched. I want it to show outputs—are there still ways to improve it? Then, let's make it better.

E: Can you say more about the Advisory Committee?

VP: I hear they're wonderful and that they throw out all these issues, it moves quickly, a lot of people give input, they rip it apart and put it back together. Then they walk away. At the same time, it is almost as if it's paternalistic: The staff wait to be told what to do and don't know if they have to report to the committee if they've made the requested changes.

E: What do you hope to learn from the evaluation?

VP: I wouldn't have chosen to do the evaluation now. Here we go again—let's get more information, get more data, ask more questions—let's evaluate it. I have not told anyone that it's being evaluated. However, since we are having it evaluated, I think it's critical to get to these issues. You can get at these tough issues and give recommendations. I want you to be brave and courageous with the recommendations—don't be nice or hold back. I want to get the best process to meet all of our needs, increase the speed of new product development, and show real outcomes. But the process has to be feasible and simple.

Discussion Questions

1. In what ways does this interview excerpt represent the political nature of evaluation?
2. Do you think the vice president is supportive of the new product development process? What makes you think so?
3. Should the evaluator have asked any additional questions regarding the politics of the new product development process or its evaluation? Why? Why not?
4. What implications might there be for the evaluator? What should the evaluator pay close attention to in future interviews or in writing the evaluation report?
5. Have any of you experienced this kind of situation?

Activity 7

The Political Nature of Evaluation

Overview

This activity asks participants to consider the political influences they may have experienced (or are currently experiencing) in their own evaluation work.

Instructional Objectives

Participants will

- Understand why evaluation is a political act
- Consider why and how programs they have evaluated, or will evaluate, are influenced by internal and external politics
- Consider how they might manage the influence of politics in future evaluations they conduct

Number of Participants

- Minimum number of participants: 3
- Maximum number of participants: unlimited when participants are in groups of 3 to 5

Time Estimate: 45 to 60 minutes

In addition to providing the necessary background information on the political nature of evaluation, this activity requires approximately 45 to 60 minutes, depending on the number of participants (or groups) and the time available for discussion.

Materials Needed

- Pens/pencils
- Handout "The Influence of Politics on Evaluation"

Instructional Method

Individual work/large-group discussion

Procedures

Facilitator's tasks:

- Distribute the handout "The Influence of Politics on Evaluation."
- Instruct participants to individually complete the handout.
- As a large group, debrief the activity with the following questions:
  - What did you discover as you thought about the program being evaluated and the politics surrounding it?
  - If the program was one in which you were involved, to what extent were you aware that the evaluation was political?
  - How did the political nature of the evaluation affect the evaluation's progress and outcomes?
  - How might you begin a new evaluation given what you know about the politics of evaluation?
  - If you were to mentor a new evaluator concerning the politics of evaluation practice, what advice might you offer?

The Influence of Politics on Evaluation

Handout for Activity 7

Directions:

Consider a program (or process, product, system) in your organization or community that has recently been evaluated or one that may be evaluated in the near future. As you think about this program, note your answers to the following questions:

Name of Program (Process, Product, System) Being Evaluated:	
Questions to Consider	*Notes*
How did it come into being?	
Who supported its development and implementation?	
In response to what and whose need was it developed?	
What and whose values are reflected in the program (process, product or system)?	
Who has a vested interest in the continuation of the program (process, product, system)? Whose purpose does the program serve?	
What resources are being allocated to the program (process, product, system)?	
Who would stand to gain or lose from the evaluation if the findings were used to make changes to the program (process, product, system)?	
Which individuals or groups have responsibility for the program's (process, product, system) success?	

Now, after considering each of the questions, describe how and why you think an evaluation of this program could be (or is) political. Note your response in the following table.

Below, indicate what you could do to enhance the likelihood of the evaluation's success despite these political influences.

From Thinking to Action	*Notes*
How and why might the evaluation be political? Use your responses from Questions to Consider in the previous table.	
What will you, as the evaluator, do to maximize the evaluation's success within this political climate?	

Activity 8

Ethical Dilemmas for Evaluators

Overview

This activity asks participants to consider various ethical dilemmas faced by evaluators and to identify relevant evaluation standards and principles.

Instructional Objectives

Participants will

- Gain familiarity with the *Program Evaluation Standards*
- Gain familiarity with the American Evaluation Association's *Guiding Principles*
- Apply these principles and standards to an ethical dilemma

Number of Participants

- Minimum number of participants: 3
- Maximum number of participants: unlimited when participants are in groups of 3 to 5

Time Estimate: 45 to 60 minutes

In addition to providing the necessary background information on the *Program Evaluation Standards* and the American Evaluation Association's *Guiding Principles,* this activity requires 45 to 60 minutes, depending on the number of participants (or groups) and the time available for discussion.

Materials Needed

- Pens/pencils
- Flipchart, markers, tape
- Handout "The Good News at Gee-Gaws"
- Handout "Ethical Dilemmas in Evaluation"

Instructional Method

Case scenario

Procedures

Facilitator's tasks:

- Ask participants to get into groups of three to five people.
- Distribute the handout "The Good News at Gee-Gaws."
- Distribute the handout "Ethical Dilemmas in Evaluation."
- Instruct the groups to read their case scenario and complete the handout "Ethical Dilemmas in Evaluation."
- Request that each group write its ideas on a piece of flipchart paper.
- Ask each group to attach its flipchart page to a wall.
- Invite participants to share their ideas with the larger group.
- Debrief the activity with the following questions:
  - What surprised you about this case?
  - What, if anything, could the evaluator have done to avoid this ethical dilemma?
  - What problems do you anticipate the evaluator will face in carrying out the recommended actions?

The Good News at Gee-Gaws

Handout for Activity 8

Gee-Gaws R Us, a small but prestigious New England manufacturer of baubles and trinkets, has hired you, an external consultant, to conduct a formative evaluation of its Employee Assistance Program (EAP), which was established nearly 1.5 years ago. The entry/contracting phase of this evaluation went smoothly and was uneventful. You met with representatives of key stakeholder groups (e.g., upper-level management, the human resources staff who oversees the program, EAP service providers, shift supervisors, rank-and-file employees) and worked with them to develop an overall framework that would guide the evaluation.

For the past several weeks, you've been collecting data through interviews, questionnaires, and a review of program records and documents. As this process unfolded, your curiosity was piqued and your suspicions aroused. Specifically, there has been a conspicuous lack of variation among Gee-Gaws's respondents in their answers to many of the interview and survey questions. (All of the survey data are in, and you've completed about half of the interviews.) Very few negative—or even neutral— comments about the program have been offered, a result that contrasts sharply with what you've found over the years when evaluating new EAP's in other settings. Glowing endorsements of virtually every aspect of the Gee-Gaws program abound, and recommendations for program change have been rare, even when you've probed extensively for them. Indeed, the EAP at Gee-Gaws appears to be too good to be true.

This afternoon, as you are in the parking lot preparing to leave for the day, an employee you recently interviewed approaches you. He asks how the data look so far, and you give him a polite but noncommittal response. He then says, "To be honest, I don't think you're gonna get much that's useful outta those interviews and surveys. Right before the evaluation started, the HR people told all of us that we should make the program look really good if we wanted the company to keep supporting it. Look, we're a small, nonunion outfit here, sort of like an extended family. Heck, a lot of our parents and grandparents worked here. The company has been good to us for a long time. Nobody is gonna wanna rock the boat, even if there are a few things they're unhappy with."

The employee wishes you good luck with "your study" and departs. As you get into your car and start buckling up, the question you're pondering is, "OK, what now?"

SOURCE: Reprinted from the following with permission granted from Elsevier.

Morris, M. (1999). The good news at Gee-Gaws. *American Journal of Evaluation, 20*(3), 584.

Commentaries on this case can be found in the following:

Posavac, E. J. (1999). Commentary: Can we help Gee-Gaws stay a family? *American Journal of Evaluation, 20*(3), 585-589.

Russ-Eft, D. (1999). Commentary: Can this evaluation be saved? *American Journal of Evaluation, 20*(3), 590-597.

Ethical Dilemmas in Evaluation

Handout for Activity 8

Directions:

After reading the scenario, identify one or more specific dilemmas in the case. Then, identify the relevant *Evaluation Standard(s)* or *Guiding Principle(s)*. Finally, describe what action should be taken.

What are the ethical dilemmas facing evaluator the evaluator?	*What are the relevant Evaluation Standards or Guiding Principles?*	*What should the evaluator do to address this dilemma?*

Activity 9

Debating an Ethical Dilemma

Overview

This activity provides an opportunity for participants to examine a case scenario and then debate two different positions concerning the recommended actions.

Instructional Objectives

Participants will

- Gain familiarity with the *Program Evaluation Standards*
- Gain familiarity with the American Evaluation Association's *Guiding Principles*
- Consider two sides of an ethical dilemma and make a case for supporting one or the other

Number of Participants

- Minimum number of participants: 8
- Maximum number of participants: 24

Time Estimate: 60 to 75 minutes

In addition to providing the necessary background information on the *Program Evaluation Standards* and the American Evaluation Association's *Guiding Principles*, this activity requires 60 to 75 minutes, depending on the number of participants (or groups) and the time available for discussion.

Materials Needed

- Pens/pencils
- Flipchart, markers, tape
- Handout "Opportunity Knocks"
- Handout "Ethical Dilemma Debate Notes"

Instructional Method

Debate

Procedures

Facilitator's tasks:

- Ask participants to get into two groups.
- Distribute the handout "Opportunity Knocks."
- Distribute the handout "Ethical Dilemma Debate Notes."
- Assign one group to take the position that the evaluator should provide outcomes data and the other group to take the position that the evaluator should not provide outcomes data.
- Instruct each group to read the scenario and to complete the handout "Ethical Dilemma Debate Notes." (If the group is large, each group could be divided into two smaller groups; they could then come back together to share their work before the debate begins.)
- Explain the rules of the debate:
  - Each group will select four members to be the debaters. The rest of the team will be in a support position. The role of supporters is to provide the debaters with information as needed. This information can be shared only by writing notes—they are not allowed to talk to the debaters during the debate.
  - Each side will have 3 minutes to make an opening statement.
  - For the next 16 minutes, each side will take 1-minute turns making its case or rebuttal (8 minutes each).
  - Each team will then have 3 minutes to make its closing arguments.
- Debrief the activity with the following questions:
  - What did you experience in preparing for the debate?
  - What other arguments might have been offered to support your own position?
  - What other arguments might have been offered to support the opposing group's position?
  - In what ways did you find the opposing group's comments to be sound?
  - What would you have done in this situation?
  - What issues, questions, and insights did this case scenario raise for you?

Opportunity Knocks

Handout for Activity 9

You have been working on an evaluation of a community-based program designed to support Pacific Islander youth in gaining a college education. The program, functioning as an after-school activity, receives funding from local churches and other community groups. Adult volunteers from those groups and from the community come to the school to help with special programs, to assist students with their homework, and to provide emotional support, when needed.

After several meetings with the program's executive director and with the funding groups, the primary stakeholders agreed it was important to conduct a formative evaluation. Given that the program has only been in operation for a year, the executive director and funding groups thought it would be important to focus the evaluation on how the program could be refined and improved. A more summative type of evaluation that will focus on the program's outcomes and impacts will take place in 3 years.

During the last 2 months, you have been gathering data from a variety of sources. You have reviewed a variety of program documents and have conducted interviews with the director, the adult volunteers, the youth participants, and the participants' parents. In addition, you have observed some of the program's after-school activities.

One day, the executive director calls and asks to meet with you as soon as possible to discuss a wonderful opportunity. When you arrive, the executive director tells you that a potential funding source has been identified and that the funder is inviting the program to submit a proposal. Since the program has a great need for additional funding at this point, the executive director is quite excited about this possibility. As part of the proposal, they would like to see some of the evaluation results, highlighting the outcomes of the program.

You immediately explain that the focus of the evaluation has been formative—not determining the program's outcomes or impacts. The executive director says, "Yes, I know we agreed on that, but I'm sure that you have some evidence as to the good effects of this program." You say, "We have just begun to analyze the formative evaluation data, and, again, the focus has been on finding out how to refine or improve the program. In addition, we have only been collecting data for a couple of months. How can we possibly say that any of the positive outcomes are a result of the program?"

The executive director says, "Yes, I know that you have a reputation for good, thorough, and fair work, but this is such an opportunity! The additional funding will allow us to strengthen and expand the program. In particular, we will be able to make whatever improvements you recommend from the formative evaluation. I'm counting on your good work to help us with this effort and to provide us with some outcomes data we can put into the proposal."

Ethical Dilemma Debate Notes

Handout for Activity 9

Directions:

After reading the case scenario, identify one or more specific dilemmas and discuss what recommendations you would make based on whether your position is to have the evaluator include or not include outcomes data.

What are the ethical dilemmas facing the evaluator?	*What would you recommend, and why?*

3

Multicultural and Cross-Cultural Aspects of Evaluation

BACKGROUND

This section includes activities that address

- Understanding the importance of recognizing the cultural contexts of evaluation
- Defining cultural competency within an evaluation context
- Understanding how one's culture and history potentially affect evaluation practice

The following information is provided as a brief introduction to the topics covered in these activities.

When conducting evaluations in any community or organizational context, it is critical that evaluators understand what it means to be culturally aware and sensitive and to have some level of cultural competence. The first step toward achieving this goal is for evaluators to know themselves—their roots, histories, biases, prejudices, and assumptions about race, culture, and ethnicity. Only then can they begin to understand, and possibly confront, long-held beliefs that may support or impede their working within a multicultural environment.

DEFINITIONS

The following definitions are useful when discussing different aspects of culture with regard to evaluation practice.

Cultural Knowledge. Familiarization with selected cultural characteristics, history, values, belief systems, and behaviors of the members of another ethnic group (Adams, 1995).

Cultural Awareness. Developing sensitivity and understanding of another ethnic group and involving changes in attitudes and values. It also reflects an openness and flexibility in working with others of another culture (Adams, 1995).

Cultural Sensitivity. Knowing that there are differences and similarities among cultures without making value judgments of good or bad, better or worse, right or wrong (Texas Department of Health, National Maternal and Child Health Resource Center on Cultural Competency, 1997).

Cultural Competence. A set of congruent behaviors, attitudes, and policies that come together in a system, agency, or among professionals that enables that system, agency, or those professionals to work effectively in cross-cultural situations (Cross, Bazron, Dennis, & Isaacs, 1989). Cultural competency is the ability to effectively operate in different cultural contexts.

RESOURCES

Adams, D. L. (Ed.). (1995). *Health issues for women of color: A cultural diversity perspective.* Thousand Oaks, CA: Sage.

American Psychological Association. (2002). *Guidelines on multicultural education, training, research, practice, and organizational change for psychologists.* Washington, DC: Author.

Brookfield, S., & Preskill, S. (2001). *Discussion as a way of teaching.* San Francisco: Jossey-Bass.

Cross, T., Bazron, B., Dennis, K., & Isaacs, M. (1989). *Towards a culturally competent system of care: Volume I.* Washington, DC: Georgetown University Child Development Center, CASSP Technical Assistance Center.

Edno, T., Joh, T., & Yu, H. C. (2003). *Voices from the field: Health and evaluation leaders on multicultural evaluation.* Oakland, CA: Social Policy Research Associates.

Fort, L., Martínez, B. L., & Mukhopadhyay, M. (2001). *Integrating a gender dimension into monitoring and evaluation of rural development projects.* Washington, DC: World Bank.

Frierson, H. T., Hood. S., & Hughes, G. (2002). Strategies that address culturally responsive evaluation. In J. F. Westat (Ed.), *2002 user-friendly handbook for project evaluation* (pp. 63-73). Arlington, VA: NSF, Directorate for Education and Human Resources.

Guzman, B. L. (2003). Examining the role of cultural competency in program evaluation: Visions for new millennium evaluators. In S. I. Donaldson & M. Scriven (Eds.), *Evaluating social programs and problems: Visions for the new millennium* (pp. 167-182). Mahwah, NJ: Lawrence Erlbaum.

Harbour, P. M. (1996). *Spiritual, moral, and cultural dimensions of cultural diversity.* Kalamazoo, MI: Fetzer Institute.

Hood, S. (1999). Culturally responsive performance-based assessment: Conceptual and psychometric considerations. *Journal of Negro Education, 67*(3), 187-197.

Hood, S., & Frierson Jr., H. (Eds.). (1994). Beyond the dream: Meaningful program evaluation and assessment to achieve equal opportunity at predominantly White universities. In R. Stake (Ed.), *Advances in program evaluation* (Vol. 2, pp. 47-60). Greenwich, CT: JAI Press.

Hood, S., & Johnson, S. (Eds.). (1998). Assessment in the context of culture and pedagogy [Special issue]. *Journal of Negro Education, 67*(3).

Kirkhart, K. E. (1995). Seeking multicultural validity: A postcard from the road. *Evaluation Practice, 16*(1), 1-12.

Mertens, D. M. (1999). Inclusive evaluation: Implications of transformative theory for evaluation. *American Journal of Evaluation, 20*(1), 1-14.

Patton, M. Q. (1994). Developmental evaluation. *Evaluation Practice, 15*(2), 311-320.

Patton, M. Q. (2001). *Qualitative research and evaluation methods* (3rd ed.). Thousand Oaks, CA: Sage.

Seigart, D., & Brisolara, S. (Eds.). (2002). *Feminist evaluation: Explorations and experiences* (New Directions for Evaluation, Vol. 96). San Francisco: Jossey-Bass.

Stanfield, J. (1999). Slipping through the front door: Relevant social scientific evaluation in the people-of-color century. *The American Journal of Evaluation, 20*(2), 414-342.

Stevens, F. I. (2000). Reflections and interviews: Information collected about training minority evaluators of math and science projects. In G. Hughes (Eds.), *The cultural context of educational evaluation. The role of minority professionals, NSF01-43.* Arlington, VA: NSF, Directorate for Education and Human Resources.

Sue, D. W., Arrendondo, P., & McDavis, R. J. (1992). Multicultural counseling competencies and standards: A call to the profession. *Journal of Counseling and Development, 70,* 477-486.

Symonette, H. (in press). Minority issues in evaluation. In S. Mathison (Ed.), *Encyclopedia of evaluation.* Thousand Oaks, CA: Sage.

Texas Department of Health, National Maternal and Child Health Resource Center on Cultural Competency. (1997). *Journey towards cultural competency: Lessons learned.* Vienna, VA: Maternal and Children's Health Bureau Clearinghouse.

World Bank. (1989). *Project monitoring and evaluation.* Retrieved April 1, 2004, from http://wbln0018.worldbank.org/Institutional/Manuals/OpManual.nsf/0/6e513837e22b8c9a8525672c007d08f2?OpenDocument

Activity 10

Understanding the Influence of Culture in Evaluation Practice

Overview

This activity asks participants to consider how their own cultural heritage and background may influence the ways in which they design and implement evaluation studies.

Instructional Objectives

Participants will

- Identify or recognize their own cultural heritage or background
- Understand other individuals' hopes, dreams, disappointments, and tragedies as they relate to one's culture
- Consider how one's background may influence his or her evaluation practice

Number of Participants

- Minimum number of participants: 8
- Maximum number of participants: 15 *or* unlimited when participants are in groups of 8 to 10

Time Estimate: 40 to 75 minutes

This activity requires approximately 5 minutes per person. Thus, if there were 15 participants, this activity would require approximately 75 minutes.

SOURCE: This activity is adapted from Brookfield and Preskill (2001), who adapted it from an exercise developed by the Fetzer Institute as part of its work on diversity dialogues (Harbour, 1996).

Materials Needed

- Personal objects brought by participants

Instructional Method

Storytelling

Procedures

Facilitator's tasks:

Prior to Class

- Ask participants to bring an object that reflects something of their ancestry. Tell participants that they will be asked to talk briefly about the object they bring.

During the Class

- Emphasize the importance of silence when listening to each other's presentations and between presentations, when participants volunteer to describe their object.
- Present your own object first to model the behavior of self-disclosure. Spend only 2 to 3 minutes describing the object.
- Invite participants to volunteer to talk about their objects for up to 5 minutes. They are to speak without interruption. Explain that when they speak, they are to rise and put their objects on a table and then talk about their objects and how it links to their culture and family histories.
- Debrief the activity with the following questions:
  - What did you learn about each other from this activity?
  - What did you learn about someone else's culture?
  - When were you most uncomfortable? Why do you think you were uncomfortable?
  - How might your own background influence the way you approach an evaluation?
  - How might you design and implement an evaluation with cultural sensitivity and awareness?

References

Brookfield, S., & Preskill, S. (2001). *Discussion as a way of teaching.* San Francisco: Jossey-Bass.

Harbour, P. M. (1996). *Spiritual, moral, and cultural dimensions of cultural diversity.* Kalamazoo, MI: Fetzer Institute.

Activity 11

Defining Evaluation Within a Cultural Context

Overview

This activity asks participants to consider various definitions of evaluation and how they relate to working with culturally diverse audiences.

Instructional Objectives

Participants will

- Describe the distinguishing characteristics of various definitions of evaluation
- Determine the ways in which these evaluation definitions relate to power
- Discuss the importance of the definitions in relation to working in culturally diverse communities and the advantages and disadvantages of using the various definitions

Number of Participants

- Minimum number of participants: 3
- Maximum number of participants: unlimited when participants are in groups of 3 to 5

Time Estimate: 45 to 60 minutes

This activity requires approximately 45 to 60 minutes, depending on the number of participants (or groups) and the time available for discussion.

Materials Needed

- Pens/pencils
- Handout "Definitions of Evaluation Within a Cultural Context"

SOURCE: This activity was contributed by Donna M. Mertens, Gallaudet University.

Instructional Method

Small-group work

Procedures

Facilitator's tasks:

- Ask participants to get into groups of three to five people.
- Distribute the handout "Definitions of Evaluation Within a Cultural Context."
- Ask participants to individually read the definitions on the handout and then, as a group, discuss each of the questions.
- Ask each group to share the results of its discussion.
- Debrief the activity with the following questions:
  - What are your reactions to this activity?
  - What are the implications of the various definitions for working in culturally diverse communities?
  - What are the advantages and disadvantages of adopting each definition in a culturally complex setting?
  - To what extent, or in what ways, has your definition of evaluation shifted or changed?

Definitions of Evaluation Within a Cultural Context

Handout for Activity 11

Commonly Used Definition

Program evaluation is the systematic collection of information about the activities, characteristics, and outcomes of programs to make judgments about the program, improve program effectiveness, and/or inform decisions about future programming (Patton, 2001, p. 10).

World Bank Definition

Monitoring is defined as "the continuous assessment of project implementation in relation to agreed schedules and of the use of inputs, infrastructure, and services by project beneficiaries" (World Bank, 1989).

Evaluation is defined as "periodic assessment of the relevance, performance, efficiency, and impact (both expected and unexpected) of the project in relation to stated objectives" (Fort, Martínez, & Mukhopadhyay, 2001).

Developmental Evaluation

Developmental evaluation consists of evaluation processes and activities that support program, project, product, personnel, or organizational development, usually all five. The evaluator is part of a team whose members collaborate to conceptualize, design, and test new approaches in a long-term, ongoing process of improvement, adaptation, and intentional change. The evaluator's primary function on the team is to elucidate team discussions with evaluative data and logic and to facilitate data-based decision making in the developmental process (Patton, 1994, p. 317).

Inclusive Evaluation

Inclusive evaluation involves a systematic investigation of the merit or worth of a program or system for the purpose of reducing uncertainty in decision making and for facilitating positive social change for the least advantaged. Thus, inclusive evaluation is data based, but the data are generated from an inclusive list of stakeholders, with special efforts to include those who have been traditionally underrepresented.

It does not exclude those who have been traditionally included in evaluations (Mertens, 1999, p. 5).

Feminist Evaluation

Feminist evaluation includes judgments of merit and worth, application of social science methods to determine effectiveness, and achievement of program goals as well as tools related to social justice for the oppressed, especially, although not exclusively, for women. Its central focus is on gender inequities that lead to social injustice. It uses a collaborative, inclusive process and captures multiple perspectives to bring about social change (Seigart & Brisolara, 2002).

References

Fort, L., Martínez, B. L., & Mukhopadhyay, M. (2001). *Integrating a gender dimension into monitoring and evaluation of rural development projects.* Washington, DC: World Bank.

Mertens, D. M. (1999). Inclusive evaluation: Implications of transformative theory for evaluation. *American Journal of Evaluation, 20*(1), 1-14.

Patton, M. Q. (1994). Developmental evaluation. *Evaluation Practice, 15*(2), 311-320.

Patton, M. Q. (2001). *Qualitative research and evaluation methods* (3rd ed.). Thousand Oaks, CA: Sage.

Seigart, D., & Brisolara, S. (2002). *Feminist evaluation: Explorations and experiences* (New Directions for Evaluation, Vol. 96). San Francisco: Jossey-Bass.

World Bank. (1989). *Project monitoring and evaluation.* Retrieved April 1, 2004, from http://wbln0018.worldbank.org/Institutional/Manuals/OpManual.nsf/0/6e513837e22b8c9a8525672c007d08f2?OpenDocument

Discussion Questions

1. What is the essence of each definition?
2. What similarities and differences do you see among the definitions? What distinguishes one definition from the other?
3. What kinds of power rest in these definitions, and how might such definitions affect the design and implementation of an evaluation?

Activity 12

Cultural Sensitivity in Evaluation

Overview

This activity asks participants to consider how various aspects of culture affect an evaluation's design and implementation.

Instructional Objectives

Participants will

- Reflect on their own values, assumptions, and experiences as they relate to working with different cultures
- Develop greater awareness of how ignoring the topic of cultural differences may affect an evaluation's design and implementation
- Determine ways in which various data collection methods can reflect cultural considerations

Number of Participants

- Minimum number of participants: 3
- Maximum number of participants: unlimited when participants are in groups of 3 to 5

Time Estimate: 60 to 90 minutes

In addition to providing the necessary background information on cultural sensitivity, cultural awareness, and cultural competence, this activity requires approximately 60 to 90 minutes, depending on the number of participants (or groups) and the time available for discussion.

Materials Needed

- Pens/pencils
- Flipchart, markers, tape

- Handout "Cultural Influences"
- Handout "Strategies for Making Evaluation More Culturally Sensitive"

Instructional Method

Small-group work

Procedures

Facilitator's tasks:

- Ask participants to get into groups of three to five people.
- Distribute the handout "Cultural Influences."
- Instruct participants to discuss their responses to the questions on the handout.
- Ask groups to share the highlights of their discussions and to write key themes on a piece of flipchart paper. If possible, sorts responses into thematic categories. A variation would be to list all of the responses and have the large group develop thematic categories.
- Distribute the handout "Strategies for Making Evaluation More Culturally Sensitive" and discusses each strategy. Invite participants to add other strategies to this list.
- Debrief the activity with the following questions:
  - What have you learned from this exercise that will influence future evaluations on which you work?
  - What else do you need to do to build cultural sensitivity in your evaluation work?
  - What are the implications of not being culturally aware, sensitive, or competent?
  - How do you think evaluators can develop these competencies?

Cultural Influences

Handout for Activity 12

1. How might each of the following influence or affect an evaluation's design and implementation?
    - The language of the participants (how and what language is used in an evaluation study)
    - The role of food and eating
    - How evaluators dress when interacting with a culture(s)
    - The concept of time
    - Communication styles
    - Importance of relationships, family, friends
    - Values and norms regarding individualism, independence, and conflict
    - Work habits and practices (e.g., task emphasis vs. emphasis on relationships)
    - Mental processes and learning styles (e.g., linear, logical, sequential vs. lateral, holistic, simultaneous)

2. How might you ensure that the following data collection activities are culturally sensitive and appropriate?
    - Observations
    - Interviews
    - Mailed surveys

Strategies for Making Evaluation More Culturally Sensitive

Handout for Activity 12

- Assess your own attitudes, beliefs, and values; be aware of your own biases.
- During the initial stages of the evaluation, explore any cultural issues that could affect the evaluation's design and implementation.
- Learn all you can about the cultural group(s) involved in the evaluation.
- Incorporate culturally diverse groups and perspectives throughout the evaluation process (e.g., obtain feedback on the evaluation's design, methods, and draft reports).
- Recognize that the evaluation may take more time to conduct if you are negotiating access and building trust in working with community groups and organizations.
- Use as little jargon as possible.
- Demystify evaluation for program staff and clients. Build buy-in.
- Include representatives of culturally diverse groups on evaluation advisory committees.
- Be flexible in your choices of methods and activities.
- Use multiple data collection sources and methods.

SOURCE: Adapted from a presentation by Valerie S. Nelkin, Bear Enterprises, Ltd.

Activity 13

Defining Cultural Competence: Evaluation in Multicultural Settings

Overview

This activity asks participants to consider the concept of cultural competence and how it relates to evaluation practice in diverse settings.

Instructional Objectives

Participants will

- Understand various definitions of cultural competency
- Determine why it is important for evaluators to consider definitions of cultural competence
- Understand the relationship between cultural competence and issues of social justice in evaluation

Number of Participants

- Minimum number of participants: 3
- Maximum number of participants: unlimited when participants are in groups of 3 to 5

Time Estimate: 60 to 75 minutes

In addition to providing any necessary background on the cultural context of evaluation, this activity requires approximately 60 to 75 minutes, depending on the number of participants (or groups) and the time available for discussion.

SOURCE: This activity was contributed by Donna M. Mertens, Gallaudet University.

Materials Needed

- Pens/pencils
- Handout "Constructing a Definition of Cultural Competence in an Evaluation Context"

Instructional Method

Small-group work

Procedures

Facilitator's tasks:

- Ask participants to get into groups of three to five people.
- Distribute the handout "Constructing a Definition of Cultural Competence in the Evaluation Context."
- Ask participants to first read the definitions and then, in their groups, respond to the questions on the handout.
- Ask groups to share highlights from their discussions.
- Debrief the activity with the following questions:
  - To what extent, or in what ways, has your view of cultural competence shifted?
  - What does cultural competency look like? In other words, what would you see evaluators doing that exemplified cultural competence?
  - What will you do to increase your own cultural competency?

Constructing a Definition of Cultural Competence in an Evaluation Context

Handout for Activity 13

Within an evaluation context, the concept of culture includes shared behaviors, values, beliefs, attitudes, and languages and is broadly construed to be multidimensional in nature, based on such characteristics as race/ethnicity, gender, disability, economic class, and sexual orientation.

- Based on your experiences, how would you define cultural competence in an evaluation context?
- Now, consider the following definitions of cultural competence as they relate to evaluation practice:
  - *Cultural competence* refers to an ability to provide services that are perceived as legitimate for problems experienced by culturally diverse populations. "This definition denotes the ability to transform knowledge and cultural awareness into interventions that support and sustain healthy participant-system functioning within the appropriate cultural context" (Guzman, 2003, p. 171).
  - "As an agent of prosocial change, the culturally competent psychologist carries the responsibility of combating the damaging effects of racism, prejudice, bias, and oppression in all their forms, including all of the methods we use to understand the populations we serve. . . . A consistent theme . . . relates to the interpretation and dissemination of research findings that are meaningful and relevant to each of the four populations and that reflect an inherent understanding of the racial, cultural, and sociopolitical context within which they exist" (American Psychological Association, 2002, p. 1).
  - "A set of congruent behaviors, attitudes, and policies that come together in a system, agency, or among professionals and enables that system, agency, or those professionals to work effectively in cross cultural situations" (Cross, Bazron, Dennis, & Isaacs, 1989, cited in Edno, John, & Yu, 2003, p. 5).
  - Many health and evaluation leaders are careful to point out that a simple checklist cannot determine cultural competence, but rather it is an attribute that develops over time. The root of cultural competency in evaluation is a genuine respect for communities being studied and openness to seek

depth in understanding different cultural contexts, practices, and paradigms of thinking. This includes being creative and flexible to capture different cultural contexts, and a heightened awareness of power differentials that exist in an evaluation context. Important skills include the ability to build rapport across difference, gain the trust of community members, and self-reflect and recognize one's own biases. (Edno, Joh, & Yu, 2003, pp. 6-7).

References

American Psychological Association. (2002). *Guidelines on multicultural education, training, research, practice, and organizational change for psychologists.* Washington, DC: Author.

Cross, T., Bazron, B., Dennis, K., & Isaacs, M. (1989). *Towards a culturally competent system of care: Volume I.* Washington, DC: Georgetown University Child Development Center, CASSP Technical Assistance Center.

Edno, T., Joh, T., & Yu, H. C. (2003). *Voices from the field: Health and evaluation leaders on multicultural evaluation.* Oakland, CA: Social Policy Research Associates.

Guzman, B. L. (2003). *Examining the role of cultural competency in program evaluation: Visions for new millennium evaluators.* In S. I. Donaldson & M. Scriven (Eds.), Evaluating social programs and problems: Visions for the new millennium (pp. 167-182). Mahwah, NJ: Lawrence Erlbaum.

Discussion Questions

1. How would you describe the cultural context in which you work?
2. Why is it important to consider the concept of cultural competence in evaluation?
3. What are the skills, attitudes, and knowledge necessary for evaluators to be considered culturally competent?
4. How can improved understandings of cultural competence be linked to furthering the goals of social justice?
5. In what ways are social justice goals important in the context of evaluating programs and processes in organizations and communities?

Activity 14

Exploring the Role of Assumptions in Evaluation Practice

Overview

This activity provides an opportunity for participants to think about the assumptions we make about other people based on how they look or act and how these might influence the ways in which we design and implement evaluations.

Instructional Objectives

Participants will

- Discover how one's assumptions influence how he or she perceives other individuals
- Reflect on how their own assumptions influence the design and implementation of an evaluation
- Discuss the ways in which their own assumptions can be tested and corrected within an evaluation context

Number of Participants

- Minimum number of participants: 4
- Maximum group size: 25

Time Estimate: 30 to 45 minutes

This activity requires approximately 30 to 45 minutes, depending on the number of participants (or groups) and the time available for discussion.

Materials Needed

- Flipchart, markers, tape

SOURCE: This activity was contributed by Joan F. Slick, Program Manager, Extended University, University of New Mexico, Albuquerque, NM.

Instructional Method

Round robin

Procedures

Facilitator's tasks:

- Write one of the following statements at the top of each of four flipchart pages:
  - I can't write my name.
  - I want my father to come to the interview with me.
  - I'm afraid to drive a car.
  - I want my paycheck cashed in quarters.
- Post the flipchart pages on the walls around the room and place markers near each page.
- Explain that this activity is about understanding how our assumptions influence our thinking and behavior.
- Go to the flipchart page that says, "I can't write my name."
- Say, "If you asked someone to write his or her name and the person told you he or she could not write, you might get irritated and think the person was just trying to make you work harder or was just being difficult. However, stop and think about the reasons why a person might not be able to write his or her name. What are some reasons?" (Let participants suggest one or two ideas and write one of them on the flipchart—e.g., he might be paralyzed, she might not know English, he might be blind, she might not know how to write.)
- Refer to the statements on the other flipchart pages (but do not ask for examples at this time).
- Ask participants to get into groups of three to five people (if possible, have participants get into groups where they don't know each other).
- Instruct each of the groups to go to one of the flipchart pages and to write the reasons people might make the statement (spend 5 minutes per chart or until the group runs out of ideas).
- Call time and ask the groups to rotate so that each group has a chance to write ideas on another chart. Each group keeps the same color marker for all charts. Call time again after 5 minutes and ask participants to go to the next flipchart. Continue this process until all groups have written on each of the four flipchart pages.

- Ask the groups to go back to their seats. Read each flipchart to the class (or asks for volunteers to read each chart). Possible responses might include
  - I want my father to come to the interview with me (first job, a female from another culture).
  - I'm afraid to drive a car (may have epilepsy, may not be able to afford a car, may have been in bad car wreck).
  - I want my paycheck cashed in quarters (laundry, gambling, parking, bus).
- Debrief the activity with the following questions:
  - In two words or less, describe your experience with this activity.
  - What kinds of assumptions might we make about evaluation and those whom we evaluate?
  - What are the implications of conducting an evaluation with a certain set of assumptions about a group of people, a program, or a geographic area?
  - How can evaluators learn to test and correct these assumptions in their practice?

4

Focusing the Evaluation

BACKGROUND

This section includes activities that address

- Using logic models to focus an evaluation
- Developing an evaluation purpose statement
- Identifying stakeholders for an evaluation
- Developing an evaluation's key questions

The following information is provided as a brief introduction to the topics covered in these activities.

Logic models can be used to understand a program's theory of action during the focusing phase of an evaluation. A logic model is "a systematic and visual way to present and share your understanding of the relationships among the resources you have to operate your program, the activities you plan to do, and the changes or results you hope to achieve" (W. K. Kellogg Foundation, 2000, p. 1). Logic models describe how a program, process, or system is supposed to work—as well as its underlying theory and assumptions and desired outcomes. Using a logic model to focus an evaluation helps stakeholders understand various aspects of the program, which can then aid in determining the evaluation's background, purpose, intended users (other stakeholders), and the guiding questions. In developing a logic model, it is important to involve as many stakeholders as possible so that all views and experiences with a program are represented.

While there are various versions of logic models, most include the following components:

- *Assumptions:* The underlying values, beliefs, and assumptions that influence the program's design, implementation, or goals
- *Resources/Inputs:* The human, financial, organizational, and community resources that are needed to accomplish the program's objectives
- *Activities:* The things the program does with the resources to meet its objectives, interventions that are expected to produce changes or results
- *Outputs:* The direct products of the program's activities, evidence that the program was actually implemented
- *Outcomes:* The specific short-term (immediate) and long-term changes in program participants' knowledge, behavior, skills, status, and level of functioning as a result of the program
- *Impact:* The intended or unintended change that occurs in the organization or community as a result of program activities several years later

Every evaluation should include an evaluation plan that clearly articulates why, how, when, where, and with whom the evaluation will be conducted. For external evaluators, the evaluation plan often serves as a contract between the evaluator and the client. For internal evaluators, an evaluation plan helps clarify the scope and depth of the evaluation and the personnel and financial resources that will be required. The following information is usually provided at the beginning of an evaluation plan:

- The background and rationale of the program (or whatever is being evaluated)
- The purpose of the evaluation, which also often implies the type of evaluation that will be undertaken (e.g., needs assessment, developmental evaluation, formative evaluation, summative evaluation, or some combination of these, as well as the intended uses of the evaluation's findings)
- The stakeholders and audiences for the evaluation (the intended users of the evaluation's findings)
- The evaluation's key questions—the broad, overarching questions that guide the evaluation study

RESOURCES

Bickman, L. (Ed.). (1987). *Using program theory in evaluation* (New Directions for Program Evaluation, Vol. 33). San Francisco: Jossey-Bass.

McLaughlin, J. A., & Jordan, G. B. (1999). Logic models: A tool for telling your program's performance story. *Evaluation and Program Planning 22,* 65-72.

Patton, M. Q. (1997). *Utilization-focused evaluation: The new century text.* Thousand Oaks, CA: Sage.

Preskill, H., & Torres, R. T. (1999). *Evaluative inquiry for learning in organizations.* Thousand Oaks, CA: Sage.

Russ-Eft, D., & Preskill, H. (2001). *Evaluation in organizations: A systematic approach to enhancing learning, performance, and change.* Cambridge, MA: Perseus Press.

United Way of America. (1996). *Measuring program outcomes: A practical approach.* Arlington, VA: Author.

W. K. Kellogg Foundation. (2000). *Logic model development guide.* Battle Creek, MI: Author.

Wholey, J. S. (1994). Assessing the feasibility and likely usefulness of evaluation. In J. S. Wholey, H. P. Hatry, & K. E. Newcomer (Eds.), *Handbook of practical program evaluation* (pp. 15-39). San Francisco: Jossey-Bass.

Worthen, B. R., Sanders, J. R., & Fitzpatrick, J. L. (1997). *Program evaluation: Alternative approaches and practice guidelines* (2nd ed., pp. 215-268). New York: Longman.

Activity 15

Using a Logic Model to Focus an Evaluation

Overview

This activity provides an opportunity for participants to develop a logic model for an evaluation they may be currently working on or for one they might conduct in the future.

Instructional Objectives

Participants will

- Understand the concept and use of logic models for focusing an evaluation
- Develop a logic model for a program or process
- Use a logic model to develop an evaluation's purpose, list of stakeholders, and key questions

Number of Participants

- Minimum number of participants: 3
- Maximum number of participants: unlimited when participants are in groups of 3 to 5

Time Estimate: 60 to 90 minutes

In addition to providing the necessary background information on logic models and their use in evaluation planning, this activity requires approximately 60 to 90 minutes, depending on the number of participants (or groups) and the time available for discussion.

Materials Needed

- Pens/pencils
- Flipchart, markers, tape
- Handout "Developing a Logic Model to Focus an Evaluation: Example A"
- Handout "Developing a Logic Model to Focus an Evaluation: Example B"
- Handout "Developing a Logic Model: Example of Buying a First House"

Instructional Method

Small-group work

Procedures

Facilitator's tasks:

- Ask participants to get into groups of three to five people.
- Explain that there are a number of ways logic models can be represented. Distribute handouts "Developing a Logic Model to Focus an Evaluation: Example A" and "Developing a Logic Model to Focus an Evaluation: Example B." Describe similarities and differences between the two versions.
- Distribute the handout "Developing a Logic Model: Example of Buying a First House" and discuss each of the model's components.
- Determine a topic for which a logic model can be developed and used to focus an evaluation. You could also ask participants to identify a topic of common interest.
- Explain that participants are to develop a logic model based on the chosen topic (e.g., "We are going to evaluate the ABC Reading Program for students in Grades 4 to 6.").
- Tell participants that they are to develop a logic model for this program and that they should be prepared to share their logic model with the larger group.
- Ask participants to write their logic model on flipchart paper and attach their paper to a wall.
- Invite participants to present their logic models.
- If time allows, ask participants (either in small groups or as a large group) to develop a list of evaluation key questions based on the short- and long-term objectives of the program that could guide an evaluation of the program.
- Debrief the activity with the following questions:
  - What similarities and differences do you see in the different logic models?
  - As you developed the logic model, what did you learn about the topic you were working on? Was anything unexpected or surprising?
  - What challenges did you face as you were developing the logic model?
  - What are the benefits of developing a logic model?
  - What are the limitations of logic models?

Developing a Logic Model to Focus an Evaluation: Example A

Handout for Activity 15

Resources	*Activities*	*Outputs*	*Short-Term Outcomes*	*Long-Term Outcomes*	*Impact*
Human, financial, organizational, and community resources needed to achieve the program's objectives	Things the program does with the resources to meet its objectives	Direct products of the program's activities; evidence that the program was actually implemented	Short-term (immediate) changes in participants' knowledge, behavior, skills, status, and level of functioning as a result of the program	Long-term changes in program participants' knowledge, behavior, skills, status, and level of functioning as a result of the program	Intended or unintended change that occurs in the organization or community as a result of program activities several years later

Developing a Logic Model to Focus an Evaluation: Example B

Handout for Activity 15

Assumptions	*Resources*	*Activities*	*Outputs*	*Short-Term Outcomes*	*Long-Term Outcomes*
The underlying assumptions that influence the program's design, implementation, or goals	Human, financial, organizational, and community resources needed to achieve the program's objectives	Things the program does with the resources to meet its objectives	Direct products of the program's activities; evidence that the program was actually implemented	Short-term (immediate) changes in participants' knowledge, behavior, skills, status, and level of functioning as a result of the program	Long-term changes in program participants' knowledge, behavior, skills, status, and level of functioning as a result of the program

Developing a Logic Model: Example of Buying a First House

Handout for Activity 15

Resources	*Activities*	*Outputs*	*Short-Term Outcomes*	*Long-Term Outcomes*	*Impact*
Human, financial, organizational, and community resources needed to achieve the program's objectives	Things the program does with the resources to meet its objectives	Direct products of the program's activities; evidence that the program was actually implemented	Short-term (immediate) changes in participants' knowledge, behavior, skills, status, and level of functioning as a result of the program	Long-term changes in program participants' knowledge, behavior, skills, status, and level of functioning as a result of the program	Intended or unintended change that occurs in the organization or community as a result of program activities several years later
• Newspaper information on current mortgage rates • Realtor listings of homes in the area • Friends, family, coworkers' recommendations • Internet sites on first-time home buying • Sunday newspaper ads with current listings • Available down payment ($$)	• Drive through different neighborhoods to identify preferred location • Obtain credit report • Determine eligibility for VHA or FHA bank loan • Determine affordability of purchasing a home • Determine preferred size of home • Go to open houses to determine housing preferences • Attend a community center workshop on how to buy a home • Choose a realtor	• Obtained mortgage at desired rate • Looked at 15 houses in price range • Bid on one house we liked—bid was accepted	• Moved into new home	• Decided to move into larger home 7 years later—used what was learned in buying first home to locate and negotiate second home	• Ability to obtain mortgages, locate and move into new homes over the next 30 years

Activity 16

Creating a Flowchart Logic Model

Overview

This activity engages participants in developing a flowchart type of logic model.

Instructional Objectives

Participants will

- Represent a program's logic using a flowchart
- Discuss the uses of logic models for developing an evaluation's purpose and key questions
- Consider the ways in which involving stakeholders in developing a logic model affects the design and implementation of an evaluation

Number of Participants

- Minimum number of participants: 3
- Maximum number of participants: unlimited when participants are in groups of 3 to 5

Time Estimate: 45 to 60 minutes

In addition to providing the necessary background information on developing evaluation logic models, this activity requires approximately 45 to 60 minutes, depending on the number of participants (or groups) and the time available for discussion.

Materials Needed

- Pens/pencils
- Flipchart, markers, tape
- Adhesive notes
- Handout "Creating a Flowchart Logic Model"

Instructional Method

Small-group work

Procedures

Facilitator's tasks:

- Ask participants to get into groups of three to five people.
- Distribute the handout "Creating a Flowchart Logic Model."
- Explain that each group will create a logic model of one of the following programs (you may either assign one of these to each group or groups may be asked to pick one):
  - Drivers' education program
  - New employee orientation program
  - Health and fitness program
  - Other program that is familiar to the participants
- Ask groups to first complete the handout with the particular program in mind.
- Ask each group to create a flowchart showing the linkages between and among the various logic model elements on the handout
- Ask groups to present their logic model
- Debrief the activity with the following questions:
  - How would you describe your group's experience in developing the flowchart logic model? What went well? What was difficult?
  - What did this activity teach you about focusing an evaluation?
  - What do you think it would be like if stakeholders were involved in developing the logic model?
  - What are some of the benefits of including stakeholders in this process? What do you think they learn?
  - How might a logic model help develop an evaluation's purpose and key questions?

Creating a Flowchart Logic Model

Handout for Activity 16

Assumptions
Resources
Activities
Outputs
Short-Term Outcomes
Long-Term Outcomes

Activity 17

Developing an Evaluation's Purpose Statement

Overview

This activity asks participants to critique a variety of evaluation purpose statements and to develop a purpose statement for an evaluation they are currently working on or have recently completed.

Instructional Objectives

Participants will

- Identify key components of an evaluation purpose statement
- Critique several evaluation purpose statements
- Write a purpose statement for an evaluation they are currently working on or have recently completed

Number of Participants

- Minimum number of participants: 3
- Maximum number of participants: unlimited when participants are in groups of 3 to 5

Time Estimate: 45 to 60 minutes

In addition to providing the necessary background information on developing evaluation purpose statements and the concepts of developmental, formative, and summative evaluation, this activity requires approximately 45 to 60 minutes, depending on the number of participants (or groups) and the time available for discussion.

Materials Needed

- Pens/pencils
- Handout "Sample Evaluation Purpose Statements"
- Handout "Critiquing Evaluation Purpose Statements"

Instructional Method

Small-group work/individual work

Procedures

Facilitator's tasks:

- Ask participants to get into groups of three to five people.
- Distribute the handout "Sample Evaluation Purpose Statements."
- Distribute the handout "Critiquing Evaluation Purpose Statements."
- Instruct participants to consider each of the purpose statements and to answer the questions on the handout "Critiquing Evaluation Purpose Statements."
- Invite groups to share their thoughts about one of the purpose statements they worked on. Ask other participants if they came up with any different ideas for that particular purpose statement.
- As an individual task, ask participants to write an evaluation purpose statement for an evaluation they are planning or one that they have recently completed.
- Ask participants to pair up with another participant and to share their purpose statement to obtain constructive feedback.
- Debrief the activity by asking the following questions:
  - In what ways does the purpose statement shape the evaluation?
  - What was your experience in writing the purpose statement?
  - How might you approach writing an evaluation's purpose statement in the future?

Sample Evaluation Purpose Statements

Handout for Activity 17

1. The purpose of the evaluation is to determine employees' level of awareness of the new vision for the organization. This information will be used to decide whether further training or communication about the new vision is needed.
2. The purpose of this evaluation is to understand the knowledge and skills needed by customer service representatives as they prepare to implement a new order entry system. This information will be used to develop a training program for teaching customer service representatives how to use the new system.
3. The purpose of the evaluation is to determine the cost-effectiveness of providing online word-processing training. The results will be used to determine whether this approach serves the organization's needs better than providing the training in a traditional classroom format.
4. The purpose of the evaluation is to determine whether the listening skills course should continue to be offered.
5. The purpose of the evaluation is to identify the strengths and weaknesses of the newly developed online course on healthy communities. The results will be used to modify and refine the design and content of the course.
6. The purpose of the evaluation is to determine if students' test scores have increased as a result of teachers' involvement in the new professional development program.
7. The purpose of the evaluation is to determine the extent to which supervisors followed the procedures for employees' performance review as presented in the New Supervisors Workshop. In addition to concerns about the design and content of the workshop, the evaluation will examine the factors that support or prevent the use of these skills. The results will be used to modify the workshop design and content, identify interventions to support the use of these skills, or both.
8. The purpose of the evaluation is to obtain the reactions of employees to the newly established program development process. The results will be presented to the Executive Team.

Critiquing Evaluation Purpose Statements

Handout for Activity 17

What is being evaluated?	*How will the results be used?*	*What kind of evaluation does this represent (developmental, formative, summative)?*	*How could the purpose statement be improved?*
1.			
2.			
3.			
4.			
5.			
6.			
7.			
9.			

Activity 18

Identifying Stakeholders and Developing Key Evaluation Questions

Overview

This activity asks participants to identify an evaluation's stakeholders and key questions based on an evaluation plan's background, rationale, and purpose statement.

Instructional Objectives

Participants will

- Discuss elements covered in an evaluation's background, rationale, and purpose statement
- Determine who might be the primary, secondary, and tertiary stakeholders for a given evaluation scenario
- Practice writing key evaluation questions

Number of Participants

- Minimum number of participants: 3
- Maximum number of participants: unlimited when participants are in groups of 3 to 5

Time Estimate: 45 to 60 minutes

In addition to providing the necessary background information on developing an evaluation plan that includes stakeholders and key questions, this activity requires approximately 45 to 60 minutes, depending on the number of participants (or groups) and the time available for discussion.

Materials Needed

- Pens/pencils
- Flipchart, markers, tape
- Handout "Evaluation Plans 1, 2, or 3"
- Handout "Identifying Stakeholders and Developing Key Questions"

Instructional Method

Case scenario

Procedures

Facilitator's tasks:

- Ask participants to get into groups of three to five people.
- Depending on the number of groups, distribute one or more evaluation plans to each group.
- Distribute the handout "Identifying Stakeholders and Developing Key Questions."
- Instruct participants to complete the handout in their groups and to put their ideas on a piece of flipchart paper.
- Invite each group to share its ideas with the larger group.
- Debrief the activity with the following questions:
  - What were your experiences in trying to identify the evaluation's stakeholders?
  - What were your experiences in developing the key evaluation questions?
  - Why do you think this process is so important?
  - To what extent do you think stakeholders should be involved in developing the evaluation's questions?
  - What impact would (or does) stakeholder involvement have in determining the evaluation's questions?
  - What would it mean if you ended up with 20 evaluation questions?

Evaluation Plan 1: The Effectiveness of Using Advanced Electrical Fundamentals for Teaching Professional Development Skills

Handout for Activity 18

Background and Rationale

The National Automotive Technicians Educational Foundation (NATEF) is an accrediting agency that certifies automotive technology education programs nationwide. In 2002, the NATEF standards were revised to require more training hours in the areas of electrical and electronic systems. At the same time, XYZ Community College began requiring all certificate and degree programs to develop program outcomes. One outcome identified was the need for technicians to continue developing their skills after graduation.

As a result of these two influences, the Automotive Department at XYZ decided to offer the course, AU 315, Advanced Electrical Fundamentals. The course was designed so that students would attain the following two outcomes:

1. Develop skills and knowledge to advance as automotive technicians
2. Develop the ability to diagnose electronic devices

Traditionally, the Automotive Technology Department at XYZ has provided competency-based instruction designed to teach specific diagnostic and procedural skills. In this course, students learn to diagnose electronic sensors and actuators with a lab scope through the use of a variety of learning resources readily available to professional automotive technicians. Figure 4.1 shows the logic model for this course.

Purpose Statement

The purpose of this evaluation is to determine the extent to which AU 315 is helping students use multiple resources for learning how to diagnose electronic devices with a lab scope. The results will also be used to improve the effectiveness of future course offerings.

SOURCE: Adapted from an evaluation plan developed by Phil Krolick, Automotive Instructor, Linn-Benton Community College, Albany, Oregon. Used with permission.

Figure 4.1 Logic Module for AU 315, Advanced Electrical Fundamentals

Course Inputs (Resources)	*Course Activities*	*Short-Term Outcomes*	*Long-Term Outcomes*
2002 NATEF requirements	Form study teams to become subject-matter experts for one classification of electronic control devices	Use multiple resources to learn how to diagnose electronic devices using a lab scope	Develop skills and knowledge to advance as automotive technicians
Newly identified program outcomes	Participate in an online forum to learn from other subject-matter experts		Develop the ability to diagnose electronic control devices
Use of the lab scope as a new technology	Use electronic repair database information systems to gather relevant information and test data		
Instructor's skill at supporting learning independently and from peers	Research trade journals on lab scope testing techniques and applications		
Auto faculty input	Experiment with lab scopes and interpretation of patterns		
Collaboration and research skills of students	Brainstorm alternative resources for learning about electronic controls and their diagnoses		
Access to Internet and print resources	Share Internet resources and personal experiences through online forums		
Access to lab scope equipment and vehicle electronics	Build a portfolio of resources and professional development activities used to become more efficient technicians		

Evaluation Plan 2: Development of Questioning Techniques Training Module

Handout for Activity 18

Background and Rationale

The Human Resources Department of the nonprofit organization Helping Society received grant funding from the Kellogg Foundation to conduct a leadership series called *Journey Into Leadership.* The *Journey* program consisted of eight modules related to various facets of leadership skills, knowledge, and application. During the *Journey* program, the evaluator helped create, design, and compile the evaluations for each module's session.

Some of the feedback received from the program participants indicated a greater need for training on topics related to communication. As a result, the training manager and the evaluator discussed the idea of conducting breakout training sessions on other communications topics. Due to time constraints, only a listening skills breakout session was developed. Now that the leadership program has been completed, the training manager is considering the possibility of developing another communication training module. Such a module would provide a follow-up to the feedback received from the leadership program as well as allow for further work on topics mentioned but not fully discussed in the program itself. One topic that was a continual focus during the program was the acknowledgment that a "good" leader has a well-developed communication style that includes the ability to ask appropriate questions.

The evaluator will conduct a training needs assessment (developmental evaluation) not only to determine if a need exists but also to design and implement a possible Questioning Techniques Training Module. The factors that led to the need for or interest in this evaluation are the following:

1. Direct feedback from leadership program participants indicates a greater need for communications-type trainings.

SOURCE: Adapted from an evaluation plan developed by Laura Boehme, Oregon State University, Managing Editor of *Human Resource Development Quarterly.* Used with permission.

2. The *Journey* program and sessions, while discussing frequently the need for "great" communication skills in leaders, fails to highlight specific elements of how to improve communication skills.

3. Some uncertainty exists as to specific training areas to target.

If the questioning techniques training proves to be needed, it will be sponsored by the Human Resource Training and Development Department. The training will also have a direct relationship and benefit to the leadership program participants as a follow-up session. Those who participate in the future training will benefit by moving conversational skills to a deeper and more critical level of thinking and interaction.

Purpose of the Evaluation

The purpose of this evaluation is to determine if there is sufficient interest and need within the Helping Society to warrant the development of a communication skills training specifically focused on questioning techniques. The audience for this training will be participants of the leadership program as well as any other interested employees. The results might be used to create a Questioning Techniques Training Module that will enhance effective communication strategies and skills. A course outcome guide will also be developed using the evaluation results.

Evaluation Plan 3: Evaluation of Volunteer Management Series

Handout for Activity 18

Background and Rationale

In the field of volunteer management, there are few opportunities for comprehensive training for people interested in becoming volunteer managers or who have had the duties incorporated into their job description. Volunteer managers can be described as either paid or unpaid workers who work with a volunteer workforce. Participants come from nonprofit or government programs, community seasonal events, one-time community projects, or for personal interests, but the important aspect is that the person manages or plans to manage a volunteer workforce.

The Volunteer Management Series consists of 10 workshops offered over 10 weeks to a maximum of 15 participants. Each workshop examines a different aspect of volunteer management. Participants are given the opportunity to explore concepts and to develop resources and skills in each area during the series. At the end of the program each participant has developed a comprehensive volunteer management plan and a resource notebook to use in the workplace. The training is designed to prepare participants to develop a volunteer program and manage volunteers in any workplace.

Since this is a new series, an evaluation is needed to determine the effectiveness of the current training structure and to suggest future workshop modifications and improvements. Participants' feedback about the workshops will help determine which activities deliver the intended learning outcomes and which activities need modification to increase learning possibilities. The workshop designer and the funding organization commissioned the evaluation.

Purpose of the Evaluation

The purpose of the evaluation is to determine the strengths and weaknesses of the Volunteer Management Series, a 10-week course on volunteer management that prepares participants to effectively implement a volunteer program within any organization and to manage a volunteer workforce within legal and ethical guidelines. The results of the evaluation will be used to determine the effectiveness of the current model and to modify the workshop series prior to future implementation.

SOURCE: Adapted from an evaluation plan developed by Glenis Chapin, Coordinator of Volunteer Services, Marion County, Oregon. Used with permission.

Identifying Stakeholders and Developing Key Questions

Handout for Activity 18

Directions:

Identify the primary, secondary, and tertiary stakeholders for the evaluation, and determine how each group might use or be affected by the evaluation's results. Then, develop possible key evaluation questions.

Who are the stakeholders for this evaluation?	*How might they use or be affected by the evaluation's results?*
Primary stakeholders	
Secondary stakeholders	
Tertiary Stakeholders	
What questions should the evaluation address? (Develop three to five questions.)	

Activity 19

Developing Evaluation Questions

Overview

This activity engages participants in developing evaluation questions that will focus and guide an evaluation study.

Instructional Objectives

Participants will

- Understand the importance of developing broad, overarching questions that will guide an evaluation study
- Experience a method that can be used to involve stakeholders in developing evaluation questions
- Be able to explain what makes a good evaluation question

Number of Participants

- Minimum number of participants: 3
- Maximum number of participants: 24

Time Estimate: 45 to 60 minutes

In addition to providing the necessary background information on developing an evaluation's purpose and the concept of stakeholders, this activity requires approximately 45 to 60 minutes, depending on the number of participants (or groups) and the time available for discussion.

Materials Needed

- Pens/pencils
- Flipchart, markers, tape
- Adhesive notes

Instructional Method

Small-group work

Procedures

Facilitator's tasks:

- Ask participants to get into groups of three to four people.
- Either pre-identify a topic on which to focus an evaluation or invite participants to choose a topic of common interest.
- Place three to four pages of flipchart paper on a wall (this is where participants place their adhesive notes). Label the pages with the title of the evaluation study.
- Develop a purpose statement for the evaluation with input from participants.
- Provide each group with a small stack of adhesive notes.
- Ask groups to construct three to seven questions that an evaluation on the chosen topic might seek to answer. Explain that each question should be written on a separate adhesive note.
- Tell participants that when they have finished writing their questions, they are to place them on the flipchart pages placed on the wall. Instruct them to place them next to other questions that are similar in content.
- Read each question on the flipchart pages and ask for clarification if necessary. Ask participants if those grouped together are similar enough so that they form a theme. Reposition any adhesive notes as determined by the participants.
- Ask participants to develop a label for each category of questions. Reposition any questions that do not fit within the identified categories.
- Explain that when using this approach with a group of stakeholders, they might ask them to prioritize the questions and the categories depending on their information needs, any constraints within the organization or community, and the resources available.
- Debrief the activity with the following questions:
  - What was your experience in developing the questions?
  - What did you learn about developing evaluation key questions?
  - How might this activity work with a group of stakeholders? What benefits might it have to collectively develop the evaluation's questions? Are there any disadvantages of using this process with a group of stakeholders?
  - What makes a good evaluation question?

5

Evaluation Models, Approaches, and Designs

BACKGROUND

This section includes activities that address

- Understanding and selecting evaluation models and approaches
- Understanding and selecting evaluation designs

The following information is provided as a brief introduction to the topics covered in these activities.

EVALUATION MODELS AND APPROACHES

The following models and approaches are frequently mentioned in the evaluation literature.

Behavioral Objectives Approach. This approach focuses on the degree to which the objectives of a program, product, or process have been achieved. The major question guiding this kind of evaluation is, "Is the program, product, or process achieving its objectives?"

The Four-Level Model. This approach is most often used to evaluate training and development programs (Kirkpatrick, 1994). It focuses on four levels of training outcomes: reactions, learning, behavior, and results. The major question guiding this kind of evaluation is, "What impact did the training have on participants in terms of their reactions, learning, behavior, and organizational results?"

Responsive Evaluation. This approach calls for evaluators to be responsive to the information needs of various audiences or stakeholders. The major question guiding this kind of evaluation is, "What does the program look like to different people?"

Goal-Free Evaluation. This approach focuses on the actual outcomes rather than the intended outcomes of a program. Thus, the evaluator has minimal contact with the program managers and staff and is unaware of the program's stated goals and objectives. The major question addressed in this kind of evaluation is, "What are all the effects of the program, including any side effects?"

Adversary/Judicial Approaches. These approaches adapt the legal paradigm to program evaluation. Thus, two teams of evaluators representing two views of the program's effects argue their cases based on the evidence (data) collected. Then, a judge or a panel of judges decides which side has made a better case and makes a ruling. The question this type of evaluation addresses is, "What are the arguments for and against the program?"

Consumer-Oriented Approaches. The emphasis of this approach is to help consumers choose among competing programs or products. *Consumer Reports* provides an example of this type of evaluation. The major question addressed by this evaluation is, "Would an educated consumer choose this program or product?"

Expertise/Accreditation Approaches. The accreditation model relies on expert opinion to determine the quality of programs. The purpose is to provide professional judgments of quality. The question addressed in this kind of evaluation is, "How would professionals rate this program?"

Utilization-Focused Evaluation. According to Patton (1997), "utilization-focused program evaluation is evaluation done for and with specific, intended primary users for specific, intended uses" (p. 23). As such, it assumes that stakeholders will have a high degree of involvement in many, if not all, phases of the evaluation. The major question being addressed is, "What are the information needs of stakeholders, and how will they use the findings?"

Participatory/Collaborative Evaluation. The emphasis of participatory/collaborative forms of evaluation is engaging stakeholders in the evaluation process, so they may better understand evaluation and the program being evaluated and ultimately use the evaluation findings for decision-making purposes. As with utilization-focused evaluation, the major focusing question is, "What are the information needs of those closest to the program?"

Empowerment Evaluation. This approach, as defined by Fetterman (2001), is the "use of evaluation concepts, techniques, and findings to foster improvement and self-determination" (p. 3). The major question characterizing this approach is, "What are the information needs to foster improvement and self-determination?"

Organizational Learning. Some evaluators envision evaluation as a catalyst for learning in the workplace (Preskill & Torres, 1999). Thus, evaluation can be viewed as a social activity in which evaluation issues are constructed by and acted on by organization members. This approach views evaluation as ongoing and integrated into all work practices. The major question in this case is, "What are the information and learning needs of individuals, teams, and the organization in general?"

Theory-Driven Evaluation. This approach to evaluation focuses on theoretical rather than methodological issues. The basic idea is to use the "program's rationale or theory as the basis of an evaluation to understand the program's development and impact" (Smith, 1994, p. 83). By developing a plausible model of how the program is supposed to work, the evaluator can consider social science theories related to the program as well as program resources, activities, processes, and outcomes and assumptions (Bickman, 1987). The major focusing questions here are, "How is the program supposed to work? What are the assumptions underlying the program's development and implementation?"

Success Case Method. This approach to evaluation focuses on the practicalities of defining successful outcomes and success cases (Brinkerhoff, 2003) and uses some of the processes from theory-driven evaluation to determine the linkages, which may take the form of a logic model, an impact model, or a results map. Evaluators using this approach gather stories within the organization to determine what is happening and what is being achieved. The major question this approach asks is, "What is really happening?"

EVALUATION DESIGNS

Evaluation designs that collect quantitative data fall into one of three categories:

1. Preexperimental
2. Quasi-experimental
3. True experimental designs

The following are brief descriptions of the most commonly used evaluation (and research) designs.

One-Shot Design. In using this design, the evaluator gathers data following an intervention or program. For example, a survey of participants might be administered after they complete a workshop.

Retrospective Pretest. As with the one-shot design, the evaluator collects data at one time but asks for recall of behavior or conditions prior to, as well as after, the intervention or program.

One-Group Pretest-Posttest Design. The evaluator gathers data prior to and following the intervention or program being evaluated.

Time Series Design. The evaluator gathers data prior to, during, and after the implementation of an intervention or program.

Pretest-Posttest Control-Group Design. The evaluator gathers data on two separate groups prior to and following an intervention or program. One group, typically called the experimental or treatment group, receives the intervention. The other group, called the control group, does not receive the intervention.

Posttest-Only Control-Group Design. The evaluator collects data from two separate groups following an intervention or program. One group, typically called the experimental or treatment group, receives the intervention or program, while the other group, typically called the control group, does not receive the intervention. Data are collected from both of these groups only after the intervention.

Case Study Design. When evaluations are conducted for the purpose of understanding the program's context, participants' perspectives, the inner dynamics of situations, and questions related to participants' experiences, and where generalization is not a goal, a case study design, with an emphasis on the collection of qualitative data, might be most appropriate. Case studies involve in-depth descriptive data collection and analysis of individuals, groups, systems, processes, or organizations. In particular, the case study design is most useful when you want to answer *how* and *why* questions and when there is a need to understand the particulars, uniqueness, and diversity of the case.

RETURN-ON-INVESTMENT DESIGNS

Many evaluations, particularly those undertaken within an organizational setting, focus on financial aspects of a program. Typically in such evaluations, the questions involve a program's "worth." Four primary approaches include cost analysis, cost-benefit analysis, cost-effectiveness analysis, and return on investment (ROI).

Cost analysis involves determining all of the costs associated with a program or an intervention. These need to include trainee costs (time, travel, and productivity loss), instructor or facilitator costs, materials costs, facilities costs, as well as development costs. Typically, a cost analysis is undertaken to decide among two or more different alternatives for a program, such as comparing the costs for in-class delivery versus online delivery.

Cost analyses examine only costs. A cost-effectiveness analysis determines the costs as well as the direct outcomes or results of the program. As with cost analyses, the costs are measured in dollars or some other monetary unit. The effectiveness measure may include such things as reduced errors or accidents, improved customer satisfaction, and new skills. The decision maker must decide whether the costs justify the outcomes.

A cost-benefit analysis transforms the effects or results of a program into dollars or some other monetary unit. Then the costs (also calculated in monetary terms) can be compared to the benefits. As an example, let us assume that a modification in the production system is estimated to reduce errors by 10%. Given that production errors cost the company $1,000,000 last year, the new system should save the company $100,000 in the first year and the succeeding year. Assuming that the modification would cost $100,000 and the benefits would last for 3 years, we can calculate the benefit/cost ratio as follows:

Benefit/cost ratio = Program benefits/program costs

Benefit/cost ratio = $300,000/$100,000

Benefit/cost ratio = 3:1

This means that for each dollar spent, the organization would realize three dollars of benefits.

The ROI calculation is often requested by executives. Using the previous example, the formula is as follows:

ROI = [Net program benefits/Program costs] × 100%

ROI = [(Program benefits – Program costs)/Program costs] × 100%

ROI = [($300,000 – $100,000)/$100,000] × 100%

ROI = [$200,000/$100,000] × 100%

ROI = 2 × 100%

ROI = 200%

This means that the costs were recovered, and an additional 200% of the costs were returned as benefits.

RESOURCES

Alkin, M. C. (Ed.). (2004). *Evaluation roots: Tracing theorists' views and influences.* Thousand Oaks, CA: Sage.

Bickman, L. (1987). The function of program theory. In P. J. Rogers, T. A. Haccsi, A. Petrosino, & T. A. Huebner (Eds.), *Using program theory in education* (New Directions for Program Evaluation, Vol. 33, pp. 5-18). San Francisco: Jossey Bass.

Bloom, B. S., Engelhart, M. D., Furst, E. J., Hill, W. H., & Krathwohl, D. R. (1956). *Taxonomy of educational objectives: Handbook I: Cognitive domain.* New York: David McKay.

Brigham, E. F., Gapenski, L. C., & Ehrhart, M. C. (1998). *Financial management: Theory and practice* (9th ed.). New York: Thomson.

Brinkerhoff, R. O. (2003). *The success case method: Find out quickly what's working and what's not.* San Francisco: Berrett-Koehler.

Chen, H. T. (1990). *Theory-driven evaluations.* Newbury Park, CA: Sage.

Cousins, J. B., & Whitmore, E. (1998). Framing participatory evaluation. In E. Whitmore (Ed.), *Understanding and practicing participatory evaluation* (New Directions for Evaluation, Vol. 80, pp. 5-23). San Francisco: Jossey-Bass.

Fetterman, D. M. (2001). *Foundations of empowerment evaluation.* Thousand Oaks, CA: Sage.

House, E. R. (1993). *Professional evaluation: Social impact and political consequences.* Thousand Oaks, CA: Sage.

Kee, J. E. (1994). Benefit-cost analysis in program evaluation. In J. S. Wholey, H. P. Hatry, & K. E. Newcomer (Eds.), *Handbook of practical program evaluation* (pp. 456-488). San Francisco: Jossey-Bass.

Kirkpatrick, D. (1994). *Evaluating training programs: The four levels.* San Francisco: Berrett-Koehler.

Levin, H. M., & McEwan, P. J. (2001). *Cost-effectiveness analysis: Methods and applications* (2nd ed.). Thousand Oaks, CA: Sage.

Mager, R. F. (1962). *Preparing instructional objectives.* Palo Alto, CA: Fearon Press.

Mark, M. M., Henry, G. T., & Julnes, G. (2000). *Evaluation: An integrated framework for understanding, guiding, and improving policies and programs.* San Francisco: Jossey-Bass.

Patton, M. Q. (1997). *Utilization-focused evaluation: The new century text.* Thousand Oaks, CA: Sage.

Phillips, J. J. (1997). *Return on investment in training and development programs.* Houston, TX: Gulf Publishing.

Preskill, H., & Torres, R. T. (1999). *Evaluative inquiry for learning in organizations.* Thousand Oaks, CA: Sage.

Russ-Eft, D., & Preskill, H. (2001). *Evaluation in organizations: A systematic approach to learning, performance, and change.* Boston: Perseus.

Scriven, M. (1973). Goal-free evaluation. In E. R. House (Ed.), *School evaluation* (pp. 319-328). Berkeley, CA: McCutchan.

Scriven, M. (1994). Product evaluation—The state of the art. *Evaluation Practice, 15*(1), 45-62.

Shadish, W. R., Cook, T. D., & Leviton, L. C. (1995). *Foundations of program evaluation: Theories of practice.* Thousand Oaks, CA: Sage.

Smith, N. L. (1994). Clarifying and expanding the application of program theory-driven evaluations. *Evaluation Practice, 15*(1), 83-87.

Stake, R. E. (1995). *The art of case study research.* Thousand Oaks, CA: Sage.

Stake, R. E. (2004). *Standards-based and responsive evaluation.* Thousand Oaks, CA: Sage.

Stufflebeam, D. L. (Ed.). (2001). *Evaluation models* (New Directions for Evaluation, Vol. 89). San Francisco: Jossey-Bass.

Swanson, R. A., & Holton, E. F., III (1999). *Results: How to assess performance, learning, and perceptions in organizations.* San Francisco: Berrett-Koehler.

Wolf, R. L. (1975). Trial by jury: A new evaluation method. *Phi Delta Kappan, 57,* 185-187.

Worthen, B. R., Sanders, J. R., & Fitzpatrick, J. L. (1997). *Program evaluation: Alternative approaches and practice guidelines* (2nd ed.). New York: Longman.

Yin, R. K. (2002). *Case study research: Design and methods* (3rd ed.). Thousand Oaks, CA: Sage.

Activity 20

Determining When and Where to Use Various Evaluation Models and Approaches

Overview

This activity provides participants with an understanding of various evaluation models and approaches and how they can be used.

Instructional Objectives

Participants will

- Describe the conditions under which certain evaluation models or approaches may be most effective or appropriate
- Discuss the implications of using various evaluation models and approaches for an evaluation study
- Discuss when and how one chooses to use a particular evaluation model or approach

Number of Participants

- Minimum number of participants: 3
- Maximum number of participants: unlimited when participants are in groups of 3 to 5

Time Estimate: 45 to 60 minutes

In addition to providing the necessary background information on various evaluation models and approaches, this activity requires approximately 45 to 60 minutes, depending on the number of participants (or groups) and the time available for discussion.

Materials Needed

- Pens/pencils
- Flipchart, markers, tape
- Handout "Evaluation Models and Approaches"

Instruction Method

Small-group work

Procedures

Facilitator's tasks:

- Ask participants to get into groups of three to five people.
- Depending on the number of groups, distributes one or two different handouts (models and approaches) to each group.
- Instruct participants, as a group, to complete the handout.
- Invite groups to share their ideas with the larger group. Ask other participants to add their ideas if they worked on this model or approach.
- Debrief the activity with the following questions:
  - Which models or approaches seem similar or compatible? In what ways are they similar or compatible?
  - Which models or approaches have different orientations? How might these differences manifest themselves in an evaluation?
  - Which of the models or approaches would fit within the context of the organization or organizations with which you typically work?
  - How do you think one decides which models and approaches to use for any one evaluation? What criteria would you use to determine the most appropriate model and approach for a given evaluation context?

Evaluation Models and Approaches

Handout for Activity 20

Behavioral Objectives

This approach focuses on the degree to which the objectives of a program, product, or process have been achieved. The major question guiding this kind of evaluation is, "Is the program, product, or process achieving its objectives?"

What are some examples or situations in which you would use this approach?	*What conditions need to exist to use this approach?*	*What are some limitations of this approach?*

Evaluation Models and Approaches

Handout for Activity 20

The Four-Level Model

This approach is most often used to evaluate training and development programs (Kirkpatrick, 1994). It focuses on four levels of training outcomes: reactions, learning, behavior, and results. The major question guiding this kind of evaluation is, "What impact did the training have on participants in terms of their reactions, learning, behavior, and organizational results?"

What are some examples or situations in which you would use this approach?	*What conditions need to exist to use this approach?*	*What are some limitations of this approach?*

Reference

Kirkpatrick, D. (1994). *Evaluating training programs: The four levels.* San Francisco: Berrett-Koehler.

Evaluation Models and Approaches

Handout for Activity 20

Responsive Evaluation

This approach calls for evaluators to be responsive to the information needs of various audiences or stakeholders. The major question guiding this kind of evaluation is, "What does the program look like to different people?"

What are some examples or situations in which you would use this approach?	*What conditions need to exist to use this approach?*	*What are some limitations of this approach?*

Evaluation Models and Approaches

Handout for Activity 20

Goal-Free Evaluation

This approach focuses on the actual outcomes rather than the intended outcomes of a program. Thus, the evaluator has minimal contact with the program managers and staff and is unaware of the program's stated goals and objectives. The major question addressed in this kind of evaluation is, "What are all the effects of the program, including any side effects?"

What are some examples or situations in which you would use this approach?	*What conditions need to exist to use this approach?*	*What are some limitations of this approach?*

Evaluation Models and Approaches

Handout for Activity 20

Adversary/Judicial

These approaches adapt the legal paradigm to program evaluation. Thus, two teams of evaluators representing two views of the program's effects argue their case based on the evidence (data) collected. Then, a judge or a panel of judges decides which side made a better case and makes a ruling. The question this type of evaluation addresses is, "What are the arguments for and against the program?"

What are some examples or situations in which you would use this approach?	*What conditions need to exist to use this approach?*	*What are some limitations of this approach?*

Evaluation Models and Approaches

Handout for Activity 20

Consumer-Oriented

The emphasis in this approach is to help consumers choose among competing programs or products. *Consumer Reports* provides an example of this type of evaluation. The major question addressed by this evaluation is, "Would an educated consumer choose this program or product?"

What are some examples or situations in which you would use this approach?	*What conditions need to exist to use this approach?*	*What are some limitations of this approach?*

Evaluation Models and Approaches

Handout for Activity 20

Utilization-Focused

According to Patton (1997), "utilization-focused program evaluation is evaluation done for and with specific, intended primary users for specific, intended uses" (p. 23). As such, it assumes that stakeholders will have a high degree of involvement in many, if not all, phases of the evaluation. The major question being addressed is, "What are the information needs of stakeholders, and how will they use the findings?"

What are some examples or situations in which you would use this approach?	*What conditions need to exist to use this approach?*	*What are some limitations of this approach?*

Reference

Patton, M. Q. (1997). *Utilization-focused evaluation: The new century text.* Thousand Oaks, CA: Sage.

Evaluation Models and Approaches

Handout for Activity 20

Expertise/Accreditation

The accreditation model relies on expert opinion to determine the quality of programs. The purpose is to provide professional judgments of quality. The question addressed in this kind of evaluation is, "How would professionals rate this program?"

What are some examples or situations in which you would use this approach?	*What conditions need to exist to use this approach?*	*What are some limitations of this approach?*

Evaluation Models and Approaches

Handout for Activity 20

Participatory/Collaborative

The emphasis of participatory/collaborative forms of evaluation is engaging stakeholders in the evaluation process, so they may better understand evaluation and the program being evaluated and ultimately use the evaluation findings for decision-making purposes. As with utilization-focused evaluation, the major focusing question is, "What are the information needs of those closest to the program?"

What are some examples or situations in which you would use this approach?	*What conditions need to exist to use this approach?*	*What are some limitations of this approach?*

Evaluation Models and Approaches

Handout for Activity 20

Empowerment

This approach, as defined by Fetterman (2001), is the "use of evaluation concepts, techniques, and findings to foster improvement and self-determination" (p. 3). The major question characterizing this approach is, "What are the information needs to foster improvement and self-determination?"

What are some examples or situations in which you would use this approach?	*What conditions need to exist to use this approach?*	*What are some limitations of this approach?*

Reference

Fetterman, D. M. (2001). *Foundations of empowerment evaluation.* Thousand Oaks, CA: Sage.

Evaluation Models and Approaches

Handout for Activity 20

Organizational Learning

Some evaluators envision evaluation as a catalyst for learning in the workplace (Preskill & Torres, 1999). Thus, evaluation can be viewed as a social activity in which evaluation issues are constructed by and acted on by organizational members. This approach views evaluation as ongoing and integrated into all work practices. The major question in this case is, "What are the information and learning needs of individuals, teams, and the organization in general?"

What are some examples or situations in which you would use this approach?	*What conditions need to exist to use this approach?*	*What are some limitations of this approach?*

Reference

Preskill, H., & Torres, R. T. (1999). *Evaluative inquiry for learning in organizations.* Thousand Oaks, CA: Sage.

Evaluation Models and Approaches

Handout for Activity 20

Theory-Driven

This approach to evaluation focuses on theoretical rather than methodological issues. The basic idea is to use the "program's rationale or theory as the basis of an evaluation to understand the program's development and impact" (Smith, 1994, p. 83). By developing a plausible model of how the program is supposed to work, the evaluator can consider social science theories related to the program as well as program resources, activities, processes, and outcomes and assumptions (Bickman, 1987). The major focusing questions of this approach are, "How is the program supposed to work? What are the assumptions underlying the program's development and implementation?"

What are some examples or situations in which you would use this approach?	*What conditions need to exist to use this approach?*	*What are some limitations of this approach?*

References

Bickman, L. (1987). The function of program theory. In P. J. Rogers, T. A. Haccsi, A. Petrosino, & T. A. Huebner (Eds.), *Using program theory in education* (New Directions for Program Evaluation, Vol. 33, pp. 5-18). San Francisco: Jossey Bass.

Smith, N. L. (1994). Clarifying and expanding the application of program theory-driven evaluations. *Evaluation Practice, 15*(1), 83-87.

Evaluation Models and Approaches

Handout for Activity 20

Success Case Method

This approach to evaluation focuses on the practicalities of defining successful outcomes and success cases (Brinkerhoff, 2003) and uses some of the processes from theory-driven evaluation to determine the linkages, which may take the form of a logic model, an impact model, or a results map. Evaluators using this approach then gather success stories within the organization to determine what is happening and what is being achieved. The major question this approach asks is, "What is really happening?"

What aspects of the training will you evaluate?	*What variables will you focus on?*	*What are some potential limitations of the evaluation and its findings?*

Reference

Brinkerhoff, R. O. (2003). *The success case method: Find out quickly what's working and what's not.* San Francisco: Berrett-Koehler.

Activity 21

Recommending an Evaluation Approach

Overview

This activity asks participants to consider several evaluation approaches and to choose one or more that would serve the stakeholders' information needs.

Instructional Objectives

Participants will

- Learn about and discuss various approaches to conducting an evaluation and the relative merits of each one
- Read a case scenario and choose one or more approaches that address the questions posed in the case
- Present the reasons for selecting a particular evaluation approach

Number of Participants

- Minimum number of participants: 6
- Maximum number of participants: 25

Time Estimate: 45 to 90 minutes

In addition to providing the necessary background information about different approaches to conducting an evaluation, this activity requires approximately 45 to 90 minutes, depending on the number of participants (or groups) and the time available for discussion.

Materials Needed

- Pens/pencils
- Flipchart, markers, tape

- Handout "Program Evaluation Approaches"
- Handout "Evaluating a Sales Training Program"
- Handout "Evaluating a Great Books Reading Program"

Instructional Method

Case scenario

Procedures

Facilitator's tasks:

- Decide whether to have participants work on one of the case scenarios, let participants choose one of the scenarios in their small groups, or divide the group in half and assign one scenario to each group.
- Ask participants to get into groups of three to five people.
- Provide participants with the handout "Program Evaluation Approaches" and either or both of the case scenarios: "Evaluating a Sales Training Program" and "Evaluating a Great Books Program."
- Ask groups to read their case scenarios and answer the questions posed on the handout.
- Instruct groups that they will have 3 minutes to make their presentations to the vice president of sales and the director of marketing.
- Invite groups to make their presentations.
- Debrief the activity by asking the following questions:
  - What did you learn from this activity?
  - What other information would have helped you choose your approach?
  - To what extent do you think the choice of approach affects the outcomes of an evaluation?
  - How does one choose an evaluation approach? What criteria drove your choices?

Program Evaluation Approaches

Handout for Activity 21

Behavioral Objectives Approach. This approach focuses on the degree to which the objectives of a program, product, or process have been achieved. The major question guiding this kind of evaluation is, "Is the program, product, or process achieving its objectives?"

The Four-Level Model. This approach is most often used to evaluate training and development programs (Kirkpatrick, 1994). It focuses on four levels of training outcomes: reactions, learning, behavior, and results. The major question guiding this kind of evaluation is, "What impact did the training have on participants in terms of their reactions, learning, behavior, and organizational results?"

Responsive Evaluation. This approach calls for evaluators to be responsive to the information needs of various audiences or stakeholders. The major question guiding this kind of evaluation is, "What does the program look like to different people?"

Goal-Free Evaluation. This approach focuses on the actual outcomes rather than the intended outcomes of a program. Thus, the evaluator has minimal contact with the program managers and staff and is unaware of the program's stated goals and objectives. The major question addressed in this kind of evaluation is, "What are all the effects of the program, including any side effects?"

Adversary/Judicial Approaches. These approaches adapt the legal paradigm to program evaluation. Thus, two teams of evaluators representing two views of the program's effects argue their case based on the evidence (data) collected. Then, a judge or a panel of judges decides which side made a better case and makes a ruling. The question this type of evaluation addresses is, "What are the arguments for and against the program?"

Consumer-Oriented Approaches. The emphasis in this approach is to help consumers choose among competing programs or products. *Consumer Reports* provides an example of this type of evaluation. The major question addressed by this evaluation is, "Would an educated consumer choose this program or product?"

Expertise/Accreditation Approaches. The accreditation model relies on expert opinion to determine the quality of programs. The purpose is to provide professional

---

SOURCE: From Russ-Eft and Preskill (2001).

judgments of quality. The question addressed in this kind of evaluation is, "How would professionals rate this program?"

Utilization-Focused Evaluation. According to Patton (1997), "utilization-focused program evaluation is evaluation done for and with specific, intended primary users for specific, intended uses" (p. 23). As such, it assumes that stakeholders will have a high degree of involvement in many, if not all, phases of the evaluation. The major question being addressed is, "What are the information needs of stakeholders, and how will they use the findings?"

Participatory/Collaborative Evaluation. The emphasis of participatory/collaborative forms of evaluation is engaging stakeholders in the evaluation process, so they may better understand evaluation and the program being evaluated and ultimately use the evaluation findings for decision-making purposes. As with utilization-focused evaluation, the major focusing question is, "What are the information needs of those closest to the program?"

Empowerment Evaluation. This approach, as defined by Fetterman (2001), is the "use of evaluation concepts, techniques, and findings to foster improvement and self-determination. It is attentive to empowering processes and outcomes" (p. 3). The major question characterizing this approach is, "What are the information needs to foster improvement and self-determination?"

Organizational Learning. Some evaluators envision evaluation as a catalyst for learning in the workplace (Preskill & Torres, 1999). Thus, evaluation can be viewed as a social activity in which evaluation issues are constructed by and acted on by organizational members. This approach views evaluation as ongoing and integrated into all work practices. The major question in this case is, "What are the information and learning needs of individuals, teams, and the organization in general?"

Theory-Driven Evaluation. This approach to evaluation focuses on theoretical rather than methodological issues. The basic idea is to use the "program's rationale or theory as the basis of an evaluation to understand the program's development and impact" (Smith, 1994, p. 83). By developing a plausible model of how the program is supposed to work, the evaluator can consider social science theories related to the program as well as program resources, activities, processes, and outcomes and assumptions (Bickman, 1987). The major focusing questions with this approach are, "How is the program supposed to work? What are the assumptions underlying the program's development and implementation?"

Success Case Method. This approach to evaluation focuses on the practicalities of defining successful outcomes and success cases (Brinkerhoff, 2003). The approach uses some of the processes from theory-driven evaluation to determine the linkages, which may take the form of a logic model, an impact model, or a results map. Evaluators using this approach then gather stories within the organization to determine what is happening and what is being achieved. The major question this approach asks is, "What is really happening?"

References

Bickman, L. (1987). The function of program theory. In P. J. Rogers, T. A. Haccsi, A. Petrosino, & T. A. Huebner (Eds.), *Using program theory in education* (New Directions for Program Evaluation, Vol. 33, pp. 5-18). San Francisco: Jossey Bass.

Brinkerhoff, R. O. (2003). *The success case method: Find out quickly what's working and what's not.* San Francisco: Berrett-Koehler.

Fetterman, D. M. (2001). *Foundations of empowerment evaluation.* Thousand Oaks, CA: Sage.

Kirkpatrick, D. (1994). *Evaluating training programs: The four levels.* San Francisco: Berrett-Koehler.

Patton, M. Q. (1997). *Utilization-focused evaluation: The new century text.* Thousand Oaks, CA: Sage.

Preskill, H., & Torres, R. T. (1999). *Evaluative inquiry for learning in organizations.* Thousand Oaks, CA: Sage.

Smith, N. L. (1994). Clarifying and expanding the application of program theory-driven evaluations. *Evaluation Practice, 15*(1), 83-87.

Evaluating a Sales Training Program

Handout for Activity 21

You are an external consultant bidding on a request for proposals. In your conversation with the vice president of sales, you learn the following:

> The Velocom Company is a global enterprise providing electronic products and services to businesses throughout the world. Because of increasing competition and recent turnover among the sales staff, the vice president of sales and the director of marketing have designed and implemented a new sales training program for all recently hired sales personnel. The sales training is 3 days long and is scheduled to occur twice a year. The program was designed by the two internal trainers who also serve as the program's instructors. The content of the training covers basic sales topics, such as how to begin the sales discussion, how to ask the right questions, and how to ask for the sale. Fifty salespeople have completed the training program in the last 12 months.
>
> Although the vice president of sales and the director of marketing believe this training program is successful, they wish to conduct a more systematic evaluation of its impact on the new sales force. They are therefore looking for an evaluator (evaluation team) to conduct the sales training evaluation.

In Your Groups

1. Discuss each of the evaluation approaches on the handout "Program Evaluation Approaches."
2. Determine which of these approaches you think would best serve this evaluation (you may recommend a hybrid of approaches).
3. Develop a 3-minute presentation outlining your reasons for selecting this particular approach—be prepared to present your idea to the vice president of sales and the director of marketing. (You may use whatever tools or props might be helpful.)

Evaluating a Great Books Reading Program

Handout for Activity 21

The mission of the Tecolote Group at St. John's College in Santa Fe, New Mexico, is to "acknowledge the dignity of New Mexico's teachers at all levels by providing occasions for building ideas through structured discussion of centrally important texts, thus bringing to life the idea that great books make great teachers." Several different foundations and individual contributors have provided funding for Tecolote.

The Tecolote Group invites approximately 40 teachers per session to attend a series of four all-day Saturday seminars, where they discuss books selected on a particular topic. For example, the theme for the 2003–2004 colloquium series, Phenomenon of Learning, began with Plato's *Meno* and was followed with the work of Aristotle, John Dewey, and Stephen Pinker.

The colloquia are characterized by the following:

- They are designed to be noncompetitive so that participants may explore and learn through shared inquiry.
- They target no particular discipline or grade level but focus on books and questions that all teachers can profitably discuss.
- Participants are chosen with attention to diversity of experience, location, ethnicity, gender, and age.
- All books, other materials, and meals are provided at no charge.
- There is no tuition, and participants receive a modest honorarium for attendance.

The expected outcomes of the program are that teachers return to their classrooms with a renewed sense of their vocation and motivation to develop new initiatives, which they are willing to share with others.

The Tecolote Group has been providing these colloquia for 3 years and has now decided to evaluate the program. They have hired you to conduct the evaluation. The first thing they want to know is what evaluation approach you will use.

SOURCE: February, 2003, colloquia synopsis of The Tecolote Group at St. John's College, Santa Fe, New Mexico.

In Your Groups

1. Discuss each of the evaluation approaches on the handout "Program Evaluation Approaches."
2. Determine which of these approaches you think would best serve this evaluation (you may recommend a hybrid of approaches).
3. Develop a 3-minute presentation outlining your reasons for selecting this particular approach—be prepared to present your idea to the executive director of the Tecolote Group. (You may use whatever tools or props might be helpful.)

Activity 22

Applying Kirkpatrick's Four-Level Approach to Evaluating Training

Overview

This activity helps participants understand appropriate uses of the Kirkpatrick (1994) four-level approach to evaluating training and development programs.

Instructional Objectives

Participants will

- Apply Kirkpatrick's four-level approach to an evaluation case scenario
- Consider and discuss the advantages and disadvantages of using this four-level approach to evaluating training and development programs
- Discuss the reasons why the Kirkpatrick approach has been so popular in the training and development field

Number of Participants

- Minimum number of participants: 4
- Maximum number of participants: 24

Time Estimate: 45 to 60 minutes

In addition to providing the necessary background information on Kirkpatrick's four-level approach to evaluating training and development programs, this activity requires approximately 45–60 minutes, depending on the number of participants and the time available for discussion.

Materials Needed

- Pens/pencils
- Flipchart, markers, tape

- Handout "Sales Training at the Verkauf Company"
- Handout "Variables That Affect the Outcomes of Learning, Performance, and Change Initiatives"

Instructional Method

Case scenario

Procedures

Facilitator's tasks:

- Divide participants into four groups and assign each group one of Kirkpatrick's four-levels: 1. Reactions, 2. Learning, 3. Behavior, or 4. Results.
- Distribute the handouts "Sales Training at the Verkauf Company," "Applying the Kirkpatrick Four-Level Approach to Evaluating Training," and "Variables That Affect the Outcomes of Learning, Performance, and Change Initiatives."
- Ask groups to complete the "Applying the Kirkpatrick Four-Level Approach to Evaluating Training" handout and to write their ideas on a piece of flipchart paper.
- Ask groups to present the information from their flipchart pages.
- Debrief the activity with the following questions:
  - What issues arose as you tried to focus the evaluation?
  - How did you decide which variables your evaluation would focus on?
  - What are the limitations of the Kirkpatrick approach?
  - What is missing from this evaluation approach?
  - Why do you think the Kirkpatrick approach has been so heavily relied on in the training and development field?
  - What could be done to make this approach be more useful, relevant, and effective?

Reference

Kirkpatrick, D. (1994). *Evaluating training programs: The four levels.* San Francisco: Berrett-Koehler.

Sales Training at the Verkauf Company

Handout for Activity 22

The Verkauf Company is a newly formed organization that provides business services to European enterprises. The vice presidents of sales and marketing decide to offer sales training to all recently hired sales personnel. The sales training takes place as part of the already scheduled regional sales meetings, and the Human Resource Development Department provides the needed trainers. The training covers basic topics, such as how to begin the sales discussion, how to ask the right questions, and how to ask for the sale. Although the two vice presidents believe that this training will be successful, they have requested that you evaluate this training program. You decide to use the Kirkpatrick four-level approach.

Applying the Kirkpatrick Four-Level Approach to Evaluating Training

Kirkpatrick level your group is working on: ______________________________

What aspects of the training will you evaluate?	*What variables will you focus on?*	*What are some potential limitations of the evaluation and its findings?*

Variables That Affect the Outcomes of Learning, Performance, and Change Initiatives

Handout for Activity 22

Organizations

- Orientation to change
- Commitment to training and learning
- Resources for training and learning
- Financial situation
- Organizational culture

Trainees

- Motivation to learn
- Readiness for training
- Motivation to transfer learning
- Attitude about and commitment to the job
- Opportunity to apply learning

Trainers

- Facilitation skills
- Content knowledge
- Level of interest/enthusiasm
- Credibility
- Listening skills

Managers

- Ability and willingness to coach on new skills
- Ability and willingness to model new skills
- Expectations of improved job performance
- Provision for time and resources for trainees to use new knowledge and skills
- Communication of the value of training and learning

SOURCE: Adapted from Russ-Eft and Preskill (2001).

Training Program Design

- Based on a needs assessment
- Clearly identified training population
- Goals and objectives that are related to identified needs
- Use of a variety of learning/teaching strategies
- Based on adult learning theories and principles

Training Program Implementation

- Appropriate materials to facilitate learning
- Adequate facilities for delivering the program effectively
- Availability of needed equipment
- Adequate schedule for content being delivered

Reference

Russ-Eft, D., & Preskill, H. (2001). *Evaluation in organizations: A systematic approach to learning, performance, and change.* Boston: Perseus.

Activity 23

Debating the Usefulness of the Kirkpatrick Four-Level Approach to Evaluating Training and Development Programs

Overview

This activity engages participants in a debate concerning the strengths and weaknesses of the Kirkpatrick four-level approach to evaluating training and development programs.

Instructional Objectives

Participants will

- Increase their understanding of the Kirkpatrick four-level approach to evaluating training and development programs
- Identify the strengths and weaknesses of the Kirkpatrick approach to evaluating training and development programs
- Discuss how the training and development field can increase its use of other evaluation models and approaches

Number of Participants

- Minimum number of participants: 8
- Maximum number of participants: 24

Time Estimate: 45 to 60 minutes

In addition to providing the necessary background information on the Kirkpatrick four-level evaluation approach, this activity requires 45 to 60 minutes, depending on the number of participants and the time available for discussion.

Materials Needed

- Pens/pencils
- Handout "The Flawed Four-Level Evaluation Model"
- Handout "Invited Reaction: Reaction to Holton Article"
- Handout "Final Word: Response to Reaction to Holton Article"
- Handout "Debating Points"

Instructional Method

Debate

Procedures

Prior to Class

Facilitator's tasks:

- Make copies of handouts for each participant:
  - Handout "The Flawed Four-Level Evaluation Model"
  - Handout "Invited Reaction: Reaction to Holton Article"
  - Handout "Final Word: Response to Reaction to Holton Article"
- Distribute articles to participants and ask them to read them before the next meeting.

During Class

Facilitator's tasks:

- Assign participants to one of two groups: 1. Pro Four-Level Approach or 2. Con Four-Level Approach.
- Ask participants to take out the Holton and Kirkpatrick articles.
- Distribute the handout "Debating Points."
- Instruct groups to first complete the handout, after which time the debate will begin.
- Explain the rules of the debate:
  - Groups will select four members of their team to be the debaters. The rest of the team will be in a support position. Their role is to provide the debaters with information as needed. This information can be shared only by writing notes—they are not allowed to talk to the debaters during the debate.
  - Each side will have 3 minutes to make an opening statement.
  - For the next 16 minutes, the two sides will take turns making their case. They will each have eight 1-minute turns for making their case or rebuttal.
  - Teams will then have 3 minutes to make their closing arguments.

- Debrief the activity with the following questions:
  - What other arguments might have been offered to support your group's position?
  - What other arguments might have been offered to support the opposing group's position?
  - To what extent do you personally agree with Holton or Kirkpatrick?
  - How might the field of training and development reconcile these two positions?
  - What can human resource development professionals do to introduce other evaluation approaches to the field?

"The Flawed Four-Level Evaluation Model"

Handout for Activity 23

Elwood F. Holton III

The lack of research to develop further a theory of evaluation is a glaring shortcoming for human resource development (HRD). In this paper, I argue that the four-level system of training evaluation is really a taxonomy of outcomes and is flawed as an evaluation model. Research is needed to develop a fully specified and researchable evaluation model. Such a model needs to specify outcomes correctly, account for the effects of intervening variables that affect outcomes, and indicate causal relationships. I propose a new model based on existing research that accounts for the impact of the primary intervening variables, such as motivation to learn, trainability, job attitudes, personal characteristics, and transfer of training conditions. A new role for participant reactions is specified. Key studies supporting the model are reviewed and a research agenda proposed.

Evaluation of interventions is among the most critical issues faced by the field of human resource development (HRD) today. Increasing global competition has led to intense pressure on HRD to demonstrate that programs contribute directly to the organization's "bottom-line." Yet the dominant evaluation model, the four-level Kirkpatrick model, has received alarmingly little research and is seldom fully implemented in organizations (Kimmerling, 1993), leaving them ill-equipped to respond to this pressure. There is a critical need for new evaluation theory and research to give organizations a more sound methodology for allocating HRD resources.

The Kirkpatrick model for training evaluation (Kirkpatrick, 1976), also known as the four-level evaluation model, is acknowledged by many practitioners as the standard in the field. A number of modifications to the model have been suggested, including adding a fifth level to reflect training's ultimate value in terms of organization success criteria, such as economic benefits or human good (Hamblin, 1974) and societal value (Kaufman & Keller, 1994), or to focus more specifically on return on investment (ROI)

Holton, E. F. III (1996). The flawed four-level evaluation model. *Human Resource Development Quarterly, 7*, 5-21.

NOTE: Elwood F. Holton III is currently professor of human resource development, Louisiana State University, Baton Rouge.

(Phillips, 1995). Brinkerhoff (1987) proposed a six-level model that, in essence, added two formative evaluation states as precursors to Kirkpatrick's four levels. Although this work has contributed greatly to our conceptual thinking about evaluation, the models have received incomplete implementation and little empirical testing.

All of them are labeled as *taxonomies,* which are simply classification schemes (Bobko & Russell, 1991). Bobko and Russell, citing Wallace (1983), noted that exploratory designs and case studies are the first steps in theory development, whereas the final steps are correlational and experimental studies. According to them, taxonomies are the link between the initial stages and the final confirmatory stages of developing theory. Although the Kirkpatrick model is elegant in its simplicity and has contributed greatly to HRD, the lack of research to develop further a theory of evaluation is a glaring shortcoming for the field. If HRD is to continue to grow as a profession, an evaluation model grounded in research is necessary.

One shortcoming of taxonomies is that they do not fully identify all constructs underlying the phenomena of interest, thus making validation impossible. Not surprisingly, Alliger and Janak (1989), in their comprehensive review of research on the four-level model, note that the implied causal relationships between each level of this taxonomy have not been demonstrated by research. Their search of the relevant academic literature located only 12 articles since 1959 reporting 26 correlations between levels in training programs out of 203 articles that reported *any type* of evaluation results. Furthermore, only three studies (Clement, 1982; Noe & Schmitt, 1986; Wexley & Baldwin, 1986) reported full four-level evaluations with correlations. The reported correlations varied widely, casting doubt on assumptions of linear causal relationships.

It can be argued that the correlations reported in these studies were not really a test of the model but rather an alternate approach to analyzing outcomes. For example, if only the four levels of outcomes are measured and a weak correlation is reported between levels two and three, all we really know is that learning from training was not associated with behavior change. In the absence of a fully specified model, we don't know if the correlation is weak because some aspect of the training effort was not effective or because the underlying evaluation model is not valid. Weak correlations might represent a well-functioning model reporting a poorly functioning training effect.

It is not surprising that the reported correlations were weak because the model is really only a taxonomy of training (and HRD) outcomes. Attempts to test causal assumptions within a taxonomy are futile because, by definition, taxonomies classify rather than define causal constructions. Kirkpatrick (1994) is unclear about causal linkages in his model. On the one hand, he discusses the influence of other factors such as organizational climate and motivation to learn on training outcomes, suggesting that the relationships between levels are not simple, linear ones. On the other hand, he makes statements that clearly imply a simple causal relationship between levels. For example, he says that "if training is going to be effective, it is important that trainees react favorably" (p. 27) and that "without learning, no change in behavior will occur" (p. 51). The problem is not that it is a taxonomy but rather that it makes or implies causal statements leading to practical decisions that are outside the bounds of taxonomies. Causal conclusions, which are a necessary part of evaluation, require a more complex model.

Klimoski (1991, pp. 254–256), building upon Dubin (1976), noted that theories or models should have at least six components:

1. *Elements* or *units*—represented as constructs—are the subject matter.
2. There are *relationships* between the constructs.
3. There are *boundaries* or *limits* of generalization.
4. *System states* and *changes* are described.
5. *Deductions* about the theory in operation are expressed as propositions or hypotheses.
6. *Predictions* are made about units.

The four-level model does not meet any of these criteria. First, essential elements are not present. Noticeably absent are the major intervening variables that affect learning and transfer processes such as trainee readiness and motivation, training design, and reinforcement of training on the job (Clement, 1982). Others have proposed models of how individual differences affect training outcomes (Noe, 1986; Noe & Schmitt, 1986) and how factors affect the transfer of training (Baldwin & Ford, 1988; Broad & Newstrom, 1992). Previous evaluation studies identified by Alliger and Janak (1989) did not attempt to measure any intervening variables, which is one likely reason for the wide variation in the correlations reported. No evaluation model can be validated without measuring and accounting for the effects of intervening variables.

Because all of the elements are not present, the relationships between constructs are not fully specified. Considering the third criteria, the four-level model seems to have no limits of generalization within HRD specified. Without full specification of the elements and the relationships, it is questionable whether the model can be applied universally. Furthermore, the missing elements and relationships prohibit making accurate statements about system states, developing propositions and hypotheses, and making predictions.

References

Alliger, G. M., & Janak, E. A. (1989). Kirkpatrick's levels of training criteria: Thirty years later. *Personnel Psychology, 42,* 331-340.

Baldwin, T. T., & Ford, J. K. (1988). Transfer of training: A review and directions for future research. *Personnel Psychology, 41,* 63-100.

Bobko, P., & Russell, C. (1991). A review of the role of taxonomies in human resources management. *Human Resource Management Review, 4,* 293-316.

Brinkerhoff, R. O. (1987). *Achieving results from training.* San Francisco: Jossey-Bass.

Broad, M. L., & Newstrom, J. W. (1992). *Transfer of training.* Reading, MA: Addison-Wesley.

Clement, R. W. (1982). Testing the hierarchy theory of training evaluation: An expanded role for trainee reactions. *Public Personnel Management Journal, 11,* 176-184.

Dubin, R. (1976). Theory building in applied areas. In M. D. Dunnette (Ed.), *Handbook of industrial/organizational psychology.* New York: Rand McNally.

Hamblin, A. C. (1974). *Evaluation and control of training.* New York: McGraw-Hill.

Kaufman, R., & Keller, J. M. (1994). Levels of evaluation: Beyond Kirkpatrick. *Human Resource Development Quarterly, 5,* 371-380.

Kimmerling, G. (1993, September). Gathering the best practices. *Training and Development,* 29-36.

Kirkpatrick, D. L. (1976). Evaluation of training. In R. L. Craig (Ed.), *Training and development handbook.* New York: McGraw-Hill.

Kirkpatrick, D. L. (1994). *Evaluating training programs: The four levels.* San Francisco: Berrett-Koehler.

Klimoski, R. (1991). Theory presentation in human resource management. *Human Resource Management Review, 4,* 253-271.

Noe, R. A. (1986). Trainee attributes and attitudes: Neglected influences on training effectiveness. *Academy of Management Review, 11,* 736-749.

Noe, R. A., & Schmitt, N. (1986). The influence of trainee attitudes on training effectiveness: Test of a model. *Personnel Psychology, 39,* 497-523.

Phillips, J. J. (1995). Return on investment—Beyond the four levels. In E. F. Holton III (Ed.), *Academy of Human Resource Development 1995 Conference Proceedings.*

Wallace, M. (1983). Methodology, research practice, and progress in personnel and industrial relations. *Academy of Management Review, 8,* 6-13.

Wexley, K. N., & Baldwin, T. T. (1986). Posttraining strategies for facilitating positive transfer: An empirical exploration. *Academy of Management Journal, 29,* 503-520.

"Invited Reaction: Reaction to Holton Article"

Handout for Activity 23

Donald L. Kirkpatrick

I didn't know whether to laugh or cry when I read the title to Holton's article, "The Flawed Four-Level Evaluation Model." After I read the article, I still didn't know how to feel. But when I thought about how Holton had "proved"—through various research papers—that the Kirkpatrick model wasn't really a model at all but only a "taxonomy," I decided not to do either. I will admit that I was a little upset when he listed the six components of a model described by Klimoski (1991) and Dubin (1996) and then stated that "the four-level model does not meet any of these criteria." He might at least have said that it met the second criterion of "relationships between the units" because my model (or my taxonomy, if you prefer) does show the relationships among the four levels.

I admit that Holton's article is a scholarly work. Certainly, cites to other articles are plentiful! Many of them have nothing to do with evaluation, but the list is impressive!

The funny thing is that I personally have never called my framework "a model." Someone else described it that way. For example, in a case study presented in *Evaluating Training Programs: The Four Levels* (Kirkpatrick, 1994), Dave Basarab, head of the evaluation department at Motorola, stated, "Motorola University has adopted the Kirkpatrick model for training evaluation" throughout the world. In another case study presented in the book, the authors from CIGNA Corporation called my model "The CIGNA CMD&T Impact Model." The case study by Patrick O'Hara of First Union National Bank referred to it as "the Four-Level Kirkpatrick Evaluation Model." And Eric Freitag of Intel Corporation wrote an article for the book entitled "Implementing the Kirkpatrick Model as an Up-Front Analysis and Evaluation Tool."

SOURCE: Reprinted with permission from Kirkpatrick, D. L. (1996). Invited reaction: Reaction to the Holton article. *Human Resources Development Quarterly, 7,* 23-25.

NOTE: Donald L. Kirkpatrick is professor emeritus of management, University of Wisconsin.

My purpose in offering these illustrations is to demonstrate that, in the real world where training evaluation takes place, the word "model" is commonly used to describe a systematic way of doing something. It may or may not meet the six criteria listed by Klimoski. Personally I don't care whether my work is called a model or a taxonomy as long as it helps to clarify the meaning of evaluation in simple terms and offers guidelines and suggestions on how to accomplish an evaluation. On second thought, I am glad it is not referred to as a taxonomy because if it were, trainers wouldn't know what it meant. The word "model" seems to communicate that it is something to be used as a helpful guide.

I realize that the *Human Resource Development Quarterly* is a scholarly journal that does not publish simple, practical articles. As a former full professor with a Ph.D., I also realize that publishing scholarly articles is required for promotion and recognition in academic circles. I realize too that those who use my model will probably continue to read the *Journal of the American Society of Training and Development,* where the emphasis is on helping the audience rather than on demonstrating the amount of scholarly research done.

Yet I admit I was a little upset by the word "flawed" used in Holton's title. My four-level model has been quoted and used all over the world. Training professionals find it helpful in doing something about evaluation. I have conducted sessions on it at professional conferences in the United States, Venezuela, Mexico, and Singapore. Most recently, in November 1993, I conducted four days of programming for the Arabian American Oil Company in Saudi Arabia.

Indeed, the Holton article tried to tear down the four-level model *without giving any credit to the concepts it depicts.* For example, Holton used the term *reaction,* but not as a level. And the "model" he described used the term *learning,* which is the second level of the Kirkpatrick model. It is interesting that it did not use the term *behavior* but instead a very similar term, *performance.* And, finally, it avoided the word *results* as the fourth level by substituting the words *organizational results.* It seems to me that if my model was so flawed, Holton would not have included so much of it in his concept of a true model.

Finally, in his conclusions, Holton stated that "the model presented here [in his article] is an initial step in the development and testing of a true model of HRD evaluation." He ended by stating that, "If HRD is to grow as a discipline and as a profession, it is imperative that researchers work deliberately to develop a more integrative and testable model." I note that he works at a vocational school. I don't know what qualifications or experience he has with the HRD profession. In contrast, I am a past president of the American Society for Training and Development (ASTD) as well as an author, speaker, and consultant in the field. I regularly conduct workshops at the National Convention of ASTD on the subject of evaluation. These sessions always seem to draw a full house of HRD professionals who are looking for help in evaluating training programs. I only hope that my model—or taxonomy—continues to be of help to the HRD professionals who are more interested in practical ideas than in scholarly research.

References

Dubin, R. (1976). Theory building in applied areas. In M. D. Dunnette (Ed.), *Handbook of industrial/ organizational psychology.* New York: Rand McNally.

Kirkpatrick, D. L. (1994). *Evaluating training programs: The four levels.* San Francisco: Berrett-Koehler.

Klimoski, R. (1991). Theory presentation in human resource management. *Human Resource Management Review, 4,* 253-271.

"Final Word: Response to Reaction to Holton Article"

Handout for Activity 23

Elwood F. Holton III

I appreciate Kirkpatrick's reaction to my article "The Flawed Four-Level Evaluation Model." In the spirit of advancing the profession, I will respond to the two issues he raised that relate to practice and research in the profession: the distinction between a model and a taxonomy and the value of evaluation research.

Kirkpatrick states that he never called the four-level framework "a model" and that he doesn't care whether it is called a model or a taxonomy, suggesting that the distinction is merely one of semantics. But the distinction between a taxonomy and a model is critical for both practice and research. If the four levels are truly proposed as a model, then there should be relationships among the levels. Kirkpatrick's response to my article clarifies that he does indeed believe there are. This is helpful because, as I discussed in my article's introduction, his writing has been unclear in this area. If the relationships he refers to are the linear relationships among the four levels he has suggested (see Kirkpatrick, 1994, p. 27 and p. 51, for example) then, unfortunately, the research does not support them. There are variables and relationships missing from the four-level framework, resulting in an underspecified model (Campbell, 1990). If simple linear relationships among the levels are not intended by Kirkpatrick, then a clear specification of intervening variables and relationships is needed. Finally, for the record, he has labeled it a model: "The reason I developed this four-level model . . ." (Kirkpatrick, 1994, p. xiii).

I do not intend to demean the value of taxonomies, which are quite appropriate for intermediate stages of theory development (Bobko & Russell, 1991). They are very useful, and I have developed them myself (Holton, in press). However, it is important to realize that they are just an intermediate stage in making complex phenomena more understandable. Therefore, whether considered a model or a taxonomy, the four-level evaluation framework needs updating. If it is a model, it is underspecified; if it is a taxonomy, then a true model is needed.

SOURCE: Reprinted with permission from Holton, E. F. III (1996). Final word: Response to "Reaction to Holton Article." *Human Resource Development Quarterly, 7*, 27-29.

NOTE: Elwood F. Holton III is assistant professor of human resource development, Louisiana State University, Baton Rouge.

This issue has critical implications for practitioners, even though they incorrectly use the terms synonymously. The purpose of evaluation is to make decisions about human resource development (HRD) interventions effectiveness and to decide on a course of action to change an intervention if it is not effective. Taxonomies, by definition, do not provide information about causes. Fully developed models do provide causal information, but underdeveloped models lead to wrong decisions or confusion.

Suppose a practitioner finds that learning outcomes in a training program are acceptable but the learning is not used on the job. Then what? Should the training program be canceled? Or should a meeting be called with the supervisors to have them reinforce the training? Should the training be redesigned to include more practical examples? Or should goal setting be included to increase trainee motivation to transfer? The practitioners I work with need to make these kinds of decisions and do not have the tools to do so, even if they implement the four levels.

This issue leads to the second issue I wish to address: the value of evaluation and HRD research. Kirkpatrick suggests in his response that the four levels must be correct because they are widely used. History has shown that the extent to which something is practiced is no indication that it cannot be improved upon. He further seems to suggest that scholarly research articles (such as those published in *Human Resource Development Quarterly*) are not practical or helpful. However, to quote Kirkpatrick, "Progress in evaluation of training will result if all of us will freely exchange information on objectives, methods, and criteria" (1960, p. 17). Isn't that what research does? Is he now suggesting that we should not capitalize on the excellent research that has been conducted to improve upon the four levels by building a more fully specified model? Is he suggesting that we should not conduct research on the four levels because they have been widely used for thirty-five years, essentially without validation or modification? Is he suggesting that the work of scholars in HRD is not important if that work is not first published in *Training and Development?* I hope he doesn't mean to suggest any of these things. Certainly some articles in *HRDQ* may need further refinement before widespread application, but "there is nothing so practical as good research" (Passmore, 1984, p. 24). I have confidence that practitioners in our field are capable of understanding and using models that depict the complex world of human performance in which we work, particularly if they lead to more effective HRD interventions.

In conclusion, if I appear not to have given full credit to Kirkpatrick for the contributions the four levels have made in the thirty-five years since they were first published, then let me acknowledge them right now. As Newstrom (1995) noted, Kirkpatrick is the person who long ago focused practitioners on evaluating outcomes. His four-level framework will always be a classic in the field. But, as Newstrom further noted, HRD research has advanced to the point that we can improve upon the four levels. Furthermore, the complexity of performance improvement practice today demands that we do so. I hope that we can continue to debate and discuss new approaches as scholars in our shared pursuit to improve HRD practice continuously.

References

Bobko, P., & Russell, C. (1991). A review of the role of taxonomies in human resources management. *Human Resource Management Review, 4*, 293-316.

Campbell, J. P. (1990). The role of theory in industrial and organizational psychology. In M. D. Dunnette & L. M. Hough (Eds.), *Handbook of industrial and organizational psychology* (2nd ed., pp. 39-73). Palo Alto, CA: Consulting Psychologist Press.

Holton, E. F., III. (in press). New employee development: Review and reconceptualization. *Human Resource Development Quarterly.*

Kirkpatrick, D. L. (1960, Feb.). Techniques for evaluating training programs, part 4: Results. *Journal of the ASTD*, 14-17.

Kirkpatrick, D. L. (1994). *Evaluating training programs: The four levels.* San Francisco: Berrett-Koehler.

Newstrom, J. W. (1995). Review of "Evaluating training programs: The four levels by D. L. Kirkpatrick." *Human Resource Development Quarterly, 6*, 317-319.

Passmore, D. L. (1984). Research and theory: There is nothing so practical as good research. *Performance and Instruction Journal, 22*(10), 24-26.

Debating Points

Handout for Activity 23

Group's assignment (either Pro or Con Kirkpatrick's Four-Level Approach): ________

What are the specific points made by the author?	*What does the author recommend?*	*Why does the author make this recommendation?*

Activity 24

Paradigms Exposed!

Overview

This activity engages participants in reflecting on and discussing their worldview as it pertains to inquiry.

Instructional Objectives

Participants will

- Complete a questionnaire that seeks to identify the extent to which they have a more positivist or naturalistic orientation to inquiry
- Discuss how one's worldview may influence an evaluation's key questions, design, and data collection methods
- Consider how their worldview may have affected previous evaluations with which they have been involved

Number of Participants

- Minimum number of participants: 3
- Maximum number of participants: unlimited

Time Estimate: 30 to 60 minutes

This activity requires approximately 30 to 60 minutes, depending on the number of participants and the time available for discussion.

Materials Needed

- Pens/pencils
- Handout "Evaluation Questionnaire"

Instructional Method

Questionnaire

Procedures

Facilitator's tasks:

- Distribute handout "Evaluation Questionnaire."
- Instruct participants to complete the questionnaire to the best of their ability. Explain that it might be difficult to choose one of the two statements in each pair, but not to worry; they should just pick one.
- Emphasize that there are no right or wrong answers and that you will help them score the instrument when they have finished.
- Provide instructions on how to score the instrument: Participants are to give themselves 1 point for each checkmark they have by the following responses (explain that these points do not indicate good or bad or right or wrong):
  - 1a
  - 2a
  - 3b
  - 4b
  - 5a
  - 6a
  - 7a
  - 8b
  - 9a
  - 10a
  - 11b
  - 12b
  - 13a
  - 14b
  - 15a
- Ask articipants to add up their points. Those with a higher number of points lean toward having a positivist worldview, whereas those with fewer points have a more naturalistic or qualitative worldview. Invite participants to raise their hands if they have scores of 0 to 5, 6 to 10, and 11 to 15, respectfully, to see the distribution among participants.
- Debrief the activity with the following questions:
  - What was your experience in completing the questionnaire? Was it difficult? If yes, why?
  - Did your score surprise you? If yes, why? Why not?
  - How might one's worldview affect his or her evaluation practice? How might it have affected your practice with previous evaluations?
  - How would you deal with a client who had a worldview different from yours?

Evaluation Questionnaire

Handout for Activity 24

Directions:

For each of the following 15 paired statements, put a check by the one that comes closest to what you believe. *There are no right or wrong answers.*

______ 1a. There exists a single reality independent of any person.

______ 1b. There exist multiple realities that are constructed by people.

______ 2a. Reality(ies) is governed by immutable natural laws.

______ 2b. Reality(ies) is *not* governed by natural laws.

______ 3a. An observer in an organization becomes part of that which is being observed.

______ 3b. An observer in an organization can remain detached from what she or he is observing.

______ 4a. The context of a program is needed to understand what is occurring in it.

______ 4b. A process can be investigated effectively without concern for the specific context.

______ 5a. Evaluation should be able to determine the true relationship between two variables or factors.

______ 5b. Evaluation provides tentative conclusions that are always open to interpretation and modification.

______ 6a. The truth about any relationship between two variables can be determined by testing it empirically.

______ 6b. The truth about any relationship between two variables can be determined by judgments of knowledgeable experts without further tests.

______ 7a. Facts and values are independent.

______ 7b. Facts have no meaning except in some value context.

SOURCE: Adapted from an instrument developed by Robert E. Stake, CIRCE, University of Illinois, Urbana-Champaign. This instrument was intended for promoting discussion and has not been validated as a measurement instrument. Used with permission.

______ 8a. Every action is "caused" by an infinite array of considerations that may never be known.

______ 8b. Every action or outcome has a primary cause that will be identified at some future time.

______ 9a. The value of evaluation is to predict and control behavior.

______ 9b. The value of evaluation is to increase understanding.

______ 10a. Solutions to organizational problems in one organization should be applicable to other organizations.

______ 10b. Solutions to organizational problems are unique unto themselves.

______ 11a. Meaningful organizational change is nonlinear and dependent on the active involvement of those affected by the change.

______ 11b. Change is a rational linear process that will occur naturally regardless of the specific people involved.

______ 12a. Change is the normal condition of life.

______ 12b. Change occurs only when something unusual causes it. Nonchange, or status quo, is the normal state of organizations.

______ 13a. Systematic collection of objective data about knowledge, behaviors, and physical conditions provides the most meaningful knowledge about learning.

______ 13b. Obtaining feelings, thoughts, and meanings of actions through interviews provides the most meaningful knowledge about learning.

______ 14a. The more nearly a study reflects the complexity of learning using "thick description," the more valuable it is.

______ 14b. Quantitative data analyzed with tests of significance are a necessary part of a valuable evaluation study.

______ 15a. If a study cannot be replicated, and the results verified, I would not have confidence in the study.

______ 15b. A 6-month case study of an organization carried out by a team of evaluators would provide valuable information even if it could not be replicated and results could not be verified.

Activity 25

Comparing and Contrasting Different Evaluation Designs

Overview

This activity helps participants understand the features of different evaluation designs and when and how each can be used effectively in an evaluation study.

Instructional Objectives

Participants will

- Understand how to determine an appropriate evaluation design
- Identify appropriate data collection methods for various evaluation designs

Number of Participants

- Minimum number of participants: 3
- Maximum number of participants: unlimited when participants are in groups of 3 to 5

Time Estimate: 45 to 60 minutes

In addition to providing the necessary background information on evaluation designs, this activity requires approximately 45 to 60 minutes, depending on the number of participants (or groups) and the time available for discussion.

Materials Needed

- Pens/pencils
- Flipchart, markers, tape
- Handout "Evaluation Designs"

Instructional Method

Small-group work

Procedures

Facilitator's tasks:

- Ask participants to get into groups of three to five people.
- Depending on the number of groups, distribute one or two copies of the handout "Evaluation Designs" that depicts different evaluation designs.
- Request that the groups write their ideas on a piece of flipchart paper.
- Ask the groups to share their ideas with the larger group, presenting one or two examples of when their design would be appropriate and useful and one or two examples of when they would not use the approach.
- Debrief the activity with the following questions:
  - As you considered the appropriate uses for your design, what occurred to you? What did you discuss?
  - How would you decide which design to use for an evaluation?
  - Which of the evaluation designs seems most problematic within an organizational context?
  - How would you compensate for the weaknesses of any of these designs if you wanted to use them in an evaluation?
  - How would you educate your client about these different designs if the client was intent on using one particular design that you thought was not useful or appropriate?

Evaluation Designs

Handout for Activity 25

One-Shot Design

In using this design, the evaluator gathers data *following* an intervention or program.

When would you use this design?	*What data collection methods might you use?*	*What are the limitations of this design?*

Evaluation Designs

Handout for Activity 25

Retrospective Pretest

As with the one-shot design, the evaluator collects data at one time but asks for recall of behavior or conditions *prior to,* as well as *after,* an intervention or program.

When would you use this design?	*What data collection methods might you use?*	*What are the limitations of this design?*

Evaluation Designs

Handout for Activity 25

One-Group Pretest-Posttest Design

The evaluator gathers data *prior to* and *following* the intervention or program being evaluated.

When would you use this design?	*What data collection methods might you use?*	*What are the limitations of this design?*

Evaluation Designs

Handout for Activity 25

Time Series Design

The evaluator gathers data *prior to, during,* and *after* the implementation or intervention of a program.

When would you use this design?	*What data collection methods might you use?*	*What are the limitations of this design?*

Evaluation Designs

Handout for Activity 25

Pretest-Posttest Control-Group Design

The evaluator gathers data from two separate groups *prior to* and *following* an intervention or program. One group, typically called the experimental, or treatment, group, receives the intervention. The other group, typically called the control group, does not receive the intervention.

When would you use this design?	*What data collection methods might you use?*	*What are the limitations of this design?*

Evaluation Designs

Handout for Activity 25

Post-Only Control-Group Design

The evaluator collects data from two separate groups *following* an intervention or program. One group, typically called the experimental, or treatment, group, receives the intervention or program, whereas the other group, typically called the control group, does not receive the intervention. Data are collected from both of these groups only after the intervention.

When would you use this design?	*What data collection methods might you use?*	*What are the limitations of this design?*

Evaluation Designs

Handout for Activity 25

Case Study Design

The evaluator studies an organization or program by collecting in-depth, qualitative data during a specific period of time. This design helps answer *how* and *why* questions and helps evaluators understand the unique features of a case.

When would you use this design?	*What data collection methods might you use?*	*What are the limitations of this design?*

Activity 26

Identifying Evaluation Designs

Overview

This activity asks participants to identify appropriate evaluation designs for various evaluation scenarios.

Instructional Objectives

Participants will

- Understand various evaluation designs
- Determine which evaluation design is being used in three different scenarios
- Discuss the strengths and weaknesses of the designs used in each of the scenarios

Number of Participants

- Minimum number of participants: 3
- Maximum number of participants: unlimited when participants are in groups of 3 to 5

Time Estimate: 30 to 60 minutes

In addition to providing the necessary background information on commonly used evaluation/research designs, this activity requires approximately 30 to 60 minutes, depending on the number of participants (or groups) and the time available for discussion.

Materials Needed

- Pens/pencils
- Flipchart, markers, tape
- Handout "Which Design Is It?"

Instructional Method

Case scenario

Procedures

Facilitator's tasks:

- Tell participants whether they will be working individually or in small groups of three to five people. If they choose small groups, ask participants to get into groups.
- Distribute the handout "Which Design Is It?"
- Instruct participants that, in their groups, they are to discuss each evaluation scenario and determine which evaluation design the scenario represents.
- Tell participants that they will be asked to present their ideas to the larger group and request that the groups draw or represent in some way their chosen designs on flipchart paper.
- Invite groups to share their findings with the large group.
- Debrief the activity with the following questions:
  - What are some of the strengths and weaknesses in each of the evaluation designs you identified in these scenarios?
  - What other information would have helped you make a more informed decision on your choice of design?
  - Which kinds of data would result from each of these designs? What would you know from these data? What wouldn't you know?

Which Design Is It?

Handout for Activity 26

Directions:

Based on the following descriptions, determine which design is being use for each evaluation. Be prepared to explain why you chose these designs and what other designs could be used to evaluate this program or intervention.

1. An evaluation sought to determine the effects of a seminar titled "Giving Effective Feedback" by looking at the differences between seminar trainees (who were self-selected) and a group of employees in similar positions in a department that did not participate in the training. Each group was given a posttest when the training was complete.
2. An evaluation sought to determine the impact of a 4-day workweek on employees' productivity. Measures of employees' productivity were taken prior to implementing the program. The group's productivity was then measured at 3-month intervals for 1 year. At the end of the year, conclusions were made about the program's impact.
3. An evaluation by internal evaluators was conducted to determine the effects of a nonprofit organization's restructuring effort. The evaluators conducted focus group and individual interviews and observed a sample of employees over a period of 2 months. In addition, the evaluators administered an organizational climate survey to all employees.
4. An evaluation compared the effectiveness of providing customer service training on the Web versus in a classroom. Call center staff were randomly assigned to one or the other group. Observations were made of their phone skills 1 month after training. Results were presented to the vice president with recommendations concerning future training.
5. An evaluation examined the degree of transfer of training from a pilot test of a leadership course. First-line supervisors who volunteered for the pilot test were surveyed before the sessions, immediately after the sessions, and 2 months after training.
6. An evaluation focused on a pilot test of a new-employee orientation program. All new employees in the Chicago office participated in the program, and evaluation surveys were distributed at the end of the program. The survey included questions about the facilitator's skills and the usefulness of the content.

Activity 27

Using Evaluation Questions to Guide an Evaluation's Design and Data Collection Methods

Overview

This activity asks participants to identify appropriate evaluation designs for specific evaluation key questions.

Instructional Methods

Participants will

- Understand how an evaluation's key questions influence an evaluation's design and data collection methods
- Identify appropriate evaluation designs and data collection methods for a series of evaluation key questions
- Discuss the relative strengths and weaknesses of each chosen design

Number of Participants

- Minimum number of participants: 2
- Maximum number of participants: unlimited when participants are in groups of 2 to 3

Time Estimate: 30 to 60 minutes

In addition to providing the necessary background information on several evaluation designs (e.g., preexperimental, quasi-experimental, experimental, and qualitative case studies), as well as a basic understanding of data collection methods, this activity requires approximately 30 to 60 minutes, depending on the number of participants (or pairs or triads) and the time available for discussion.

Materials Needed

- Pens/pencils
- Handout "Using Evaluation Questions to Guide an Evaluation's Design and Data Collection Methods"

Instructional Method

Small-group work

Procedures

Facilitator's tasks:

- Ask participants to get into pairs or triads.
- Distributes handout "Using Evaluation Questions to Guide an Evaluation's Design and Data Collection Methods."
- Instruct pairs or triads to read each evaluation question in the left-hand column and to discuss and note, in the right-hand column, which evaluation design and data collection methods might be best suited for answering this question.
- Go down the list of questions, asking for volunteers to share their choices for each question. Ask participants to identify the strengths and weakness of the designs they have chosen.
- Debrief the activity with the following questions:
  - What kinds of things did you consider in choosing an evaluation design?
  - What issues did this activity raise for you?
  - What do you think would happen if two evaluators chose different designs to conduct the same evaluation?

Using Evaluation Questions to Guide an Evaluation's Design and Data Collection Methods

Handout for Activity 27

Directions:

For each of the evaluation questions, choose an evaluation design that would best address the question. In addition, identify one or two data collection methods that could be used to answer the question within the chosen design's framework.

Evaluation Key Questions	*Evaluation Design/Methods*
What impact is the diabetes prevention program having on high school students?	
How does participants' learning from the distance-learning course on customer service compare to participants' learning from the course when it is delivered face-to-face?	
In what ways have program recipients changed their behaviors?	
What impact has sexual assault training had on community service providers?	
How are the program's activities being implemented?	

What are participants' most successful experiences with the program?	
What impact has the new policy had on the ways in which the program is implemented across the 10 sites?	
How are work-life balance policies being implemented and used in this organization?	
What impact is the No Child Left Behind legislation having on curriculum development in Grades K–8?	

Activity 28

Debating the Usefulness of Return on Investment

Overview

This activity involves participants in a debate concerning the strengths and weaknesses of using return on investment (ROI) to determine a program's success.

Instructional Objectives

Participants will

- Increase their understanding of what it means to conduct an ROI evaluation
- Identify the strengths and weakness of using an ROI approach to evaluation
- Determine appropriate uses for an ROI approach to evaluation

Number of Participants

- Minimum number of participants: 8
- Maximum number of participants: 24

Time Estimate: 45 to 60 minutes

In addition to providing the necessary background information on ROI and related concepts, such as cost-benefit and cost-effectiveness designs, this activity requires approximately 45 to 60 minutes, depending on the time available for discussion.

Materials Needed

- Pens/pencils
- Handout "Debating Points"

Instructional Method

Debate

Procedures

Facilitator's tasks:

- Assign participants to one of two groups: 1. For ROI or 2. Against ROI.
- Distribute the handout "Debating Points."
- Instruct groups that they will first have time to complete the handout, and then they will begin to debate the two positions.
- Explain the rules of the debate:
  - Each group will select four members of its team to be the debaters. The rest of the team will be in a support position. Their role is to provide the debaters with information as needed. This information can be shared only by writing notes—they are not allowed to talk to the debaters during the debate.
  - Each side will have 3 minutes to make an opening statement.
  - For the next 16 minutes, participants will take turns making their case or rebuttal. They will have 1 minute each time (eight turns for each team).
  - Each team will then have 3 minutes to make its closing arguments.
- Debrief the activity with the following questions:
  - What other arguments might have been offered to support your group's position?
  - What other arguments might have been offered to support the opposing group's position?
  - To what extent do you personally agree with the position that ROI is the most useful approach to determining the effectiveness or success of a program?
  - Under what conditions might an ROI approach be useful and appropriate?
  - What other kinds of evaluation approaches and designs might evaluators use to determine a program's impact or success?

Debating Points

Handout for Activity 28

Group's assignment (For or Against ROI): ______________________________

The debate focuses on the following statement:

> Determining if ROI is the best approach for evaluating the effectiveness and success of a program.

What arguments can you make to support your position?	*What evidence supports these arguments?*

Activity 29

Is It Really a Return on Investment Evaluation?

Overview

This activity asks participants to consider whether a return on investment (ROI) evaluation was accurately designed and reported.

Instructional Objectives

Participants will

- Increase their understanding of what it means to conduct an ROI evaluation
- Compare the differences between an ROI evaluation and an evaluation that calculates a program's costs
- Discuss the challenges in conducting an ROI evaluation

Number of Participants

- Minimum number of participants: 3
- Maximum number of participants: unlimited when participants are in groups of 3 to 5

Time Estimate: 30 to 45 minutes

In addition to providing the necessary background information on ROI and related concepts, such as cost-benefit and cost-effectiveness designs, this activity requires approximately 30 to 45 minutes, depending on the number of participants (or groups) and the time available for discussion.

SOURCE: This activity was contributed by Marguerite Foxon, Principal Performance Technologist, Motorola.

Materials Needed

- Pens/pencils
- Handout "Is It Really ROI?"

Instructional Method

Case scenario

Procedures

Facilitator's tasks:

- Ask participants to get into groups of three to five people.
- Distribute the handout "Is it Really ROI?"
- Instruct participants to read, in their groups, the case scenario on the handout and respond to the discussion questions.
- Invite participants to share their thoughts about the case and their responses to the discussion questions.
- Debrief the activity with the following questions:
  - This case is based on a real example that was disseminated widely on the Internet. Given this, what are your reactions?
  - How could ROI be calculated for this management-training program? What other data would be needed?
  - What challenges might the evaluator have faced if he or she had conducted a real ROI evaluation?
  - How can we help organizations understand the difference between calculating ROI and calculating a program's costs savings?

Is It Really ROI?

Handout for Activity 29

The Situation

A major U.S.-based company had a policy of training several thousand new managers each year. Managers were typically brought together from around the United States, and in some cases from overseas, to centralized locations in the United States for a 1-week management-training event. Two years ago, however, the company began to look for alternative ways of training these managers for several reasons:

- The sheer number of trainees (approximately 5,000 individuals) required a huge administrative staff just to organize and run the 1-week events.
- The cost of bringing thousands of people from multiple locations became a major budgetary issue.
- The increasing complexity of managers' jobs required more than 5 days of training.
- The company was moving into multiple countries. The additional time required to fly to the United States, and the costs of travel, were becoming prohibitive.

The company decided to use a blended approach with e-learning as the primary delivery format for the management training program. In place of the centralized classroom-based training that had been offered before, managers now entered a 6-month e-learning program, which included collaborating online with colleagues to resolve management issues. The training closed with a 5-day, face-to-face session in participants' local offices.

Calculating the Return on Investment

Some time later, the company hired a consultant to calculate the return on investment (ROI) on the new management-training program. The consultant took into account the physical costs of transitioning to e-learning (hardware, software, Internet servers) as well as other costs, such as information technology support, e-learning designers, and content development.

The final report included impressive numbers that showed the following:

- A significant reduction in program, travel, and time away from work costs
- An increase in the amount of content taught during a 6-month period

- A reduction in the cost of course and module development by providing templates for internal business groups to customize their own content rapidly
- A reduction in the time needed to learn (it was estimated that managers could learn the same material in one quarter the time it took using the classroom approach)
- An increase in managers' satisfaction with the blended approach

The consultant's report concluded that the ROI for the e-learning program was more than 2,200%.

Discussion Questions

1. Did the consultant really calculate the program's ROI? If it wasn't ROI, what was it?
2. Was the company's investment in training really paying off in terms of greater productivity and more effective management of teams? Why or why not?
3. Is the ROI figure reliable evidence that the impact on the organization is greater now that managers are trained using a blended approach (e-learning and a 5-day, face-to-face meeting in local offices), rather than the former intensive classroom approach?

Activity 30

Calculating the Return on Investment

Overview

This activity highlights appropriate uses of return on investment (ROI) and the challenges of conducting this type of evaluation within an organizational context.

Instructional Objectives

Participants will

- Understand the underlying assumptions of conducting an ROI evaluation
- Practice calculating ROI for a given situation
- Discuss situations in which calculating ROI is most appropriate
- Identify the challenges in conducting ROI evaluations within organizations

Number of Participants

- Minimum number of participants: 3
- Maximum number of participants: unlimited when participants are in groups of 3 to 5

Time Estimate: 45 to 60 minutes

This activity requires approximately 45 to 60 minutes, depending on the number of participants (or groups) and the time available for discussion.

SOURCE: This activity was contributed by Barbra Zuckerman, Evaluation Consultant, Albuquerque, New Mexico.

Materials Needed

- Pens/pencils
- Handout "What Is the Return on Investment for Going to College?"
- Small colored stickers (e.g., dots, smiley faces, stars); 80 stickers per group

Instructional Method

Small-group work

Procedures

Facilitator's tasks:

- Ask participants to get into groups of three to five people.
- Explain that they will be calculating the ROI for going to college (either undergraduate or graduate).
- Distribute 80 stickers to each group.
- Distribute the handout "What Is the Return on Investment for Going to College?"
- Explain that participants are to do the following:
  - Identify all of the benefits of going to college and list these in the first column on the handout (e.g., higher paying job, more self-confidence, more opportunities for advancement in career).
  - Identify all of the costs (both financial and nonfinancial) of going to college (e.g., less time with family, more stress, strained work relations) and write these in the second column.
  - Place one to four stickers next to each benefit and each cost, the number of stickers indicating the relative benefits and costs. Participants may not place more than four stickers next to any one benefit or cost. They do not need to use all 80 stickers. The number of stickers relates to the perceived importance or weight of each benefit or cost.
- Instruct groups to add the number of stickers in each column and to indicate the sum at the bottom of the handout.
- Instruct groups to then calculate the ROI given the formula on the handout.
- Invite groups to share some of the benefits and costs on their handout and their ROI results.
- Debrief the activity with the following questions:
  - What was your experience in trying to develop a list of the benefits and costs?
  - How difficult or easy was it to assign the number of stickers to each benefit and cost?

- Did the ROI results you obtained seem credible? If yes, why? If no, why not?
- As you think about applying ROI within an organization, what challenges might you face?
- Under what circumstances might ROI be particularly appropriate? Under what circumstances might it not be appropriate?
- If a client asked you to do an ROI evaluation and you knew it was not an appropriate approach, what would you say? What would you recommend instead?
- What other questions does this activity raise for you concerning the use of ROI in evaluation?

What Is the Return on Investment for Going to College?

Handout for Activity 30

Focus of your ROI study (check one) _____ Undergraduate _____ Graduate

Benefits	*Costs*
1.	1.
2.	2.
3.	3.
4.	4.
5.	5.
6.	6.
7.	7.
8.	8.
9.	9.
10.	10.

Total benefits (or number of stickers) = ______

Total costs (or number of stickers) = ______

ROI = ([Benefits – Costs]/Costs) × 100%

ROI for going to college = ______________________

6

Issues of Validity and Sampling

BACKGROUND

This section includes activities that address

- Understanding quantitative and qualitative definitions of reliability and validity
- Understanding various approaches and issues related to sampling

The following information is provided as a brief introduction to the topics covered in these activities.

RELIABILITY AND VALIDITY

Reliability refers to the level of measurement error that exists in the instrument or the data. If the data (or the instrument) are considered unreliable, then the data are unrelated to the phenomenon or the concept being measured. Measurement error, leading to a lack of reliability, can result from various sources. One source involves an inadequate sampling of items used to measure the phenomenon or concept. A second source of error can come from situational factors, such as the context (e.g., a noisy room), or personal factors, such as the person's mood or level of anxiety.

The *internal validity* of an evaluation effort refers to the extent to which it correctly answers the questions it claims to answer about what is being evaluated. In other words, are the data an accurate representation of how people think, feel, know, or act about the evaluand? In evaluations, whether using quantitative or qualitative approaches, one major threat to internal validity is that some unmeasured processes (also called confounding factors or variables) might account for the results that were obtained. A high level of internal validity is necessary if the evaluation results are to be used for decision-making purposes. On the other hand, internal validity need not be as great for exploratory evaluations. A certain level of internal validity is always needed to justify the collection and analysis of data.

External validity concerns the extent to which the results can be generalized to other situations. Generally, external validity is determined by sample selection, whereas internal validity is determined by sample assignment. Thus, external validity is increased to the extent that the sample selection reflects the population and the results can be generalized. In contrast, internal validity is increased through random assignment to one or more groups. The value of external validity is the ability to generalize the results to a larger population. Such generalizability, then, depends on drawing a representative sample of the population.

The *Standards for Educational and Psychological Testing* (American Educational Research Association, American Psychological Association, and National Council on Measurement in Education, 1999) is considered the definitive reference work on issues regarding testing and test validity. The Joint Committee on Educational and Psychological Tests, made up of representatives of the American Psychological Association, the American Educational Research Association, and the National Council on Measurement in Education, prepared the statement. These *Standards* define validity as the "degree to which evidence and theory support the interpretation of test scores entailed by proposed uses of tests" (p. 9). They also introduce the following concepts:

- *Face Validity.* In this case, casual review suggests that the instrument measures what it claims to measure.
- *Validity Based on Test Content.* This more rigorous examination, potentially by experts or involving some data collection analysis, suggests that the instrument measures what it claims to measure.
- *Validity Based on Response Processes.* In this case, the response processes are examined to ensure that the instrument measures what it claims to measure.
- *Validity Based on Internal Structure.* In this case, statistical analyses confirm that the instrument includes certain factors and measures what it claims to measure.
- *Validity Based on Relations to Other Variables.* In this instance, statistical analyses compare the instruments to other related instruments and variables.

- *Validity Based on Consequences.* In this examination, the consequences of the instrument are examined to ensure that it measures what it claims to measure.

Note that these concepts have replaced notions of criterion, predictive, and construct validity.

The concept of validity for qualitative or naturalistic inquiry is defined somewhat differently. Lincoln and Guba (1985) suggest that it is important to establish the trustworthiness of a study and use the terms *credibility, transferability, dependability,* and *confirmability.* Through prolonged engagement, the use of thick description, and an audit of the evaluation process, the evaluator is able to verify the data and establish its value.

SAMPLING

Sampling is undertaken when it is difficult or not feasible to involve the entire population in the evaluation for the following reasons:

- *Time Constraints.* You do not have the time to interview a large number of individuals.
- *Cost Constraints.* You do not have the travel budget to visit various places to collect data.
- *Limited Accessibility.* Some people within the population are difficult to reach.
- *Compromised Accuracy.* For example, if you cannot find qualified interviewers to conduct all of the interviews, the quality of the data may be less than desired.

Things to consider when choosing a sampling method:

- Size and accessibility of the population
- The amount of money available for travel, consultants, interviewers, postage, audiotapes, and other materials
- Geographical location(s) of the population
- Availability of a sampling frame (a list of all those in the population)
- The data collection method(s)
- The amount of variance in the population

There are various approaches to selecting a sample. The extent to which you wish to generalize your findings will help determine the type of sampling strategy that is most appropriate for your study. When wanting to generalize the evaluation findings to the larger population, the following characteristics may be important:

- Sample is large enough to yield desired level of precision.
- Everyone in the population has an equal chance to be in the sample.
- The characteristics of people not in the sample are similar to those in the sample.

One approach to achieving such a sample is to use random sampling. This can be accomplished by drawing names from a hat or by assigning numbers to each person and then using a random number generator on a computer to pick the people for the sample.

There are cases, however, where simple random sampling is not appropriate or advisable. For example, you may want to include representatives from each department in the organization, but one department might have only a few people. With a simple random sample, it is possible that none of these people will be selected. In such cases, you may want to develop subcategories, or strata, and then sample from each of these. Such a sample would be called a stratified sample.

In other cases, you may want to sample from some larger units first and then sample within the selected units. For example, you may be undertaking an evaluation involving in-person interviews in an organization that has many field offices. Rather than use simple random sampling, you might first sample from among the field offices. Then, within the selected locations, you would select individuals to be interviewed. Such a sample is called a cluster sample.

In many organizations, such sampling methods are not possible. Individuals are selected simply because they are available. Such a sample is called a convenience sample. Another type of sampling is one in which specific individuals are contacted because of their particular positions, characteristics, or knowledge. For example, you may want to survey all of the regional sales vice presidents concerning a newly implemented sales tracking system. Such a sample is called a purposive sample.

When sampling is used, certain kinds of errors or biases can be introduced. These are considered sampling errors when they result from the sampling procedures or nonsampling errors arising from other sources. For example, a sampling error would appear if one were to use the telephone book to select the sample because those with no telephones or those with unlisted numbers would be eliminated from the sample. A nonsampling error occurs whenever there are nonrespondents.

RESOURCES

American Educational Research Association, American Psychological Association, and National Council on Measurement in Education. (1999). *Standards for educational and psychological testing.* Washington, DC: American Educational Research Association.

Campbell, D. T., & Stanley, J. C. (1963). *Experimental and quasi-experimental designs for research.* Boston: Houghton Mifflin.

Cook, T. D., & Campbell, D. T. (1979). *Quasi-experimentation: Design and analysis issues for field settings.* Boston: Houghton Mifflin.

Creswell, J. W. (1998). *Qualitative inquiry and research design: Choosing among five traditions.* Thousand Oaks, CA: Sage.

Fink, A. (2003). *How to sample in surveys* (2nd ed.). Thousand Oaks, CA: Sage.

Gall, M. D., Gall, J. P., & Borg, W. R. (2003). *Educational research: An introduction.* (7th ed.). Boston: Allyn & Bacon.

Guba, E. G., & Lincoln, Y. S. (1985). *Effective evaluation.* San Francisco: Jossey-Bass.

Henry, G. T. (1990). *Practical sampling* (Applied Social Research Methods Series, Vol. 21). Newbury Park, CA: Sage.

Kemper, E. A., Stringfield, S., & Teddlie, C. (2003). Mixed methods sampling strategies in social science research. In A. Tashakkori & C. Teddlie (Eds.), *Handbook of mixed methods in social and behavioral research* (pp. 241-272). Thousand Oaks, CA: Sage.

Lincoln, Y. S., & Guba, E. G. (1985). *Naturalistic inquiry.* Beverly Hills, CA: Sage.

Mathison, S. (1988). Why triangulate? *Educational Researcher, 17*(2), 13-7.

Mertens, D. M. (1998). *Research methods in education and psychology.* Thousand Oaks, CA: Sage.

Patton, M. Q. (2001). *Qualitative research and evaluation methods* (3rd ed.). Thousand Oaks, CA: Sage.

Rossi, P. H., Freeman, H. E., & Lipsey, M. W. (2003). *Evaluation: A systematic approach* (7th ed.). Thousand Oaks, CA: Sage.

Russ-Eft, D., & Preskill, H. (2001). *Evaluation in organizations: A systematic approach to enhancing learning, performance, and change.* Boston: Perseus Press.

Schwandt, T. A. (1997). *Qualitative inquiry: A dictionary of terms.* Thousand Oaks, CA: Sage.

Tashakkori, A., & Teddlie, C. (Eds.). (2003). *Handbook of mixed methods in social and behavioral research.* Thousand Oaks, CA: Sage.

Activity 31

Reliability and Validity 101

Overview

This activity engages participants in thinking about the ways in which the quality of data may affect the process and outcomes of an evaluation study.

Instructional Objectives

Participants will

- Understand the concepts of reliability and validity
- Brainstorm factors that may affect the quality of data
- Discuss strategies for improving the collection of valid data

Number of Participants

- Minimum number of participants: 3
- Maximum number of participants: 25

Time Estimate: 30 to 45 minutes

This activity requires approximately 30 to 45 minutes, depending on the number of participants and the time available for discussion.

Materials Needed

- Pens/pencils
- Flipchart, markers
- Handout "Thinking About Reliability and Validity"
- Handout "Reasons Why Data May Not Be Valid"

Instructional Method

Large-group discussion

Procedures

Facilitator's tasks:

- Distribute the handout "Thinking About Reliability and Validity" and ask participants for their answers to the questions. Ask them to support their responses with examples.
- Illustrate the concepts of reliability and validity with the following example:

  > Every day I get on the scale I have at home, and it says I weigh 115 pounds—every day it says this—and I feel pretty good about it! Regardless of what I eat, how much exercise I do or do not do, it always says 115 pounds. Last week, I went to my doctor for my annual physical exam, and, as usual, she asked me to get on the scale. Imagine my shock when her scale said I weighed 135 pounds! I told her that the scale must be broken because mine says 115 pounds—every day. She assured me that her office scale is calibrated once a month and had just been checked out a few days ago, and, indeed, her scale was accurate.

- Ask participants to imagine they are collecting data or providing data to someone else. Ask the following questions: What factors or situations might lead to the collection of data that are less credible, believable, or accurate? What things might affect the quality of the data being collected? Write participants' responses on flipchart paper.
- Distribute the handout "Reasons Why Data May Not Be Valid" and discuss each reason with participants. Ask participants for examples of when and how these situations or conditions might occur.
- Debrief the activity with the following questions:
  - What implications are there if the data collected are not valid or are less than trustworthy?
  - What are some strategies for increasing the validity of data collected for an evaluation?
  - How can evaluators help clients understand the concept of validity and its implications for an evaluation's design and implementation?

Thinking About Reliability and Validity

Handout for Activity 31

Discussion Questions

1. What does it mean for data to be reliable?

2. What does it mean for data to be valid?

3. Can data collected from an instrument be valid if they are not reliable?

4. Can data collected from an instrument be reliable if they are not valid?

Reasons Why Data May Not Be Valid

Handout for Activity 31

Reasons Why Data May Not Be Valid	*Examples*
Sample Selection. The sample may not represent the desired population.	
Concealment of the Truth. Respondents may not be truthful in their responses.	
Lack of Knowledge. Respondents may not have the information but feel compelled to provide a response.	
Nonresponse. Some people may choose not to respond.	
Processing Errors. Errors may be made in the data entry or recording processes.	
Conceptual Problems. Items may be worded in a way to elicit different interpretations.	

Activity 32

Understanding Validity

Overview

This activity helps participants become familiar with the concept of validity as used in quantitative approaches to inquiry.

Instructional Objectives

Participants will

- Understand and articulate the meaning and importance of validity within an evaluation context
- Create a mind map that represents the concept of validity

Number of Participants

- Minimum number of participants: 3
- Maximum number of participants: unlimited when participants are in groups of 3 to 5

Time Estimate: 45 to 60 minutes

In addition to providing the necessary background information on the concept of validity, this activity requires approximately 45 to 60 minutes, depending on the number of participants (or groups) and the time available for discussion.

Materials Needed

- Pens/pencils
- Flipchart, markers, tape

Instructional Method

Visual representation

Procedures

Facilitator's tasks:

- Ask participants to get into groups of three to five people.
- Ask participants to discuss, in their groups, the concept of validity and to help each other clarify any questions they may have.
- Explain that participants are to create a mind map that represents the concept of validity. They should feel free to use words, pictures, or symbols to create their mind map. (A mind map is a visual method that is used to organize thoughts, identify key ideas, link themes, and remember materials using both words and pictures. Participants should create their mind map in a way that makes the most sense to them.)
- Ask groups to represent their mind maps on a piece of flipchart paper and attach it to a wall.
- Invite groups to present their mind maps to the larger group.
- Debrief the activity with the following questions:
  - What similarities and differences did you see in the various mind maps?
  - What do you now understand about validity that you might not have understood before this activity?
  - Why is validity so important within an evaluation context?
  - What surprised you about this task?
  - If you had to summarize the concept of validity in three words or less, what would you say?

Activity 33

Detecting Threats to Validity

Overview

This activity asks participants to consider the ways in which the quality of data collected during an evaluation study might be compromised or considered invalid.

Instructional Objectives

Participants will

- Become familiar with threats to internal validity
- Determine which threats to internal validity are present in various evaluation designs
- Discuss the implications of collecting data that are not valid

Number of Participants

- Minimum number of participants: 3
- Maximum number of participants: unlimited when participants are in groups of 3 to 5

Time Estimate: 45 to 60 minutes

In addition to providing the necessary background information on evaluation/research designs, this activity requires approximately 45 to 60 minutes, depending on the number of participants (or groups) and the time available for discussion.

Instructional Method

Case scenario

Materials Needed

- Pens/pencils
- Flipchart, markers, tape
- Handout "Threats to Internal Validity"
- Handout "Detecting Threats to Validity"

Procedures

Facilitator's tasks:

- Distribute the handout "Threats to Internal Validity" and discuss each threat with participants. Ask participants for examples from their own experience. Provide other examples as needed.
- Ask participants to get into groups of three to five people, and distribute the handout "Detecting Threats to Validity."
- Explain that for each case scenario, they are to identify the evaluation design represented in the case and describe any threats to internal validity that may be present in the design.
- Ask groups to write their responses on flipchart paper.
- Invite participants to share their responses. Ask other groups if they agree or have additional or different results.
- Debrief the activity with the following questions:
  - What did this activity highlight for you?
  - What impact does collecting invalid data have on an evaluation's outcomes?
  - What insights did you gain about ensuring the validity of data?
  - To what extent do you think it is the evaluator's responsibility to report problems with the data's validity?

Threats to Internal Validity

Handout for Activity 33

- *History.* Relates to specific and unexpected events affecting the variables of interest; any change between a pretest measure and posttest measure that is not attributable to the intervention

- *Maturation.* Occurs when there is a passage of time that leads to changes in attitudes or behavior; any changes in responses due to changes in the respondent that are not related to the intervention (e.g., boredom, aging, becoming hungry or tired)

- *Testing.* Effects of one data collection effort on later data collection; when a pretest affects respondents' future responses

- *Instrumentation.* Occurs when there are changes in the data collection instruments or the observers that may affect the manner in which measurements are taken; changes in the measurement due to fatigue, increased observational skills, and changes in data collection methods or instrument items

- *Mortality.* Attrition from the sample; bias introduced into the study by some respondents leaving the study

- *Statistical Regression.* Occurs when a group's extremely high pretest scores move toward the average on the posttest

- *Selection.* Occurs when there are systematic biases represented in groups that are being studied

Reference

Campbell, D. T., & Stanley, J. C. (1963). *Experimental and quasi-experimental designs for research.* Boston: Houghton Mifflin.

SOURCE: Adapted from Campbell and Stanley (1963).

Detecting Threats to Validity

Handout for Activity 33

For each one of the evaluation scenarios, answer the following questions:

1. Which evaluation design was used?
2. What threats to internal validity are present in that particular design?
3. What would you do to minimize these threats to the data's validity, or how would you manage those threats during the evaluation's design and implementation?

Scenario 1

A large insurance company has developed a new communication skills training program for middle-level managers. Within days of posting this opportunity, the Training Department is flooded with interested managers. Given this huge, unanticipated response, the Training Department decides to offer two 6-week training programs—one to begin in May, the second one to begin in September. They randomly assign the interested managers to either the May or September sessions.

Two weeks before the May workshop, the subordinates of all the registered managers (those who will take the course in May and September) are asked to complete an assessment instrument asking them to rate their managers on a variety of verbal and written communication skills.

In July, after the first group of managers has completed the program and before the second group has taken the program, both groups of managers' subordinates complete the communication skills assessment instrument once again. The subordinates' ratings of the May group are then compared to those of the September group. Because the ratings of the May group were statistically significantly higher than those of the September group (who had not yet been through the training), the course was lauded as a success.

Scenario 2

A country water district introduces a water conservation campaign by sponsoring various media events. Water consumption levels for the 36 months preceding and following the campaign are studied to determine if the campaign was effective.

Scenario 3

The Staff Development Department of a local hospital decides to evaluate a new computer-based, self-instructional system on negotiation skills. The computer-based program is made available to a group of employees from the same department. Employees from another department receive the same training content but within a classroom setting. These people are not given access to the computer-based course. At the end of the instructional period, all training participants are videotaped to determine their level of negotiating skills. The results are then compared across the two groups to determine whether the computer-based approach is more effective than the classroom training approach.

Scenario 4

A consultant was called in to a large school district to help principals develop effective leadership skills. The consultant developed a 6-week program, whereby the consultant would be with the 15 principals each week for 4 hours (a total of 24 hours of staff development). At the first training meeting, the consultant administered a leadership instrument to the principals (to serve as a pretest). The principals' participation rate for the six sessions was as follows:

Week 1 = 15 principals

Week 2 = 13 principals

Week 3 = 12 principals

Week 4 = 9 principals

Week 5 = 8 principals

Week 6 = 7 principals

At the last session (Week 6), the consultant administered the same leadership assessment instrument (to the remaining seven principals). When the pre- and posttest scores were compared, the consultant was elated. The scores showed that the 6-week training program was a success.

Activity 34

Ensuring the Quality of Qualitative Data

Overview

This activity helps participants understand the concept of validity as it relates to the collection of qualitative data within an evaluation context.

Instructional Objectives

Participants will

- Understand the difference between quantitative concepts of validity and how validity is defined for qualitative, naturalistic, and ethnographic kinds of data
- Create a visual display that communicates a strategy for ensuring the quality of qualitative data
- Discuss the ways in which an evaluation study can use these different strategies

Number of Participants

- Minimum number of participants: 14
- Maximum number of participants: 35

Time Estimate: 60 to 75 minutes

In addition to providing the necessary background information on the concept of validity as it is defined for both quantitative and qualitative forms of inquiry, this activity require approximately 60 to 75 minutes, depending on the number of participants and the time available for discussion.

Materials Needed

- Pens/pencils
- Handout "Strategies for Verifying Qualitative Data"
- Handout "Discussion Questions"
- Poster board, markers, crayons, other arts and crafts materials

Instructional Method

Small-group work

Procedures

Facilitator's tasks:

- Ask participants to get into groups of 2 to 5 people to make seven groups (e.g., if there are 14 participants, there will be 2 people per group; if there are 35 participants, there will be 5 participants per group).
- Distribute the handout "Strategies for Verifying Qualitative Data."
- Explain that each group will be asked to develop a visual display of one of the seven strategies for verifying qualitative data. The display should depict the concept clearly enough so that no additional written or oral explanation is necessary.
- Instruct participants to begin working on their displays.
- Ask groups to post their display around the room.
- Provide participants with the handout "Discussion Questions."
- Ask each group to go to one of the displays and respond to the discussion questions. After 3 to 5 minutes, tell the groups to move clockwise to the next display. This is repeated until all groups have visited all of the displays.
- Debrief the activity with the following questions:
  - How has this activity increased your understanding of validity as it is applied to the collection of qualitative data?
  - What impact does ensuring the validity of qualitative data have on an evaluation's design, implementation, and budget?
  - What challenges are there to ensuring the validity of qualitative data in the course of an evaluation study?
  - Which of these strategies are you likely to use in your own evaluation work?

Strategies for Verifying Qualitative Data

Handout for Activity 34

1. *Prolonged Engagement and Persistent Observation.* Being onsite for long periods of time allows the evaluator to build trust, develop rapport with participants, learn about the organization's culture, and check for misinformation generated from participants or the evaluator.

2. *Triangulation.* This approach, which compensates for biases built into single methods, single data sources, and single theory evaluations, uses multiple theories, multiple methods, multiple sources for data collection, and multiple evaluators to provide corroborating information.

3. *Peer Review or Debriefing.* This approach involves conducting an external check of the evaluation process (similar to interrater reliability in quantitative forms of inquiry) and might involve the evaluator sharing various design and implementation challenges with trusted colleagues, who provide advice on how to proceed.

4. *Negative Case Analysis or Rival Explanations.* Seeking data that do not conform to emerging themes and patterns ensures that all possible interpretations are offered. Seeking rival explanations involves looking for data that support alternative explanations.

5. *Clarifying Evaluator Bias.* This approach involves identifying the evaluator's experiences, perceptions, assumptions, and positions prior to the evaluation to determine the ways in which these biases may impact the evaluation.

6. *Member Checks.* This strategy involves soliciting respondents' views of the credibility of the evaluation's findings and the interpretations made by the evaluator. Member checks often involve asking respondents for feedback on the accuracy of interview transcripts, summarized data, or draft reports (also known as confirmability).

7. *Rich, Thick Description.* This approach involves writing in such a way as to provide readers with a vicarious experience of the program and often includes participants' quotes and detailed information about the context and program. This strategy increases the transferability of information to other contexts and situations (similar to external validity).

SOURCE: Lincoln, Y. & Guba, E. (1985). *Naturalistic inquiry.* Thousand Oaks, CA: Sage.

Discussion Questions

Handout for Activity 34

As you look at each display, discuss and answer the following questions:

1. What does this display tell you about how to verify qualitative data, and how to ensure qualitative data's trustworthiness, quality, accuracy, credibility?

2. How would you use this strategy in an evaluation study? (Give one example.)

Activity 35

Sampling Matters

Overview

This activity helps participants understand the issues of using a small sample, as well as using a sampling strategy that is unfocused and undefined.

Instructional Objectives

Participants will

- Understand the implications of using an inadequate sample in an evaluation study
- Understand how one's choices about sample size and sampling strategy may influence an evaluation's findings
- Consider how issues related to sampling are currently affecting or may affect an evaluation they may conduct in the future

Number of Participants

- Minimum number of participants: 3
- Maximum number of participants: unlimited when participants are in groups of 3 to 5

Time Estimate: 30 to 45 minutes

In addition to providing the necessary background information on sampling, this activity requires approximately 30 to 45 minutes, depending on the number of participants (or groups) and the time available for discussion.

Materials Needed

- Pens/pencils
- Handout "The Taste Test"
- Handout "Organizational Culture and School Reform"

Instructional Method

Case scenario

Procedures

Facilitator's tasks:

- Distribute one or both of the handouts, "The Taste Test" and "Organizational Culture and School Reform."
- Ask participants to get into groups of three to five people.
- Instruct groups to discuss their case scenario and the related discussion questions.
- Invite groups to describe the key points of their own discussion.
- Debrief the activity with the following questions:
  - What did this activity confirm for you with regard to sampling?
  - After participating in this activity, what implications can you see for an evaluation you are currently working on or one you will be conducting in the near future?
  - What is one tip you would share with someone who needed to better understand sampling? State this tip in the form of a bumper sticker quip.

The Taste Test

Handout for Activity 35

Going into an ice cream store and being able to taste test different ice creams is one of life's greatest little pleasures—at least for those of us who enjoy eating ice cream. Now, some of us always go right for the Mocha Java, or the Vanilla, or the Chocolate Chip Cookie Dough, regardless of the other choices available. In this situation, we do not look at the freezer as an endless array of possibilities. Yet some of us like to try something different every once in a while and have to make a choice about which ice cream to order. Given that we don't indulge in ice cream very often, this choice of flavor becomes quite important—we wouldn't want to choose an ice cream and not like it once we paid for it. So, to narrow down our choices, we take advantage of the free samples offered by most ice cream parlors.

Now, imagine you have decided to try a flavor you have not had before. After you take a quick scan of the other 25 flavors in the freezer, you ask for a sample of the Rocky Road (chocolate ice cream with nuts, marshmallows, and little pieces of fudge). The person helping you takes a small wooden stick and scrapes off a small taste of the Rocky Road ice cream. With great anticipation, you taste the ice cream.

Discussion Questions

1. Under what circumstances or conditions would the sample of Rocky Road ice cream you were given provide *incorrect* information?
2. If, based on your taste test, you decided not to order this ice cream, what are the chances you would have made the wrong decision?
3. If you concluded that you made the wrong decision, what could you do to reduce the likelihood of this problem occurring again if you asked for another sample?
4. How does this example of sampling relate to sampling within the context of an evaluation study?

Organizational Culture and School Reform

Handout for Activity 35

A team of evaluators was contracted to evaluate school culture(s) in a state's seven elementary schools that were experimenting with different school reform initiatives. To identify the cultures of the school and their relationship to educational reform, evaluators decided to use a nonparticipant observer approach (they also collected test score data as well as teachers' lesson plans). Each school was to be observed by one member of the evaluation team. The following list describes their efforts:

- The evaluators were on site in their respective schools for 6 hours.
- Some of the evaluators stayed in one classroom the entire time; others changed classrooms throughout the day.
- Some of the evaluators talked with the students; others had no interaction with the students.
- Some of the evaluators took copious notes, using complete sentences, and included drawings of the school's layout and student–teacher interactions; other evaluators wrote down thoughts, phrases, and a few comments they overheard.
- Some of the evaluators took photographs of bulletin boards and posters in the hallway and signs posted in the teachers' lounge.
- Some of the evaluators had lunch with the teachers in the cafeteria; others went to the closest fast food restaurant to grab a bite to eat.
- One of the evaluators observed the Communities of the Future after-school club.

Discussion Questions

1. What sampling issues does this case scenario raise?
2. How comparable are the data collected?
3. If, based on these observations, your team determined that these schools failed to implement a culture supportive of educational reform, what are the chances your team would be wrong?
4. If you concluded that you made the wrong decision, what could you do to reduce the likelihood of this problem occurring again?

Activity 36

Making the Case for Using a Random Sample

Overview

This activity helps participants understand appropriate uses of random sampling within an evaluation context.

Instructional Objectives

Participants will

- Understand issues related to selecting a random sample
- Identify appropriate applications of random sampling within an evaluation context

Number of Participants

- Minimum number of participants: 4
- Maximum number of participants: 25

Time Estimate: 30 to 45 minutes

In addition to providing the necessary background information on sampling methods, this activity requires approximately 30 to 45 minutes, depending on the number of participants and the time available for discussion.

Materials Needed

- Pens/pencils
- Flipchart, markers, tape
- Handout "Random Sampling Examined"

Instructional Method

Large-group discussion

Procedures

Facilitator's tasks:

- Distribute the handout "Random Sampling Examined."
- Write "Agree" on one flipchart paper and "Disagree" on another piece of flipchart paper.
- Attach each piece of flipchart paper to a different wall in the room.
- Read aloud the following statement, noting that this also appears on the handout: "Random sampling is the most appropriate sampling method for most evaluations."
- Ask participants to decide if they agree or disagree with the statement and to stand before the flipchart paper that represents their opinion.
- Ask the two groups to discuss why they agree or disagree with the statement and to list their reasons on the flipchart paper.
- Ask groups to share their reasons for either agreeing or disagreeing with the statement.
- Debrief the activity with the following questions:
  - What surprised you about the positions people took?
  - As a result of this activity, have you changed your position?
  - What are some of the challenges of selecting a random sample within an evaluation context?
  - What have you learned about sampling that you will be able to use in a current or future evaluation?

Random Sampling Examined

Handout for Activity 36

Directions:

Indicate whether you agree or disagree with the following statement:

Random sampling is the most appropriate sampling method for most evaluations.

__________ Agree

__________ Disagree

Go to the flipchart page that represents your opinion. As a group, list the reasons that justify your opinion.

Agree	*Disagree*

Activity 37

Choosing an Appropriate Sample

Overview

This activity asks participants to apply their knowledge of sampling to two case scenarios.

Instructional Objectives

Participants will

- Understand various probability and nonprobability sampling methods
- Determine an appropriate sampling method given an evaluation's purpose and key question
- Justify their reasons for choosing a particular sampling method

Number of Participants

- Minimum number of participants: 3
- Maximum number of participants: unlimited when participants are in groups of 3 to 5

Time Estimate: 45 to 90 minutes

In addition to providing the necessary background information on sampling, this activity requires approximately 45 to 90 minutes, depending on the number of participants (or groups) and the time available for discussion.

Materials Needed

- Pens/pencils
- Flipchart, markers, tape
- Handout "Sampling at Always Comfortable Furniture"

Instructional Method

Case scenario

Procedures

Facilitator's tasks:

- Ask participants to get into groups of three to five people.
- Distribute the handout "Sampling at Always Comfortable Furniture."
- Ask participants to read the case scenario and complete the task outlined on the handout.
- Request that participants note their responses on flipchart paper.
- Invite groups to present their sampling choices to the larger group.
- Debrief the activity with the following questions:
  - What did you learn about sampling from this activity?
  - When conducting an evaluation, what are the implications of obtaining a low response rate from a sample?
  - What could you do to prevent obtaining a low response rate (in the context of the case or from current practice)?
  - Reflecting on your past evaluation experiences, what problems have you observed in how samples were determined or selected?

Sampling at Always Comfortable Furniture

Handout for Activity 37

Background

Always Comfortable Furniture is a furniture manufacturing company that specializes in ergonomic furniture for home and office use. It employs 1,750 employees; 116 employees are supervisors and managers who supervise other employees. Of these 116 individuals, 90 are floor supervisors and 26 are department managers (from seven different operational units). As part of its effort to ensure that managers are effective facilitators of their employees' learning and development, the organization has designed, developed, pilot tested, and implemented a new 8-hour workshop for the 116 supervisors. Over the past 9 months, all of the supervisors and managers have participated in the training (four sessions were offered; 25 to 30 individuals were in each session).

The director of organizational learning now wants to evaluate the extent to which the training has affected the trainees' ability to effectively support their employees' learning and development goals. You were asked to evaluate the workshop and have developed the following key evaluation question to focus and guide the evaluation:

In what ways have the supervisors and managers used their learning from the workshop?

In your group, complete the following tasks:

1. Identify one data collection method that you would use to answer the evaluation question.
2. Recommend two different sampling methods (one probability and one non-probability) and identify the advantages and disadvantages of each method. Use the following table to organize your thoughts. Be prepared to justify your recommendations.

Sampling Method	*Advantages*	*Disadvantages*

Activity 38

Sampling With Bias

Overview

This activity asks participants to identify specific biases and errors in a sampling plan or from a drawn sample.

Instructional Objectives

Participants will

- Understand different approaches to sampling
- Understand the kinds of error that can occur in sampling
- Determine strategies that can be used to address sampling bias or error

Number of Participants

- Minimum number of participants: 3
- Maximum number of participants: unlimited when participants are in groups of 3 to 5

Time Estimate: 30 to 60 minutes

In addition to providing the necessary background information on sampling and sampling error, this activity requires approximately 30 to 60 minutes, depending on the number of participants (or groups) and the time available for discussion.

Materials Needed

- Pens/pencils
- Flipchart, markers, tape
- Handout "Problem Samples"

Instructional Method

Case scenario

Procedures

Facilitator's tasks:

- Ask participants to get into groups of three to five people.
- Distribute the handout "Problem Samples."
- Instruct participants to discuss each scenario with their group and determine which sampling problem occurred and what could be done to improve the sample.
- Ask participants to write their responses on a piece of flipchart paper.
- Invite groups to share their findings with the larger group.
- Debrief the activity with the following questions:
  - What other information would have helped you make a more informed decision in terms of the error or its solution?
  - If you were the evaluator in these cases, what would you tell the client about the error?
  - If you were the client, to what extent would you trust the information coming from these evaluations?
  - What are some challenges in sampling when working within an organizational context?
  - What, if any, ethical issues are there when sampling?

Problem Samples

Handout for Activity 38

Directions:

For each of the following scenarios, identify what problems exist with the sample and how the evaluator could have improved the sample.

1. An evaluation in a manufacturing plant sought to determine employee satisfaction with the Employee Assistance Program (EAP). The external evaluator decided to conduct telephone interviews. Because many employees in the plant were not accessible by phone during their shifts, the evaluator planned to call employees at home. The organization had a policy of not releasing employee home phone numbers, so the evaluator decided to obtain whatever phone numbers were available from the local phone directory.

What is the problem with this sample?	*What could the evaluator have done to improve the sample?*

2. The focus of this evaluation is on determining the degree to which teachers are using the school district's newly revised discipline policy. Surveys were distributed to all elementary, middle, and high school teachers. All elementary school and middle school teachers returned the surveys, but only about 30% of the high school teachers did so.

What is the problem with this sample?	*What could the evaluator have done to improve the sample?*

3. The variety of languages spoken by employees in a high-tech company has led to several problems during the production phase of the company's products. As a result, the organization has been implementing an English as a second language (ESL) program for non-English-speaking employees. The evaluator decides to conduct interviews in English with employees to determine the program's effectiveness. However, because of the production schedule, which limits access to employees, the evaluator agrees to conduct the interviews with the third-shift employees—many of whom do not speak English and, as a group, do not share a common language.

What is the problem with this sample?	*What could the evaluator have done to improve the sample?*

4. This evaluation focuses on a new door-to-door transportation service being offered throughout the metropolitan area. The agency decides to use a telephone-interviewing firm to conduct the interviews. The firm says that they plan to use the random-digit dialing system to contact community members. If no one answers, then the dialer will call another number.

What is the problem with this sample?	*What could the evaluator have done to improve the sample?*

7

Collecting Evaluation Data

BACKGROUND

This section includes activities that address the following:

- Choosing among data collection methods
- Understanding how to design effective surveys and questionnaires
- Conducting individual and focus group interviews
- Collecting observation and archival (documents and records) data

The following information is provided as a brief introduction to the topics covered in these activities.

CHOOSING AMONG DATA COLLECTION METHODS

It is important to recognize that the choice of data collection methods should come after determining an evaluation's purpose and key questions. Only then can one determine which methods are best suited to addressing the evaluation's concerns. Because each data collection method has inherent weaknesses, it is prudent to use multiple methods that collect both quantitative and qualitative data, whenever possible and appropriate. Using multiple methods with different data sources guards against apparently consistent but actually inaccurate findings.

SURVEYS AND QUESTIONNAIRES

One of the first decisions to make when creating a survey involves the types of questions to be asked. These include questions that are either open-ended or closed-ended. Open-ended questions ask respondents to write a response using their own words and are particularly effective when you are uncertain as to the entire range of alternative answers or when you wish to obtain examples, stories, lists, or descriptions. Respondents' answers to open-ended questions often result in insights into their experiences, attitudes, values, and beliefs.

Closed-ended items ask the respondent to choose from two or more alternatives. Such items include fill-in-the-blank questions, dichotomous or two-choice questions (such as a yes-no or true-false question), multiple-choice questions, rating scales, and ranking. Likert-type scales (a type of rating scale) are frequently used because they can be highly reliable and can be adapted to measure many different phenomena. To obtain valid information, however, closed-ended items must be carefully worded, and a full range of alternatives must be provided. The following are some guidelines for reviewing and improving the quality of survey items:

- Avoid leading or loaded questions.
- Avoid questions that ask for two or more pieces of information (also called double-barreled questions).
- Avoid wording that indicates bias or suggests a specific answer.
- Use response categories that are mutually exclusive.
- Use words that survey respondents will understand.
- Avoid jargon, slang, and abbreviations.
- Avoid negative and double-negative questions.
- With closed-ended items, provide a full range of responses.

A goal of any survey is to have a high enough response rate so that there is sufficient confidence that the findings represent the total population and thus can be used to make decisions or take action. To encourage individuals to respond to a self-administered survey, various incentives may be used. When choosing an incentive, it is important to consider its cost, logistical requirements, ethical implications, respondent reactions, as well as the likelihood that the incentive will lead to a higher response rate than if no incentive were used. In particular, consider how appropriate various incentives might be for different respondent groups.

INDIVIDUAL AND FOCUS GROUP INTERVIEWS

Conducting individual interviews can provide rich and valuable data for the evaluator. Through the telling of stories, examples, and critical incidents, rich, contextual information can be collected. Evaluators who wish to conduct individual interviews as part of an evaluation's strategy should consider several issues when employing this method of data collection. For example, the act of interviewing requires the evaluator to become part of the context being studied. Understanding this context includes understanding one's own role in it, as well as the individual filters or lenses through which one views the world. Another issue relates to the concern for obtaining trustworthy (valid) data. How do we ensure that the interviewees' responses truly represent their opinions, attitudes, or experiences and that they are not providing false or inaccurate information? With regard to documentation, evaluators also need to consider the ways in which interview data are recorded.

A focus group interview typically consists of 6 to 12 participants who share a common experience and can collectively address a set of evaluation questions. Keeping the size of the group to a manageable number increases the likelihood that all participants will have an opportunity to speak. A major advantage of using focus group interviews is the opportunity it provides participants to hear a variety of experiences and opinions on a particular topic. This not only helps the interviewer come away with richer data, but it also often provides participants with a greater understanding of the evaluation issue. To ensure that participants feel safe and comfortable talking with one another, it is usually wise to structure the focus group interviews so that people of similar position, experience, tenure, or need are within the same group. Focus group interviews generally range in time from 1.5 to 3 hours. Focus group interviews allow for the gathering of data from a large number of people at a relatively low cost.

OBSERVATION AND ARCHIVAL DATA

The power of using observation methods is that observation engages all of our senses, not just our sight. Unlike other data collection methods, observation data can provide us with a more holistic understanding of the phenomenon we are studying. Sources of observational data include the following:

- The program setting
- The human social environment
- The program implementation activities and formal interactions
- Identification of participants and their level of engagement
- Participants' language
- Nonverbal communications
- Unobtrusive indicators
- Program documents
- Observations of what does not happen

Various issues should be considered when conducting observations within an evaluation context:

- The observer's role
- What to disclose to those being observed
- The focus of the observations
- How data will be collected and recorded
- The location of the observations
- Who will conduct the observations and what training, if any, this person will need
- The duration and frequency of the observations

Observing physical traces of behavior is another type of observation that requires little to no interaction with individuals. Called unobtrusive measures, this method has been widely used by anthropologists and sociologists. The data collected are referred to either as erosion or accretion measures and are a result of a human activity that either accumulates (accretion) or is depleted (erosion).

Examples of accretion measures include the following:

- Sticky or dirty computer keyboards (to determine usage)
- Notes made on handouts and in manuals (to determine level of engagement and interest in material)
- Number of grievances filed after a workshop on sexual harassment

Erosion measures, on the other hand, provide evidence of the wearing away or wearing down of a thing. Examples include the following:

- Pages missing in a training manual or book (to determine use and interest)
- Materials requested or taken by employees, for example, brochures, catalogs, schedules (to determine interest in subject matter)
- Broken equipment (to determine degree of usage or quality)

Although unobtrusive measures can provide interesting data that are often useful to evaluation studies, one must be very cautious not to overinterpret their meaning. Given the multiple interpretations one may make from these kinds of data, this method is best used in conjunction with other data gathering techniques.

Documents and records (archival data) can be very useful for obtaining facts and artifacts as an evaluation data collection method. A document is "a written or printed paper that bears the original, official, or legal form of something and can be used to furnish decisive evidence or information." A record is "an account, as of information or facts, set down especially in writing as a means of preserving knowledge; information or data on a particular subject collected and preserved; the known history of performance, activities, or achievement" (Guba & Lincoln, 1981, p. 239). The value of documents and records lies in their credibility: Do they only represent truth and reality (validity)? Or are they also credible to others? Guba and Lincoln (1981) suggest that evaluators consider the following questions to determine the veracity and usefulness of documents and records they collect as part of an evaluation effort:

- What is the history of the document?
- What guarantee is there that it is what it pretends to be?
- Is the document complete, as originally constructed? Has it been tampered with or edited?
- Under what circumstances and for what purposes was it produced?
- Who is the author? What was he or she trying to accomplish? For whom was the document intended?
- To what extent was the writer likely to want to tell the truth?
- Do other documents exist that might shed additional light on the same story, event, project, program, context? If so, are they available? Accessible? Who holds them?

RESOURCES

Bader, G. E., & Rossi, C. A. (2002). *Focus groups: A step-by-step guide* (3rd ed.). San Diego, CA: Bader Group.

Bouchard, T. J., Jr. (1976). Unobtrusive measures. *Sociological Methods and Research, 4*(3), 267-300.

Denzin, N. K., & Lincoln, Y. S. (Eds.). (2000). *Handbook of qualitative research* (2nd ed.). Thousand Oaks, CA: Sage.

Dillman, D. A. (1999). *Mail and Internet surveys: The tailored design method* (2nd ed.). New York: Wiley.

Fern, E. F. (2001). *Advanced focus group research.* Thousand Oaks, CA: Sage.

Fink, A. (2003). *The survey kit* (2nd ed.). Thousand Oaks, CA: Sage.

Fowler, F. J. (2001). *Survey research methods* (3rd ed.). Thousand Oaks, CA: Sage.

Greenbaum, T. L. (1999). *Moderating focus groups: A practical guide for group facilitation.* Thousand Oaks, CA: Sage.

Greene, J. C., & Caracelli, V. J. (Eds.). (1997). *Advances in mixed method evaluation: The challenges and benefits of integrating diverse paradigms* (New Directions for Evaluation, Vol. 74). San Francisco: Jossey-Bass.

Guba, E. G. & Lincoln, Y. S. (1981). *Effective evaluation.* San Francisco: Jossey-Bass.

Hatry, H. P. (1994). Collecting data from agency records. In J. S. Wholey, H. P. Hatry, & K. E. Newcomer (Eds.), *Handbook of practical program evaluation* (pp. 374-386). San Francisco: Jossey-Bass.

Holstein, J., & Gubrium, J. F. (Eds.). (2003). *Inside interviewing: New lenses, new concerns.* Thousand Oaks, CA: Sage.

Krueger, R. A., & Casey, M. A. (2000). *Focus groups: A practical guide for applied research* (3rd ed.). Thousand Oaks, CA: Sage.

Morgan, D. L., & Kruger, R. A. (1997). *The focus group kit* (Vol. 1–6). Thousand Oaks, CA: Sage.

Patton, M. Q. (1997). *Utilization-focused evaluation: The new century text* (3rd ed.). Thousand Oaks, CA: Sage.

Patton, M. Q. (2001). *Qualitative research & evaluation methods* (3rd ed.). Thousand Oaks, CA: Sage.

Payne, S. L. (1980). *The art of asking questions.* Princeton, NJ: Princeton University Press.

Prior, L. (2003). *Using documents in social research.* Thousand Oaks, CA: Sage.

Rubin, I., & Rubin, H. J. (1995). *Qualitative interviewing: The art of hearing data.* Thousand Oaks, CA: Sage.

Russ-Eft, D., & Preskill, H. (2001). *Evaluation in organizations: A systematic approach to enhancing learning, performance, and change.* Boston: Perseus.

Spradley, J. P. (1997). *Participant observation.* Boston: Thomson Publishing.

Sudman, S., & Bradburn, N. M. (1982). *Asking questions: A practical guide to questionnaire design.* San Francisco: Jossey-Bass.

Webb, E., Campbell, D. T., Schwartz, R., & Sechrest, L. (2000). *Unobtrusive measures: Nonreactive research in the social sciences* (rev. ed.). Thousand Oaks, CA: Sage.

Activity 39

Choosing Data Collection Methods

Overview

This activity provides participants an opportunity to discuss, select, and justify the use of various data collection methods with regard to a particular evaluation study.

Instructional Objectives

Participants will

- Discuss various types of data collection methods as they are applied to evaluation practice
- Discuss several criteria that can be used to determine which data collection methods are best suited for a particular evaluation
- Determine the strengths and weaknesses, as well as the level of intrusiveness, of several data collection methods

Number of Participants

- Minimum number of participants: 3
- Maximum number of participants: unlimited when participants are in groups of 3 to 5

Time Estimate: 45 to 90 minutes

In addition to providing the necessary background information about various data collection methods, this activity requires approximately 45 to 90, minutes depending on the number of participants (or groups) and the time available for discussion.

Materials Needed

- Pens/pencils
- Flipchart, markers, tape
- Handout "Evaluating the GEAR UP Program"
- Handout "Matrix of Data Collection Methods"

Instructional Method

Small-group work/case scenario

Procedures

Facilitator's tasks:

- Ask participants to get into groups of three to five people. Provide each group with a piece of flipchart paper.
- Assign each group one of the following data collection methods:
  - Mailed survey
  - Online survey
  - Individual, face-to-face interview
  - Focus group interview
  - Phone survey or interview
  - Observation
  - Archival data (records and documents)
  - Test

  If there are fewer than eight groups, some groups can be asked to work on two or three of these methods.
- Ask participants to write their method on the flipchart paper.
- Instruct each group to draw a line down the middle of the flipchart paper and to label one side "Advantages" and the other side "Disadvantages."
- Instruct participants to discuss the relative advantages and disadvantages of the methods they are assigned and to note these on the flipchart paper.
- Ask groups to attach their flipchart paper to the wall.
- Invite groups to briefly describe their methods' advantages and disadvantages.
- Distribute the handout "Evaluating the GEAR UP Program" and ask participants to individually read the case scenario (participants could also take turns reading the scenario aloud).
- Distribute the handout "Matrix of Data Collection Methods."

- Tell participants that, in their groups, they are to complete the matrix by choosing the best data collection methods for this evaluation scenario.
- Ask for volunteers to share their group's chosen data collection methods and their reasons for choosing them.
- Debrief the activity with the following questions:
  - What information influenced your decisions?
  - What additional information about the program's context would have been helpful?
  - What challenges might the evaluator face using the data collection methods you chose?
  - How would you support your choices with the stakeholders?
  - What "ah-ha's," if any, did you have as a result of working on this activity?

Evaluating the GEAR UP Program

Handout for Activity 39

Background

The GEAR UP program is a federally funded early intervention program that provides information on higher education, financial aid, and student services to low-income middle school students. The mission of GEAR UP is "to accelerate the academic achievement of cohorts of disadvantaged middle and secondary school students so that increasing numbers will graduate from high school, enroll in college, and succeed."

GEAR UP accomplishes its mission by providing a myriad of services through its seven component areas:

1. Early college awareness activities
2. Statewide clearinghouse of outreach programs
3. Tutoring Plus program through community colleges
4. Enhanced academics
5. Statewide college awareness outreach
6. College access via online admissions applications
7. Professional development

During the first year of one state's GEAR UP grant, targeted services were provided to schools in two rural towns. The second year, it added schools from an additional seven towns. And, in the project's third year, it added another six towns. GEAR UP is currently providing targeted services to 15 schools in this state and has partnered with six community colleges to provide tutoring and other educational assistance.

Based on conversations with GEAR UP liaisons, families, students, and community members, the GEAR UP staff members are confident that the activities their sites provide are having a positive impact on the students' interest in completing high school and pursing higher education.

Throughout the year, liaisons collect data and submit information about their GEAR UP activities to the state's GEAR UP staff members. This information is included in the annual report submitted to the United States Department of Education. However, the staff members would like to collect additional data that provide more in-depth information concerning what is working well and what changes might be needed regarding the program's administration and the design and implementation of specific site activities. The staff believe that not only will this additional evaluation data help to support continuous improvement but having such data will also support their future funding efforts.

Purpose of the Evaluation

The purpose of the evaluation is to better understand the ways in which GEAR UP is being implemented, to identify the extent to which it is successful, and to determine how it might be improved.

Stakeholders

The primary stakeholders in this evaluation include the state's GEAR UP project director, and an advisory group made up of 16 principals, teachers, counselors, and GEAR UP liaisons. As intended users of the evaluation results, they will determine what actions, if any, to take based on the results of this evaluation. In addition, they may be invited to review and provide feedback on this evaluation plan, the data collection instruments, and the resulting aggregated data.

The secondary stakeholders consist of the United States Department of Education, which funds the program; community college service providers; and other local site staff who are responsible for implementing GEAR UP.

Tertiary stakeholders are other teachers and administrators at the GEAR UP sites who are not currently involved in the program but who might be in future years.

Evaluation Key Questions

Based on a meeting with the advisory group, the following questions were developed to guide this evaluation:

1. In what ways and how well is GEAR UP's mission and purpose communicated to students, parents, staff members, local administration, and community members?
2. What activities are local sites designing and implementing to achieve GEAR UP's objectives (e.g., college tours, journaling, after-school programs, enrichment, tutoring)?
3. In what ways and why are the various GEAR UP activities successful? What advice do local site staff members have for others implementing these activities?

4. What are the barriers to student participation in GEAR UP activities, and how have site staff members been able to increase student participation?
5. To what extent and in what ways has GEAR UP affected students' interest in and willingness to finish high school?
6. To what extent and in what ways has GEAR UP influenced students' interest in pursuing higher education?
7. To what extent and in what ways have the professional development activities funded by GEAR UP affected the creation of a college-bound culture in the schools?

Additional Information

- The evaluation must be completed between June and December (6 months).
- The federal government is not requiring this evaluation (they do require quantitative data on the number of participants and the number of activities, which are already being provided by the stakeholders).
- Students from one of the sites will be participating in a youth college tour at one of the state's universities for 5 days in August.
- There is a national conference for GEAR UP staff members around the country in July in Washington, DC. Several GEAR UP staff members from the state will be attending.
- The stakeholders believe it is important to see the program's participants and activities firsthand.
- The evaluator has been conducting evaluations for 7 years. She learned evaluation by taking several workshops and a graduate-level course at a nearby university.
- The budget for the evaluation is $20,000.

Matrix of Data Collection Methods

Handout for Activity 39

Methods / *Criteria*	*Mailed Survey*	*Online Survey*	*Individual Face-to-Face Interview*	*Focus Group Interview*	*Phone Survey or Interview*	*Observation*	*Archival Data (Records & Documents)*	*Test (Computer, Pencil, Simulation)*
Evaluation questions								
Evaluator skills								
Resources								
Stakeholders' preferences								
Level of acceptable intrusiveness								
Validity								
Availability								
Timeliness								
External requirements								

Activity 40

Comparing and Contrasting Open-Ended and Closed-Ended Survey Formats

Overview

This activity helps participants understand the differences in developing and administering closed-ended and open-ended survey items.

Instructional Objectives

Participants will

- Understand the advantages and disadvantages of open- and closed-ended survey items
- Practice writing both open- and closed-ended survey items
- Collect survey data
- Practice analyzing open- and closed-ended survey data
- Understand when to use each type of survey item

Number of Participants

- Minimum number of participants: 2
- Maximum number of participants: unlimited when participants work in pairs

Time Estimate: 90 to 120 minutes (over two sessions)

This activity requires two consecutive meeting times. Approximately 45 to 60 minutes are needed for the first meeting; less time may be needed if the group is small. After the first meeting and outside of class, participants need approximately 1 hour to administer the survey and analyze the resulting data. The second meeting may last from 45 to 60 minutes, depending on the number of participants.

Materials Needed

- Pens/pencils
- Handout "Comparing and Contrasting Open- and Closed-Ended Surveys: Part 1"
- Handout "Comparing and Contrasting Open- and Closed-Ended Surveys: Part 2"

Instructional Method

Small-group work/fieldwork

Procedures

Class 1 (approximately 45 to 60 minutes)

Facilitator's tasks:

- Introduce the activity explaining that participants will be exploring the use of open- and closed-ended survey questions. Describe the purpose of the activity and distribute the handout "Comparing and Contrasting Open- and Closed-Ended Surveys: Part 1."
- Ask participants to pair up with one other person.
- Instruct pairs to choose a topic for which they will develop a survey. The topic should be one of common interest or experience.
- Instruct pairs to create five to seven open-ended questions that relate to the topic they have chosen.
- Instruct pairs to convert each open-ended question into a Likert-scale question or other closed-ended type of question. Explain that they must have the same number of closed-ended items as they have open-ended items.
- Instruct participants that they are to administer their surveys to a sample of 5 individuals. Discuss who would be an appropriate sample. For example, if they have chosen a topic relating to family, they may administer the survey to family members. On the other hand, if the survey questions are work related, they should plan on asking a sample of colleagues to complete the survey. Explain that one person in the pair is to administer the open-ended survey to 5 people, and the other person is to administer the closed-ended survey to a different sample of 5 people.

Out-of-Class Assignment (approximately 1 hour)

Participants' tasks:

- Administer their survey in person. This could be done as part of a staff meeting or in one-on-one sessions.
- Observe and note respondents' reactions, questions, and requests for more information or clarification.

- Note how long it takes each person to complete the survey.
- Note how many people they asked before obtaining the 5-person sample.
- Analyze the survey responses using appropriate analysis methods. These might include frequencies, means or averages, and percentages and content analysis of the qualitative responses. Participants could also develop charts and tables that display the findings.
- Note how long it takes to analyze the data.

Class 2 (approximately 45 to 60 minutes)

Facilitator's tasks:

- Ask pairs to compare the results of their surveys and the notes they took during the surveys' administration and analysis using the handout "Comparing and Contrasting Open- and Closed-Ended Surveys: Part 2."
- Ask pairs to discuss their experiences with the larger group.
- Debrief the activity with the following questions:
  - What were your experiences in converting the open-ended questions to closed-ended items?
  - What kinds of information were generated from the two surveys? Which survey seemed to provide more useful and informative findings?
  - To what extent were the findings from the two surveys similar or different?
  - When would you use open- or closed-ended items, based on your findings and experiences?
  - What surprised you the most about designing and implementing these surveys?

Comparing and Contrasting Open- and Closed-Ended Surveys: Part 1

Handout for Activity 40

Directions:

- Pair up with one other person.
- Choose a topic in which you are both interested.
- Create five to seven open-ended questions that relate to your topic.
- Convert those open-ended questions into Likert-scale questions or another kind of closed-ended question. These questions must parallel exactly the kinds of information you are seeking from the open-ended questions.
- Before the next class, one of you is to administer the open-ended survey to a sample of 5 individuals, and one of you is to administer the closed-ended survey to a sample of 5 individuals.
- As these individuals respond to the survey, please take note of the following:
  - How many people you asked before you got 5 people to participate.
  - The respondents' reactions, questions, and requests for more information (try not to give them too much information).
  - How long it takes each person to complete the survey.
- Analyze your data and be prepared to discuss your findings.
  - What information resulted?
  - How long did it take to complete the analyses?

Comparing and Contrasting Open- and Closed-Ended Surveys: Part 2

Handout for Activity 40

With your partner, discuss the following:

- How you administered your survey
- How many people were asked before you achieved your sample
- The respondents' reactions, comments, and questions
- How long it took respondents to complete the survey
- How long it took to analyze your data
- Challenges you experienced in analyzing your data
- How your findings are similar and different
- What you learned from this activity

Activity 41

Critiquing a Survey's Content and Format

Overview

This activity requires participants to use their knowledge of survey design to improve a survey's design and potential effectiveness.

Instructional Objectives

Participants will

- Identify poorly worded and formatted survey items
- Practice improving survey items
- Identify ways to improve a survey's format

Number of Participants

- Minimum number of participants: 2
- Maximum number of participants: unlimited when participants are in groups of 2 to 3

Time Estimate: 30 to 45 minutes

In addition to providing the necessary background information on survey design, this activity requires approximately 30 to 45 minutes, depending on the number of participants (or groups) and the time available for discussion.

Materials Needed

- Pens/pencils
- Handout "Human Resources Survey: Subordinate Appraisal of Management (SAM)" (Other surveys that have design flaws may be used in addition to, or instead of, this handout.)

Instructional Method

Small-group work

Procedures

Facilitator's tasks:

- Explain that participants will be critiquing a survey and determining ways in which it could be improved.
- Ask participants to get into groups of two to three people.
- Distribute the handout "Human Resources Survey: Subordinate Appraisal of Management (SAM)" and ask groups to discuss any problems they see with the survey's items, formats, and directions. Explain that they are to describe specific things they would do to improve the survey's design.
- Instruct participants to begin working on their critique of the survey.
- Invite participants to describe their suggested revisions.
- Debrief the activity with the following questions:
  - What surprised you the most about trying to improve this survey?
  - If this survey had been implemented as is, what issues might there have been with the data collected?
  - What did you learn about survey design from this activity?

Human Resources Survey: Subordinate Appraisal of Management (SAM)

Handout for Activity 41

Circle your response:

1. Are any employees in your company given the opportunity to evaluate management directly (Attitude/Climate survey excluded)?

   A. YES B. NO

2. Is management evaluated by employees in a general Attitude/Climate survey?

   A. YES B. NO

3. Are you considering Subordinate Appraisals of Management (SAM) for the future?

   A. YES B. NO

If you answered NO to both Questions 1 and 2, skip to Question 9.

4. Is your SAM direct information to the manager, training, or upper management:

   A. YES B. NO

5. How is the SAM used?

   A. Feedback B. Pay C. Promotion D. Training

6. How long have you been using SAMs?

   A. 0–1 year B. 1–5 years C. 5–10 years D. 10 years or more

7. Does your SAM have open-ended and closed-ended items?

   A. YES B. NO

8. Who receives the results of the SAM?

   A. Manager B. Upper management C. Training D. Employees
   E. General management F. Other: ____________________

9. Does your company conduct a formal management assessment or do they have an outside source do it?

   A. YES B. NO

10. Does your company practice any type of participative management (employee participation in management decisions)?

    A. YES B. NO

Activity 42

Using Incentives to Increase Survey Response Rates

Overview

This activity focuses on the appropriateness and ethical implications of using various incentives, as well as the feasibility of different incentives.

Instructional Objectives

Participants will

- Understand the reasons for using incentives as a means for increasing survey response rates
- Identify and consider a variety of incentives for increasing survey response rates
- Determine the advantages and disadvantages of various incentives

Number of Participants

- Minimum number of participants: 3
- Maximum number of participants: unlimited when participants are in groups of 3 to 5

Time Estimate: 30 to 60 minutes

In addition to providing the necessary background information on the use of incentives for increasing survey responses, as well as the ethical implications and related validity issues that may arise from using incentives, this activity requires approximately 30 to 60 minutes, depending on the number of participants (or groups) and the time available for discussion.

Materials Needed

- Pens/pencils
- Flipchart, markers, tape
- Handout "Using Incentives to Increase Survey Response Rates"

Instructional Method

Small-group work

Procedures

Facilitator's tasks:

- Ask participants to get into groups of three to five people.
- Distribute the handout "Using Incentives to Increase Survey Response Rates."
- Read the activity's directions. You might want to provide an example if the group has limited experience with survey design or the use of incentives. Sample incentives might include money, gift certificates, a copy of the final evaluation report, a cookbook, restaurant coupons, or a raffle ticket.
- Instruct participants to make notes on their handouts and then to pick three incentives they think would work best with the population(s) they have identified. Ask participants to write the incentives on a piece of flipchart paper.
- Ask groups to post their flipchart pages on a wall, and invite the participants to briefly discuss the incentives listed on the groups' flipchart pages.
- Debrief the activity with the following questions:
  - How did you decide what would be an effective survey incentive? What were your criteria?
  - What issues arose in your discussions concerning the positive and negative aspects of various incentives?
  - What ethical issues did your group discuss relative to the use of incentives?
  - Under what circumstances might the use of incentives be inappropriate?
  - Have you ever used any of these incentives in your own survey work? If yes, what impact did they have?

Using Incentives to Increase Survey Response Rates

Handout for Activity 42

Directions:

1. In the first column, make a list of possible incentives that could be used to obtain a high survey response rate. Don't worry about whether the particular incentive will work at this point—just note whatever incentives come to mind.
2. In the second column, indicate the type of respondent for whom this incentive would be best suited.
3. For the incentives your group identified, discuss and note the positive and negative aspects of each one. These might also be written and thought of as advantages and disadvantages (the third and fourth columns).
4. Highlight the incentives that you think are particularly feasible for the contexts in which you work.
5. Write your top three incentives on a piece of flipchart paper to share with the entire group.

Incentive	*Respondent Population*	*Positive Aspects or Advantages*	*Negative Aspects or Disadvantages*

Activity 43

Following Up on Survey Nonrespondents

Overview

This activity asks participants to consider several issues related to following up on a survey's nonrespondents.

Instructional Objectives

Participants will

- Become familiar with ways to follow up on survey nonrespondents to obtain a higher response rate
- Identify issues related to following up on survey nonrespondents
- Understand how following up on nonrespondents can affect an evaluation's budget, timeline, and results

Number of Participants

- Minimum number of participants: 8
- Maximum number of participants: 20

Time Estimate: 30 to 60 minutes

This activity requires approximately 30 to 60 minutes, depending on the time available for discussion.

Materials Needed

- Pens/pencils
- Flipchart, markers, tape
- Handout "Flipchart Questions"

Instructional Method

Round-robin

Procedures

Facilitator's tasks:

- Write each of the following questions on a piece of flipchart paper and post them around the room (i.e., on each of four walls or on four flipcharts placed around the room).
  - Why might people not respond to a mailed or online survey?
  - How might a low survey response rate affect an evaluation's findings?
  - What methods could be used to follow up with nonrespondents?
  - Under what circumstances might you choose not to follow up with nonrespondents?
- Ask participants to get into groups of two to five people.
- Direct each group to one of the flipchart pages and tell the groups they have a certain amount of time to spend at each flipchart station (3 to 6 minutes). Explain that when the allocated time is up, each group will move clockwise to the next flipchart page and will respond to the posted question, adding to what the previous group provided.
- After groups have written their responses on each flipchart page, ask participants to review the information on all of the flipchart pages.
- Go to each flipchart and ask for clarification and examples and add content that may have been overlooked. Invite participants to offer additional ideas.
- Debrief the activity with the following questions:
  - Is there anything to add? Did we miss anything?
  - What would it mean if we didn't follow up on nonrespondents and settled for a low response rate?
  - What implications does following up on nonrespondents have on an evaluation's budget and timeline?
  - As you consider evaluations you are now conducting or might conduct in the future, how might you approach following up on survey nonrespondents?
- If possible, tell participants that the information from the flipchart pages will be typed up and distributed to them (either in the next session or by e-mail).

Flipchart Questions

Handout for Activity 43

The following questions should be written on individual pieces of flipchart paper and placed in various parts of the room.

Flipchart A

Why might people not respond to a mailed or online survey?

Flipchart B

How might a low survey response rate affect an evaluation's findings?

Flipchart C

What methods could be used to follow up on nonrespondents?

Flipchart D

Under what circumstances might you choose not to follow up on nonrespondents?

Activity 44

Developing a Concept Map for the Use of Online Surveys

Overview

This activity engages participants in developing a concept map or mind map that reflects when and how to use online surveys for evaluation purposes. The benefits and challenges to using online surveys versus paper-pencil surveys are also addressed.

Instructional Objectives

Participants will

- Discuss strategies for developing effective surveys in general and online surveys in particular
- Collaboratively develop a concept map or mind map that depicts how and when online surveys may be effectively used in an evaluation context
- Compare and contrast the benefits and challenges of using online surveys versus paper-pencil surveys

Number of Participants

- Minimum number of participants: 3
- Maximum number of participants: unlimited when participants are in groups of 3 to 5

Time Estimate: 60 to 75 minutes

In addition to providing the necessary background information on survey design and the development and use of online surveys, this activity requires approximately 60 to 75 minutes, depending on the number of participants (or groups) and the time available for discussion.

Materials Needed

- Pens/pencils
- Markers, crayons, colored pencils

- Flipcharts, tape
- Background readings or handouts (or both) on survey design and the use of online surveys provided by the facilitator

Instructional Method

Visual representation

Procedures

Facilitator's tasks:

- Obtain recent background readings on survey design and use of online surveys.
- Ask participants to get into groups of three to five people.
- Place a variety of markers, crayons, and colored pencils and a piece of flipchart paper at each table.
- Explain that participants are going to develop a mind map (or concept map) that describes when and how to use online surveys for evaluation purposes. (A mind map is a visual method that is used to organize thoughts, identify key ideas, link themes, and remember materials, using both words and pictures. Participants should create their mind map in a way that makes the most sense to them.)
- Instruct participants to take out any of their readings, notes, or other materials they have on the topic of survey design and online surveys.
- Instruct participants to first discuss the use of online surveys (including when and how they may be used) in an evaluation context.
- Instruct participants to begin developing their maps by creating a center image or symbol that reads "Using online surveys."
- Encourage participants to use different colors and symbols to represent tips for developing online surveys, appropriate uses for online surveys, and any procedural guidelines they may wish to offer.
- Invite groups to present their concept maps.
- Debrief the activity with the following questions:
  - What issues should be considered when using an online survey versus a paper-pencil survey?
  - Under what conditions is an online survey most appropriate? Inappropriate?
  - What are the data analysis implications for using an online survey? How do these compare to analyzing data from a paper-pencil survey?
  - To what extent do you think the validity of respondents' answers is affected by the different survey delivery formats (online vs. paper-pencil)?
  - In what ways are issues of anonymity and confidentiality affected by the use of online surveys versus paper-pencil surveys?

Activity 45

Tips for Conducting Effective Interviews

Overview

This activity asks participants to recall and discuss the use of interviews as a data collection method within an evaluation context.

Instructional Objectives

Participants will

- Brainstorm various skills, techniques, and benefits of conducting interviews
- Reflect on how they might further develop their interviewing skills and knowledge

Number of Participants

- Minimum number of participants: 8
- Maximum number of participants: 20

Time Estimate: 30 to 60 minutes

In addition to providing the necessary background information on interviewing, this activity requires approximately 30 to 60 minutes, depending on the time available for discussion.

Materials Needed

- Flipchart, markers, tape
- Clock or timer
- Handout "Flipchart Categories"

Instructional Method

Round-robin

Procedures

Facilitator's tasks:

- Write each of the following on flipchart paper and post them around the room:
  - Things to Do to Prepare for Conducting an Interview
  - Essential Interviewer Skills and Characteristics
  - Barriers to Gaining Trustworthy Data/Strategies for Collecting Trustworthy Data
  - Advantages and Disadvantages of Note Taking, Tape-Recording, and Computer Recording
- Ask participants to get into groups of two to five people.
- Direct each group to one of the flipchart pages and tell participants that they have a certain amount of time to spend at each flipchart (3 to 6 minutes is usually sufficient). When the allocated time is up, each group moves clockwise to the next flipchart page and responds to the topic posted, adding to what the previous group provided.
- After groups have visited each of the four flipcharts, they are to go around one more time to review all of the responses.
- Go to each flipchart and ask for clarification and examples and add content that may have been overlooked. Invite participants to offer additional ideas.
- Debrief the activity with the following questions:
  - What do you want to remember about interviewing for your own practice?
  - What had you not thought of (regarding interviewing) before engaging in this activity?
  - What is one thing you want to make sure you do when you interview someone in the context of an evaluation?
- If possible, tell participants that the information from the flipchart pages will be typed up and distributed to them (either in the next session or by e-mail).

Flipchart Categories

Handout for Activity 45

Flipchart A

Things to Do to Prepare for Conducting an Interview

Flipchart B

Essential Interviewer Skills and Characteristics

Flipchart C

Barriers to Gaining Trustworthy Data/Strategies for Collecting Trustworthy Data

Barriers to Gaining Trustworthy Data	*Strategies for Collecting Trustworthy Data*

Flipchart D

Advantages and Disadvantages of Note Taking, Tape-Recording, and Computer Recording

	Advantages	*Disadvantages*
Note taking		
Tape-recording		
Computer recording		

Activity 46

Role-Playing Individual Interviews

Overview

This activity provides participants an opportunity to conduct and observe an individual interview.

Instructional Objectives

Participants will

- Understand the benefits and limitations of individual interviewing
- Practice conducting an interview
- Obtain feedback on their interviewing technique
- Observe and provide feedback to others who are conducting interviews

Number of Participants

- Minimum number of participants: 3
- Maximum number of participants: unlimited when participants are in groups of 3

Time Estimate: 75 to 105 minutes

In addition to providing the necessary background information on conducting individual (face-to-face) interviews, this activity requires approximately 75 to 105 minutes, depending on the number of participants (or groups) and the time available for discussion.

Materials Needed

- Pens/pencils
- Flipchart, markers, tape
- Handout "Role-Playing Interview Scenarios"

Instructional Method

Role play

Procedures

Facilitator's tasks:

- Ask participants to get into groups of three people.
- Distribute the handout "Role-Playing Interview Scenarios."
- Explain that participants will be conducting interviews with each other using three different scenarios and that for each scenario they will assign one person to be the interviewer, one person to be the interviewee, and one person to be the observer who provides feedback on the interview once it is complete.
- Instruct each group to select the interviewer, interviewee, and observer for the first scenario.
- Give participants the following instructions:
  - They will have 5 minutes to read the scenario and prepare interview questions.
  - The interview will last 5 to 10 minutes.
  - The interviewer and the interviewee will spend 5 minutes talking about their experiences.
  - The observer will have 5 minutes to provide feedback to the interviewer and interviewee.
- Ask the groups to read Scenario 1.
- Tell the groups the following:
  - When to begin the interview
  - When to end the interview
  - When the observer is to provide feedback
- Ask group members to change roles.
- Ask the groups to read Scenario 2.
- Tell the groups the following:
  - When to begin the interview
  - When to end the interview
  - When the observer is to provide feedback
- Ask group members to change roles.
- Ask the groups to read Scenario 3.
- Tell the groups the following:
  - When to begin the interview
  - When to end the interview
  - When the observer is to provide feedback
- Debrief the activity with the following questions:
  - What was it like for you when you were the interviewer? What was it like to be interviewed?
  - What were some of the most effective interviewer behaviors that you observed?
  - What nonverbal behaviors among the interviewees did you observe?
  - If you were to use interviews as a data collection method for an evaluation, what one thing would you make sure to do as you conducted the interview?

Role-Playing Interview Scenarios

Handout for Activity 46

Scenario 1

An evaluation is being undertaken of the Employee Assistance Program (EAP) within a manufacturing organization. Interviews are being conducted with a sample of managers and employees at that site. The purpose of the interview is to determine the extent to which managers and employees are using the program and their level of satisfaction with the program. Interviewers should be aware that both managers and employees might be reluctant to reveal that they have personally used the services of the program because that might indicate some degree of inability to deal with personal problems.

Scenario 2

An evaluation is being conducted of a violence prevention program within a school district. This program consists of training sessions for all teachers and administrators as well as special sessions designed for students. Interviews will be conducted with a sample of teachers at each of the schools in the district. The interviews will focus on the level of verbal and physical abuse observed by these teachers both in the classroom as well as during recess periods.

Scenario 3

This evaluation focuses on the community services provided by a senior center. This particular center has been recognized for its outstanding programs, including its meal programs, social clubs, health services, and community involvement. What is not known, however, is information regarding the services provided to homebound seniors. The purpose of the interviews is to determine the community's level of awareness of and satisfaction with these services.

Activity 47

Individual Interviewing Challenges

Overview

This activity asks participants to consider several issues related to conducting individual interviews.

Instructional Objectives

Participants will

- Discuss several issues concerning the collection of trustworthy interview data
- Articulate both challenges and solutions interviewers often face when conducting individual interviews

Number of Participants

- Minimum number of participants: 3
- Maximum number of participants: unlimited when participants are in groups of 3 to 5

Time Estimate: 30 to 45 minutes

In addition to providing the necessary background information on conducting individual (face-to-face) interviews, this activity requires approximately 30 to 45 minutes, depending on the number of participants (or groups) and the time available for discussion.

Materials Needed

- Pens/pencils
- Handout "Interviewing in Times of Change"

Instructional Method

Case scenario

Procedures

Facilitator's tasks:

- Ask participants to get into groups of three to five people.
- Distribute the handout "Interviewing in Times of Change."
- Ask participants to discuss their responses to the questions on the handout.
- Invite participants to volunteer the highlights of their groups' answers to the handout's questions.
- Debrief the activity with the following questions:
  - What were some of the challenges your group experienced in trying to answer the discussion questions?
  - What did this activity confirm for you?
  - What did this activity make you think of concerning your own evaluation practice?
  - In what situations do you think individual interviews are the most appropriate and useful data collection method?
  - If you were to give one tip to an evaluator who was going to interview someone in an evaluation context, what would that be?

Interviewing in Times of Change

Handout for Activity 47

The Evaluation Context

The company for which you work has just undergone a merger with another company. The process was long and drawn out, and there has been a marked decrease in employee morale. One outcome of the merger is that some positions will likely be eliminated or consolidated, and as a result there is some tension and anxiety among organization members. The new company's senior management has observed this situation and has asked you to administer an organizational climate survey to measure the status of employee satisfaction and morale. They want you to make recommendations for improving the organization's climate.

One of the data collection methods you have chosen is individual, face-to-face interviews with 25 employees in various departments. Your purpose for conducting these interviews is to elicit detailed descriptions of people's perceptions of the current situation. You hope to use what you learn from the interviews to develop a climate survey that you will administer to all employees.

Discussion Questions

- What problems might you have in gaining access to these potential interviewees? What strategies would you use to convince them to participate?
- What impact might your being a part of the organization have on the interviewees' willingness to participate in the interview process?
- What would you do to ensure that the data provided by the interviewees were trustworthy/valid?
- How would you document the interviews? What are some of the advantages and disadvantages of your approach?
- How would you deal with the issue of confidentiality? What would you do if the senior managers asked to see the interview transcripts or your interview notes? What are the potential implications of your decision?

Activity 48

Mock Focus Group Interviews

Overview

This activity provides participants with an experiential understanding of how to use focus group interviews as a data collection method within an evaluation context.

Instructional Objectives

Participants will

- Experience facilitating and participating in a focus group interview
- Discuss the advantages and disadvantages of using focus group interviews as an evaluation data collection method
- Compare the use of focus group interviews to other data collection methods

Number of Participants

- Minimum number of participants: 6
- Maximum number of participants: 25

Time Estimate: 60 to 90 minutes

In addition to providing the necessary background information on the use of focus group interviews, this activity requires approximately 60 to 90 minutes, depending on the number of participants (or groups) and the time available for discussion.

Materials Needed

- Pens/pencils
- Flipchart, markers, tape

Instructional Method

Role play

Procedures

Facilitator's tasks:

- Ask participants to get into groups of three to four people.
- Ask participants, in their groups, to brainstorm one topic on which everyone could answer questions in an interview context.
- Ask groups to report on the topic of their choice, listing their chosen topic on flipchart paper. Invite participants to vote on one of the suggested topics. (The topic with the most votes will be the topic of the focus group interview.)
- Ask each group to think of one question that relates to the chosen topic.
- Ask groups to report on their question, writing each question on the flipchart paper.
- Move four to six chairs into the center of the room and place them in a semicircle.
- Invite four to six participants to occupy the seats in the semicircle.
- Ask for a volunteer to be the focus group interview facilitator for the first interview question. Explain that they are to pretend this is a real focus group interview and to respond accordingly. Instruct the focus group facilitator to note the participants' responses on the flipchart paper. Inform the focus group facilitator that she or he will have approximately 5 to 7 minutes for the first question. (More time can be allocated if time is available.)
- Observe the process and make notes on participant and facilitator behaviors to provide feedback at the end of the activity.
- After the first question has been answered, invite different participants to occupy the chairs in the semicircle. Thank previous participants as they get up and go back to their original seats. Invite another volunteer to be the facilitator of Question 2. (This process is repeated until all of the focus group interview questions have been addressed.)
- Offer feedback based on noted observations.
- Debrief the activity with the following questions:
  - What was the experience like for those of you who were facilitators? What was challenging? What did you learn from being a focus group facilitator that you might apply to your own practice?
  - What was the experience like for those of you who were participants? What was challenging? What did you learn from being a participant in the focus group interview that you might apply to your own practice?
  - What knowledge and skills are necessary for conducting effective focus group interviews?
  - When would a focus group interview be an appropriate and useful data collection method?
  - What are some of the advantages and disadvantages of using focus group interviews in an evaluation context?

Activity 49

Conducting Observations

Overview

This activity provides participants an opportunity to discuss various techniques and issues associated with collecting observation data.

Instructional Objectives

Participants will

- Conduct an observation
- Understand the importance of defining the scope and purpose of collecting observation data
- Consider how one's choices in documenting observation data influence the ways in which the resulting data will be analyzed

Number of Participants

- Minimum number of participants: 2
- Maximum number of participants: unlimited when participants are organized into pairs

Time Estimate: 45 to 60 minutes

This activity requires approximately 45 to 60 minutes, depending on the number of participants (or pairs) and the time available for discussion.

Materials Needed

- Pens/pencils
- Paper for taking notes

Instructional Method

Fieldwork/large-group discussion

Procedures

Facilitator's tasks:

- Ask participants to pair up with one other person.
- Explain that as a pair they are to agree on and find a location in which to sit or stand for 10 minutes. It should be a place within 3 to 5 minutes' walking distance.
- Provide participants with the following guidelines:
  - They are to observe their environment for 10 minutes. They are to be nonparticipant observers.
  - Once the observation begins, they are not to discuss what they are observing or to discuss their observations on their way back to the room.
  - They may take paper with them to make notes if they wish.
- Write the following questions on flipchart paper. When participants return, ask them to discuss the questions with their partner:
  - What did you focus on? What did you observe?
  - What did you see, hear, and smell?
  - What did you note on your paper? Did you count things, or did you write words? How did the type of data (quantitative or qualitative) affect your findings?
  - What was this experience like? Were you comfortable, uncomfortable?
- Debrief the activity with the following questions:
  - How similar were your observations? How were they different?
  - How difficult was it to do the observation without agreeing on what you were going to look for? What implications are there for collecting observation data in a real evaluation context?
  - How similar were your notations? What impact would the quality of these notations have on your ability to analyze data from your observations?
  - Did your observation activity affect how others perceive you? What impact would this have in a real-world evaluation setting?
  - If you had been a participant observer, what would you have done differently?
  - If someone asked what you were doing, what did you disclose? How comfortable were you with this disclosure? What obligations do evaluators have for disclosing the purposes of their observations?
  - What impact did the observation's length of time have on the quality of your data? Would you have observed anything different if you had stayed there for another hour? What implications are there for the length of an observation? What about multiple observations and different times of the day?
  - To what extent did your familiarity with the environment affect what you focused on or documented? How might this affect any observations you do in a real evaluation setting?

Activity 50

Collecting Unobtrusive Measures Data

Overview

This activity asks participants to consider the advantages and disadvantages as well as the applications of collecting unobtrusive measures data within an evaluation context.

Instructional Objectives

Participants will

- Understand the use of unobtrusive measures as a form of observation data
- Consider what kinds of data can be collected as unobtrusive measures
- Understand the strengths and weakness of using unobtrusive measures as an evaluation data collection method

Number of Participants

- Minimum number of participants: 3
- Maximum number of participants: unlimited when participants are in groups of 3 to 5

Time Estimate: 30 to 60 minutes

In addition to providing the necessary background information on the use of unobtrusive measures as an observation technique, this activity requires approximately 30 to 60 minutes, depending on the number of participants (or groups) and the time available for discussion.

Materials Needed

- Pens/pencils
- Flipchart, markers, tape
- Handout "Collecting Unobtrusive Measures Data"

Instructional Method

Case scenario

Procedures

Facilitator's tasks:

- Determine which scenario(s) participants will work on. Depending on the amount of time available, participants may work on one or more of the scenarios.
- Ask participants to get into groups of three to five people.
- Distribute the handout "Collecting Unobtrusive Measures Data."
- Ask participants to address the questions posed from the scenario(s) they have been assigned and to write their responses on a piece of flipchart paper.
- Ask groups to describe the evaluation scenario they worked on and to explain which kinds of unobtrusive data they would collect for that evaluation.
- Ask participants if they want to add anything to the groups' answers.
- Debrief the activity with the following questions:
  - Under what circumstances would you want to collect unobtrusive measures data? When might this data collection method be most appropriate?
  - What concerns would you have for collecting this type of data?
  - What did you learn from answering the questions in the scenario(s)?

Collecting Unobtrusive Measures Data

Handout for Activity 50

Scenario 1

You have been asked to study the effectiveness of a newly implemented communication skills training program. In addition to interviewing participants and trainers, you decide to collect unobtrusive measures data. Which data might you collect? How will you collect these data? What will these data tell you about the training program? What are the weaknesses of these data?

Scenario 2

A committee of elementary school teachers has developed a new writing program that is supposed to excite and motivate students to write more. The committee wants to evaluate the program's effectiveness and has asked you to collect unobtrusive measures data that will inform them of the program's impact. Which kinds of unobtrusive data might you collect? What will these data tell them? What won't these data tell them?

Scenario 3

A new department manager is very interested in understanding her subordinates' views toward the company and its upper management and has asked you to do an evaluation. In addition to a survey, you decide to collect unobtrusive measures data. Which data would you collect that could address her information needs? What are potential biases in these data? What will these data tell her?

Scenario 4

A manager in a state department office is becoming concerned with the level of employee absenteeism. This situation has decreased the ability of others to complete their team projects and is limiting the amount of service the department is providing its internal and, possibly, external clients. Which kinds of unobtrusive measures data might you collect to help this manager understand why the rate of absenteeism is so high? How would you collect these data? What would you tell the manager about the strengths and weaknesses of these data?

Scenario 5

The principal of a high school is concerned with the low level of student participation in nonacademic school activities. She has asked you to develop some ways to measure student participation but does not want the students to know that these data are being collected. Which kinds of unobtrusive measures data might you collect? What would you want to make sure the principal understood once you collected these data? What won't these data tell her?

Activity 51

Collecting Documents and Records (Archival Data)

Overview

This activity helps participants understand the wide variety of documents and records that can be collected in the context of an evaluation study as well as the issues related to their use.

Instructional Objectives

Participants will

- Identify the many kinds of documents and records (archival data) that can be collected for an evaluation study
- Determine the extent to which the identified documents are credible and accessible and thus worth collecting for a particular evaluation study

Number of Participants

- Minimum number of participants: 2
- Maximum number of participants: unlimited

Time Estimate: 20 to 40 minutes

This activity requires approximately 20 to 40 minutes, depending on the number of participants (or groups) and the time available for discussion.

Materials Needed

- Pens/pencils
- Flipchart, markers, tape
- Handout "Identifying Documents and Records for an Evaluation Study"

Instructional Method

Brainstorming/individual work

Procedures

Facilitator's tasks:

- Ask participants to brainstorm a list of documents and records that exist in most organizations. Write their responses on flipchart paper, using as many pages as needed. Ask for examples when necessary.
- Distribute the handout "Identifying Documents and Records for an Evaluation Study."
- Ask participants to think of an evaluation they are currently conducting or may be conducting in the near future. Ask them to consider each of the documents and records listed on the flipchart pages and to copy those that might be relevant to their evaluation onto the handout.
- Ask participants to individually rate each of the documents and records listed on their handout in terms of the data's trustworthiness and availability. Suggest they capture any additional thoughts about using these documents and records in the column labeled "Notes."
- If time permits, ask participants to pair up to share their ideas and to obtain feedback.
- Debrief the activity with the following questions:
  - What questions did this activity raise for you?
  - What documents and records might you use that you had not thought of before?
  - What are the advantages and disadvantages of using documents and records as a data collection method within an evaluation context?
  - What are some potential weaknesses of documents and records? How might these weaknesses affect the data's validity?

Identifying Documents and Records for an Evaluation Study

Handout for Activity 51

Name or Type of Document or Record	*Validity or Trustworthiness* *1 2 3 4 5* *Low High*	*Accessibility or Availability* *1 2 3 4 5* *Low High*	*Notes*

8

Analyzing Evaluation Data

BACKGROUND

This section include activities that address

- Understanding the issues and strategies for analyzing qualitative data
- Understanding the issues and strategies for analyzing quantitative data

The following information is provided as a brief introduction to the topics covered in these activities.

QUALITATIVE DATA ANALYSIS

Often referred to as *content analysis* or *thematic analysis*, qualitative data analysis is a process for identifying themes and patterns in the data and then coding and categorizing these themes in an effort to understand and describe the phenomenon being evaluated. In most cases, evaluators must decide if it is both feasible and appropriate to organize the data around a preexisting framework, rubric, outline, agenda, or structure. For example, categories related to the program or organization goals might be developed based on the evaluation's key questions or the program's objectives. This is a useful and straightforward approach for analyzing qualitative data if such schemas are available and relevant to the evaluation. However, a preexisting framework is most often only a starting point.

There are other times when the data analysis process should not be guided by a particular preexisting set of categories. When evaluators want to see how the data can be organized without any overarching framework, they conduct the analysis by focusing on the categories and themes that emerge from the data. This approach is particularly appropriate when no other framework exists for developing the categories, when imposing a preexisting schema could limit the full range of findings, or when using a preexisting framework could be criticized for biasing the results.

QUANTITATIVE DATA ANALYSIS

Many evaluations that gather quantitative data involve calculating basic descriptive statistics, such as frequency distributions, measures of central tendency (mode, median, and mean), and measures of distribution (range, interquartile range, and standard deviation). In some cases, the data might be analyzed using statistics such as correlations, chi square, *t*-tests, and analysis of variance (ANOVA). All of these statistical methods can be found in an elementary statistics text.

RESOURCES

Barcus, F. E. (1961). A content analysis of trends in Sunday comics, 1900–1959. *Journalism Quarterly, 38*(2), 171-180.

Boyatzis, R. E. (1998). *Transforming qualitative information.* Thousand Oaks, CA: Sage.

Creswell, J. W. (2003). *Educational research: Planning, conducting, and evaluating quantitative and qualitative research.* Upper Saddle River, NJ: Merrill Prentice Hall.

Gall, M. D., Gall, J. P., & Borg, W. R. (2003). *Educational research: An introduction* (7th ed.). Boston: Allyn & Bacon.

Glaser, B. G., & Strauss, A. L. (1967). *The discovery of grounded theory: Strategies for qualitative research.* Chicago: Aldine.

Miles, M. B., & Huberman, A. M. (1994). *An expanded sourcebook: Qualitative data analysis* (2nd ed.). Thousand Oaks, CA: Sage.

Miller, D. C., & Salkind, N. J. (2002). *Handbook of research design and social measurement* (6th ed.). Thousand Oaks, CA: Sage.

Neuendorf, K. A. (2002). *The content analysis guidebook.* Thousand Oaks, CA: Sage.

Rossi, P. H., Lipsey, M. W., & Freeman, H. E. (2004). *Evaluation: A systematic approach* (7th ed.). Thousand Oaks, CA: Sage.

Russ-Eft, D. (1999). Research methods for advancing performance improvement. In R. A. Swanson (Series Ed.) & R. J. Torraco (Issue Ed.), *Performance improvement theory and practice: Vol. 1(1): Advances in developing human resources.* San Francisco: Berrett-Koehler.

Russ-Eft, D., & Preskill, H. (2001). *Evaluation in organizations: A systematic approach to enhancing learning, performance, and change.* Boston: Perseus.

Salkind, N. J., (2003). *Statistics for people who (think they) hate statistics* (2nd ed.). Thousand Oaks, CA: Sage.

Strauss, A. L. (1987). *Qualitative analysis for social scientists.* New York: Cambridge University Press.

Tashakkori, A., & Teddlie, C. (Eds.). (2003). *Handbook of mixed methods in social and behavioral research.* Thousand Oaks, CA: Sage.

Wolcott, H. F. (1994). *Transforming qualitative data.* Thousand Oaks, CA: Sage.

Activity 52

Planning for Data Analysis

Overview

This activity engages participants in determining how data from a survey might be analyzed using both quantitative and qualitative data analysis methods.

Instructional Objectives

Participants will

- Understand the importance of planning for how data will be analyzed before data are collected
- Practice planning for data analysis

Number of Participants

- Minimum number of participants: 3
- Maximum number of participants: unlimited when participants are in groups of 3 to 5

Time Estimate: 45 to 60 minutes

In addition to providing the necessary background information on various kinds of data analysis strategies and methods, this activity requires approximately 45 to 60 minutes, depending on the number of participants (or groups) and the time available for discussion.

Materials Needed

- Pens/pencils
- Flipchart, markers, tape
- A 10- to 20-item survey that has both open- and closed-ended questions
- Handout "Developing a Data Analysis Plan"

Instructional Method

Small-group work

Procedures

Prior to Class

Facilitator's task:

- Obtain a survey that has between 10 and 20 open- and closed-ended items.

During Class

Facilitator's tasks:

- Ask participants to get into groups of three to five people.
- Distribute a copy of the survey to all participants.
- Distribute the handout "Developing a Data Analysis Plan."
- Instruct groups to develop an analysis plan for the survey, using the handout.
- Ask groups to record their ideas on a piece of flipchart paper and to attach the paper to a wall.
- Ask groups to share their ideas with the larger group. Invite other participants' questions and additions.
- Debrief the activity with the following questions:
  - What insights into data analysis did you gain from this activity?
  - If you were going to administer the survey to two different groups, what other analyses might you consider?
  - What might be the impact on this evaluation if there were no data analysis plan?
  - What implications does planning for data analysis have on an evaluation budget?

Developing a Data Analysis Plan

Handout for Activity 52

Directions:

- In the first column, record the question numbers from the survey.
- In the second column, indicate the possible data analysis methods that could be undertaken with data resulting from each question.
- In the third column, describe why you would use each analysis. What would you hope to learn?

Survey Data Analysis		
Question or Item Numbers	*What data analysis methods might you use?*	*Why would you use this analysis? What would you hope to learn?*

Activity 53

Developing Qualitative Data Analysis Categories and Themes

Overview

This activity helps participants understand how to develop categories and themes when analyzing qualitative data.

Instructional Objectives

Participants will

- Experience sorting qualitative data
- Understand the importance of deciding whether a predetermined set of categories will be used to analyze qualitative data or whether such categories and themes should emerge from the data
- Consider when it is most appropriate to use a predetermined set of categories or themes to analyze qualitative data instead of having categories and themes emerge from the data

Number of Participants

- Minimum number of participants: 3
- Maximum number of participants: unlimited when participants are in groups of 3 to 5

Time Estimate: 15 to 30 minutes

This activity requires approximately 15 to 30 minutes, depending on the number of participants (or groups) and the time available for discussion.

SOURCE: This activity was contributed by Nicole Vicinanza, Aguirre International, Burlingame, California, and Bob Covert, University of Virginia.

Materials Needed

- Different kinds of wrapped candy (one bag of candy per group)
- Plastic bags to hold the candy

Instructional Method

Small-group work

Procedures

Prior to Class

Facilitator's tasks:

- Buy candy (e.g., different kinds of chocolate, hard candies of different sizes and different brands)
- Put 15 to 30 pieces of candy into each plastic bag (there should be enough bags so that each group receives a bag of candy).

During Class

Facilitator's tasks:

- Ask participants to get into groups of three to five people.
- Provide each group with a bag of candy.
- Tell participants that their group has 5 minutes to organize their bag of candy into piles.
- At the end of the 5-minute period, ask volunteers from each group to explain how they sorted the candy. (How did they decide which piles to put the candy into? Did they have any disagreements? What were the criteria they used to place a piece of candy into a particular pile?)
- Ask participants to now organize the candy into the following categories:
  - Color of wrapping or color of candy if unwrapped
  - Shape of candy
  - Degree of hardness
- Ask volunteers from each group to discuss their experiences in sorting the candy using the two different approaches. (This discussion should focus on the issue of emerging or predetermined categories of qualitative data analysis.)
- Debrief the activity with the following questions:
  - What challenges did you experience in trying to sort the candy without the predetermined activities?

- What challenges did you experience in trying to sort the candy according to the predetermined categories?
- After sorting the candy, to what extent did you reach different conclusions about the data even though the data were the same? What implications are there for evaluation practice?
- When might you use a predetermined set of categories for analyzing qualitative data? Where might the predetermined categories come from? What implications might using predetermined categories have on the evaluation's findings?
- How would you go about deriving categories or themes from the data if there were no predetermined categories?
- What are the advantages and disadvantages of these two approaches to analyzing qualitative data?

Activity 54

Using Comics to Understand Qualitative Data Analysis Processes

Overview

This activity engages participants in analyzing qualitative data by identifying themes and patterns in comic strips.

Instructional Objectives

Participants will

- Understand the process of using a predetermined set of categories to analyze qualitative data
- Recognize the importance of establishing decision rules to guide the analysis of qualitative data
- Consider the implications of using a predetermined set of categories versus allowing the categories or themes to emerge from the data

Number of Participants

- Minimum number of participants: 3
- Maximum number of participants: unlimited when participants are in groups of 3 to 5

Time Estimate: 45 to 60 minutes

This activity requires approximately 45 to 60 minutes, depending on the number of participants (or groups) and the time available for discussion.

Materials Needed

- Pens/pencils
- Copies of 7 to 10 comic strips from a local newspaper
- Handout "Comic Strip Types"
- Handout "Dominant Themes"
- Handout "Principal Characters"

Instructional Method

Small-group work

Procedures

Prior to Class

Facilitator's task:

- Cut out 7 to 10 comic strips from a local newspaper and photocopy them onto one or two pieces of paper. Title the copy "Today's Comic Strips."

During Class

Facilitator's tasks:

- Ask participants to get into groups of three to five people.
- Tell participants that in 1961, Frances Barcus published an article titled "A Content Analysis of Trends in Sunday Comics, 1900–1959." In this article, he described a study he conducted to "trace trends and patterns of major themes, comic strip types, and use of characters since the beginning of the use of comic strips in the Sunday paper" (p. 171). The article describes in detail the coding procedures and categories that were established. The findings provide some interesting insights into the social and cultural changes of the American character as seen through the eyes of emerging cartoonists and illustrators during the study's 59-year period. The following activity is based on this article.
- Distribute the handout "Today's Comic Strips" (copies of comic strips).
- Distribute the handouts "Comic Strip Types," Dominant Themes," "Principal Characters." These are the categories from Barcus's 1961 article.
- Explain that participants are to read the comic strips and, in their groups, reach consensus on how the strips should be categorized using the three handouts.
- Instruct participants to keep notes on how they select the comic strips' locations on each of the handouts.
- Ask for volunteers to report their group's decisions. Suggest that participants observe similarities and differences between the different groups' analyses. Invite participants to comment on the different analyses.
- Debrief the activity with the following questions:
  - What challenges did you experience in trying to categorize the comic strips?
  - How do you explain the similarities and differences between the groups' decision rules?

- What implications does this have for when you analyze qualitative data from interviews, open-ended survey items, or observations in the context of an evaluation study?
- How valid were these categories for analyzing today's comic strips, given that they were developed in 1961?
- How can evaluators ensure that their approach to qualitative data analysis is rigorous and thorough?

Comic Strip Types

Handout for Activity 54

Serious	*Action or Adventure*	*Humor*	*Real Life*	*Fantasy*	*Other*

Dominant Themes

Handout for Activity 54

Domestic	
Crime	
Historical	
Religion	
Love/Romance	
Supernatural	
Nature	
International	
Education	
Business	
Government	
Science	
Entertainment	
Armed Forces	
Literature	
Other	

Principal Characters

Handout for Activity 54

Adults	*Teens*	*Infants/Children*	*Animals*	*Other*

Activity 55

Analyzing and Interpreting Qualitative Data

Overview

This activity helps participants learn about and experience the processes involved in analyzing and interpreting qualitative data.

Instructional Objectives

Participants will

- Understand various approaches to qualitative data analysis
- Experience the advantages and disadvantages of working with predetermined versus emergent categories
- Experience and discuss the challenges in analyzing qualitative data
- Interpret qualitative data results and make recommendations

Number of Participants

- Minimum number of participants: 3
- Maximum number of participants: unlimited when participants are in groups of 3 to 5

Time Estimate: 45 to 60 minutes

This activity requires approximately 45 to 60 minutes, depending on the number of participants (or groups) and the time available for discussion.

Materials Needed

- Pens/pencils
- Flipchart, markers, tape
- Handout "Open-Ended Responses to Survey Questions"
- Handout "Predetermined Qualitative Data Analysis Categories"
- Handout "Analyzing and Interpreting Qualitative Data"

Instructional Method

Small-group work

Procedures

Facilitator's tasks:

- Ask participants to get into groups of three to five people.
- Distribute the handout "Open-Ended Responses to Survey Questions."
- Distribute the handout "Predetermined Qualitative Data Analysis Categories" to half of the groups. These groups will be called Group A. The remaining groups will be called Group B.
- Distribute the handout "Analyzing and Interpreting Qualitative Data."
- Give participants in Group(s) A the following instructions:
  - Review the predetermined categories and agree on their definitions.
  - Code the data from Questions 1 and 2 according to the predetermined categories.
  - Complete the handout "Analyzing and Interpreting Qualitative Data."
  - Summarize the data for each question and develop a set of recommendations based on the findings.
- Give participants in Group(s) B the following instructions:
  - Review the data from Question 1 and develop categories based on the themes and patterns in the data.
  - Code the data for Question 1 according to the categories you have developed.
  - Complete the handout "Analyzing and Interpreting Qualitative Data."
  - Summarize the data for Question 1 and develop a set of recommendations based on the findings.
- Ask participants in Group(s) A to share their findings and recommendations.
- Ask participants in Group(s) B to share their findings and recommendations.
- Debrief the activity with the following questions:
  - How similar or different were the findings among those in Group A? In Group B?
  - What were some of the similarities and differences between the results from Group A and the results from Group B?
  - How would you describe your experience in analyzing these data?
  - What surprised you about this work?
  - What insights did you gain from this activity that will be useful the next time you collect and analyze qualitative data?

Open-Ended Responses to Survey Questions

Handout for Activity 55

Question 1

What recommendations would you make to help us improve our consulting services to you?

1. Seems more difficult in past year to reach a representative on the first call or to receive a prompt response to a call. Have left voice mail messages and takes several days for return call.
2. Knowledgeable staff with high level of customer service. Very professional while being "human."
3. Hard to reach.
4. Too often all employees from the regional office are out at the same time. A receptionist is left behind who is unable to answer questions. Sometimes it is several days or a week at a time that staff is out.
5. None requested.
6. Need for improved quality and content of programs.
7. [None.]
8. The quality of the materials.
9. Did not use consultant service.
10. Consultant needs straightforward approach to problem solving.
11. You have the best service response I have ever experienced.
12. Couldn't be any better! (That's the truth!)
13. Takes several days for a response—took 3 1/2 weeks for a contact list (phone numbers of who to call for what). Requests not followed up.
14. [Didn't contact us.] We called them!
15. Applicable to different audiences (supervisors, managers, directors).
16. Consultant needs to provide opportunity for skills practice.
17. Consultant must show ability to work with a multicultural workforce.

18. Provide more information about target audiences and more specifics on suggested implementation stages.
19. As we are a mining company, consultant could relate more to a mining or construction atmosphere.
20. No opinion.
21. [Question is] redundant. [Respondent does not differentiate between the salesperson and the consultant.]
22. Quality.
23. Reputation.
24. Ease of use.
25. Need help with certification.
26. [Change our address in your files.]
27. I need to certify a trainer and have had little help in counseling or follow-up.
28. Structure and clarity.
29. Cost.
30. Lack of flexibility in recertification.
31. Help companies maximize use of products by flexible rates.
32. Very well prepared, easy to facilitate.
33. Consultant is clear, concise.
34. Expensive.
35. Have not contacted anyone for assistance.
36. Easy to reach.
37. Good service.
38. Materials shipped to wrong source, even though purchase order had correct address on it. Also asked that particular order be changed. It was not and had to return it and order again.
39. The program, materials, video, etc. People really like the material and start to use it.
40. Service is thorough, competent, and courteous.
41. Programs are well-prepared, easy, and fun to present.
42. Participants find programs valuable, very useful, and enjoyable.
43. [Nothing.]

44. [None.]
45. The quality of service is excellent.
46. The "partnership" attitude for providing services, professionalism of all staff.
47. [Nothing.]
48. [None.]
49. Real-life application.
50. [Consultants] were not familiar with our unique situation as a university using the course in an academic setting.

Question 2

What other improvements would you like to see?

1. The packaging/packing lists are very difficult to inventory against.
2. Don't split up "packages" on packing list.
3. [Dissatisfaction with the quality of videos for Program A.] They are old films. Should be more modern with modern problems and atmospheres.
4. Check up to see if we're happy with the program and if there is any way you can help us do better. Make sure we're happy and are actually getting results from the program.
5. Need more variety as to structure of skills practice.
6. Participants become bored by the same skill practice each session.
7. Excellent content.
8. Repetitive exercises.
9. Larger variety in methodologies.
10. You're doin' good.
11. I'd like to work for your organization sometime in the future.
12. Cost.
13. Cost!!
14. Keep up the good work.
15. You practice what you preach!! Keep it up.
16. Price.
17. Good material that brings to light necessary skills.

18. Some of the people I train get lost in the workbook because of the vocabulary being over their heads. Summarize the main thoughts for each specific action.
19. Need more variety and/or options for Learning Activities.
20. Making flipcharts.
21. Some of the videos are dated.
22. Materials easy to use and professional.
23. No toll-free number for placing orders.
24. No toll-free telephone number.
25. The material and content is excellent. Quality in every way.
26. Participants readily gain skills/knowledge. They feel they get their money and time's worth.
27. Ease of use.
28. Repetitive nature—gets boring to class—instructor must make major changes to alter process.
29. Salesperson is great! He compares equally well to those from other suppliers.
30. The content of the material. It has always been very relevant to the issues and concerns of our managers and supervisors.
31. The repetitive format.
32. Instead of some of the exercise suggestions, I might have an open group discussion, debate, or small-group activity.
33. Too expensive for small organization.
34. Videos are out of date—workbooks too expensive.
35. Your bias for customer service/satisfaction.
36. Cost is high.
37. Reading level too high.
38. Lower reading level.
39. Continue to send new ways to implement and evaluate the program.
40. Well-planned programs. Seems they are tested effectively. Work as promised.
41. Repetitive format of programs.
42. Complicated pricing structure.
43. Less stringent instructor certification requirements for experienced, high-quality facilitators.

44. Quality [of videos for Program A] could be improved by using actual companies and real employee situations.
45. The videotapes [for Program A] could be updated and improved.
46. Provide better presentation skills training for sales representatives.
47. Routineness of learning design.
48. Variety in quality of videos—some are good, some racially biased, some "dumb" and unrealistic.
49. Redo your videos.
50. Offer more alternative exercises to relieve boredom and predictability. (Mix and match approach.)

Predetermined Qualitative Data Analysis Categories

Handout for Activity 55

Question 1

What recommendations would you make to help us improve our consulting services to you?

- Reduce response time to requests.
- Increase consultant knowledge and skills.
- Increase consultant familiarity with specific setting and issues.
- Improve quality and content of programs.
- Reduce costs for services.
- No recommendations—pleased with services.
- Did not use consultants.

Question 2

What other improvements would you like to see?

- Update videos.
- Include more variety in programs.
- Improve packaging.
- Reduce costs for programs.
- Lower reading level in material.
- No recommendations—pleased with products and services.
- Did not use consulting.

Analyzing and Interpreting Qualitative Data

Handout for Activity 55

Category Name	*Key Findings*

If you had to make three recommendations from the results of these findings, what would you recommend?

1.

2.

3.

Activity 56

Understanding Descriptive Statistics

Overview

This activity engages participants in calculating basic descriptive statistics.

Instructional Objectives

Participants will

- Understand the application of descriptive statistics to evaluation data
- Understand how to calculate basic descriptive statistics

Number of Participants

- Minimum number of participants: 7
- Maximum number of participants: unlimited when participants are in groups of 7 to 10

Time Estimate: 30 to 45 minutes

This activity requires approximately 30 to 45 minutes, depending on the number of participants (or groups) and the time available for discussion.

Materials Needed

- Pens/pencils
- Flipchart, markers, tape
- Calculators, rulers, and tape measures, if available
- Handout "Calculating Descriptive Statistics"

Instructional Method

Small-group work

Procedures

Facilitator's tasks:

- Ask participants to get into groups of 7 to 10 people.
- Distribute the handout "Calculating Descriptive Statistics."
- Ask participants to line up according to height within their group.
- Instruct participants to work in their groups to complete the tasks listed on the handout.
- Debrief the activity with the following questions:
  - What insights did you gain from this activity?
  - What kinds of information do descriptive statistics provide?
  - What are some limitations of descriptive statistics? What don't they tell you?

Calculating Descriptive Statistics

Handout for Activity 56

Directions:

1. Line up from the shortest person to the tallest person.
2. List the heights (in inches) of all the people in the group.
3. Create a simple frequency distribution of the heights from the shortest to the tallest.
4. Identify the mode for the heights (or the most frequent score), if one exists.
5. Determine the range of the heights—from the shortest to the tallest.
6. Identify the median of the heights (or the middle-most height).
7. Calculate the mean for the heights. (Add all the heights together and divide by the number of participants in the group.)
8. Create a scatter plot showing inches of height on the x-axis and inches for foot size on the y-axis.
9. Create a class frequency distribution of these heights using the following categories:
   - Fewer than 60 in. (or fewer than 5 ft.)
   - 60 to 62 in.
   - 63 to 65 in.
   - 66 to 68 in.
   - 69 to 71 in.
   - 72 to 74 in.
   - 75 to 77 in.
   - 78 to 80 in.
   - 81 to 83 in.
   - 84 in. or greater (or 7 ft. and taller)
10. Examine the class frequency distribution and identify the mode and median.

Activity 57

Understanding Quantitative Data Analysis

Overview

This activity helps participants understand basic quantitative data analysis methods and how they may be used in an evaluation context.

Instructional Objectives

Participants will

- Become familiar with the circumstances under which various quantitative analysis methods are appropriate and useful
- Teach others about a particular quantitative data analysis method
- Discuss implications for collecting and analyzing quantitative data within an evaluation context

Number of Participants

- Minimum number of participants: 6
- Maximum number of participants: unlimited when participants are in groups of 2 to 5

Time Estimate: 60 to 90 minutes

In addition to providing the necessary background information on various statistical analyses, this activity requires approximately 60 to 90 minutes, depending on the number of participants (or groups) and the time available for discussion.

Materials Needed

- Pens/pencils
- Flipchart, markers, tape
- Professional papers, articles, or book chapters on various data analysis methods
- Handout "Understanding Quantitative Analysis Methods"

Instructional Method

Small-group work

Procedures

Prior to Class

Facilitator's tasks:

- Divide participants into the following groups:
  - Group A: Descriptive statistics
  - Group B: Correlation statistics
  - Group C: Inferential statistics
- Provide each group with professional papers, articles, or book chapters on their assigned topic and ask them to become experts in their topic prior to the next session. (These readings should focus on what the analysis means and how it is applied to quantitative data.)

During Class

Facilitator's tasks:

- Distribute the handout "Understanding Quantitative Analysis Methods."
- Instruct groups to discuss their understanding of the analysis method they have been assigned. Clarify any questions that groups have about their strategy.
- Ask groups to prepare a 10- to 15-minute presentation on their analysis method (including a question-and-answer period from the audience). Explain that the purpose is to teach others when and where to use their assigned quantitative data analysis method.
- Invite groups to make their presentations.
- Debrief the activity with the following questions:
  - Which of these analyses have you used or seen in past evaluations?
  - What insights about quantitative analysis did you gain from the presentations?
  - What implications do these various analysis methods have on a data collection instrument's development?
  - What implications do your choices about quantitative analyses have on an evaluation's budget?
  - What else do you need to know about quantitative data analysis? How might you further develop your skills and knowledge in this area?

Understanding Quantitative Analysis Methods

Handout for Activity 57

Your group's analysis method: ______________________________

1. What is the purpose of this analysis method? What will it tell you?

2. What level of data (i.e., nominal, ordinal, interval, ratio) is appropriate for this analysis?

3. Under what circumstances would you use this analysis method?

4. Under what circumstances would it be inappropriate to use this analysis method?

5. Provide one or two examples of how and when you might use this analysis method.

Activity 58

Analyzing and Interpreting Quantitative Data

Overview

This activity asks participants to analyze quantitative data using basic data analysis methods.

Instructional Objectives

Participants will

- Analyze and interpret means, frequencies, and correlation data
- Clarify their understanding of when to use certain kinds of basic quantitative data analysis methods
- Discuss the limitations of basic quantitative data analysis methods

Number of Participants

- Minimum number of participants: 3
- Maximum number of participants: unlimited when participants are in groups of 3 to 5

Time Estimate: 45 to 60 minutes

In addition to providing the necessary background information on descriptive statistics and correlations, this activity requires approximately 45 to 60 minutes, depending on the number of participants (or groups) and the time available for discussion.

Materials Needed

- Pens/pencils
- Flipchart, markers, tape
- Handout "Survey Information"

- Handout "Frequency Distribution Prior to Training"
- Handout "Frequency Distribution Following Training"
- Handout "Item Correlations of Participants Before and After Training"
- Handout "Mean Scores for Participants"
- Handout "Frequency Distribution Results"
- Handout "Mean Score Results"
- Handout "Correlation Results"

Instruction Method

Small-group work

Procedures

Facilitator's tasks:

- Ask participants to get into groups of three to five people.
- Distribute the handout "Survey Information." Explain that participants will be analyzing and interpreting quantitative data collected from a survey.
- Provide each group with one or more data handouts ("Frequency Distribution Prior to Training, "Frequency Distribution Following Training," "Item Correlations of Participants Before and After Training," and "Mean Scores for Participants").
- Provide each group with the appropriate handout, either "Frequency Distribution Results," "Correlation Results," or "Mean Score Results."
- Instruct groups to review their respective handout(s) and to complete their worksheets.
- Request that groups write their statements on a piece of flipchart paper.
- Ask groups to share their statements and thoughts with the larger group. Invite other participants to comment on and ask questions of the presenting group.
- Debrief the activity with the following questions:
  - What are the similarities and differences in the interpretations across the three groups?
  - What do these analyses say about these data?
  - What other data might the evaluator collect to increase the usefulness of these findings? In other words, what do we still not know?
  - What insights about quantitative data analysis did you gain from this activity?

Survey Information

Handout for Activity 58

- The survey was undertaken with supervisors at a manufacturing plant. It was administered before training and 2 months after training.
- Each of the questions used a 7-point Likert scale:

1	2	3	4	5	6	7
Not at all			*To some extent*			*To a great extent*

- The survey questions included the following (this is a subset of a larger group of questions):
  - How satisfied are you with the nature of your work?
  - How satisfied are you with your manager's performance?
  - How satisfied are you with coworkers' relationships?
  - To what extent will training help you better do your job?
  - To what extent will training increase productivity?

Frequency Distribution
Prior to Training

Handout for Activity 58

How satisfied are you with the nature of your work?

Scale Rating	*Frequency*	*Percentage*	*Cumulative Frequency*	*Cumulative Percentage*
3	1	2.33	1	2.33
4	4	9.30	5	11.63
5	8	18.60	13	30.23
6	20	46.51	33	76.74
7	10	23.26	43	100.00

How satisfied are you with your manager's performance?

Scale Rating	*Frequency*	*Percentage*	*Cumulative Frequency*	*Cumulative Percentage*
2	1	2.33	1	2.33
3	1	2.33	2	4.65
4	9	20.93	11	25.58
5	11	25.58	22	51.16
6	12	27.91	34	79.07
7	9	20.93	43	100.00

How satisfied are you with coworkers' relationships?

Scale Rating	*Frequency*	*Percentage*	*Cumulative Frequency*	*Cumulative Percentage*
4	2	4.65	2	4.65
5	8	18.60	10	23.26
6	25	58.14	35	81.40
7	8	18.60	43	100.00

To what extent will training help you better do your job?

Scale Rating	*Frequency*	*Percentage*	*Cumulative Frequency*	*Cumulative Percentage*
3	1	2.33	1	2.33
4	7	16.28	8	18.60
5	6	13.95	14	32.56
6	15	41.86	32	74.42
7	11	25.58	43	100.00

To what extent will training increase productivity?

Scale Rating	*Frequency*	*Percentage*	*Cumulative Frequency*	*Cumulative Percentage*
2	1	2.33	1	2.33
3	3	6.98	4	9.30
4	7	16.28	11	25.58
5	9	20.93	20	46.51
6	13	30.23	33	76.74
7	10	23.26	43	100.00

Frequency Distribution Following Training

Handout for Activity 58

How satisfied are you with the nature of your work?

Scale Rating	*Frequency*	*Percentage*	*Cumulative Frequency*	*Cumulative Percentage*
2	1	4.55	1	4.55
4	5	22.73	6	27.27
5	8	36.36	14	63.64
6	7	31.82	21	95.45
7	1	4.55	22	100.00

How satisfied are you with your manager's performance?

Scale Rating	*Frequency*	*Percentage*	*Cumulative Frequency*	*Cumulative Percentage*
3	2	9.09	2	9.09
4	10	45.45	12	54.55
5	7	31.82	19	86.36
6	1	4.55	20	90.91
7	2	9.09	22	100.00

How satisfied are you with coworkers' relationships?

Scale Rating	*Frequency*	*Percentage*	*Cumulative Frequency*	*Cumulative Percentage*
4	9	40.91	9	40.91
5	7	31.82	16	72.73
6	4	18.18	20	90.91
7	2	9.09	22	100.00

To what extent will training help you better do your job?

Scale Rating	*Frequency*	*Percentage*	*Cumulative Frequency*	*Cumulative Percentage*
2	1	4.55	1	4.55
3	1	4.55	2	9.09
4	11	50.00	13	59.09
5	6	27.27	19	86.36
6	2	9.09	21	95.45
7	1	4.55	22	100.00

To what extent will training increase productivity?

Scale Rating	*Frequency*	*Percentage*	*Cumulative Frequency*	*Cumulative Percentage*
2	1	4.55	1	4.55
3	1	4.55	2	9.09
4	10	45.45	12	54.55
5	6	27.27	18	51.82
6	3	13.64	21	95.45
7	1	4.55	22	100.00

Item Correlations of Participants Before and After Training

Handout for Activity 58

	Correlations
How satisfied are you with the nature of your work?	0.43939
How satisfied are you with your manager's performance?	0.55001
How satisfied are you with coworkers' relationships?	0.48354
To what extent will training help you better do your job?	0.38517
To what extent will training increase productivity?	0.53796

Mean Scores for Participants

Handout for Activity 58

Prior to Training

	N	*Mean*	*SD*
How satisfied are you with the nature of your work?	43	5.79	0.98
How satisfied are you with your manager's performance?	43	5.37	1.23
How satisfied are you with coworkers' relationships?	43	5.90	0.75
To what extent will training help you better do your job?	43	5.72	1.09
To what extent will training increase productivity?	43	2.39	1.32

Following Training

	N	*Mean*	*SD*
How satisfied are you with the nature of your work?	22	5.04	1.09
How satisfied are you with your manager's performance?	22	4.59	1.05
How satisfied are you with coworkers' relationships?	22	4.95	0.99
To what extent will training help you better do your job?	22	4.45	1.05
To what extent will training increase productivity?	22	4.54	1.10

Frequency Distribution Results

Handout for Activity 58

What questions arose in your discussions about these findings?

What are the key findings? Write three statements that summarize these results.	*What do you find interesting about these data?*
1.	
2.	
3.	

Mean Scores Results

Handout for Activity 58

What questions arose in your discussions about these findings?

What are the key findings? Write three statements that summarize these results.	*What do you find interesting about these data?*
1.	
2.	
3.	

Correlation Results

Handout for Activity 58

What questions arose in your discussions about these findings?

What are the key findings? Write three statements that summarize these results.	*What do you find interesting about these data?*
1.	
2.	
3.	

9

Communicating and Reporting Evaluation Processes and Findings

BACKGROUND

This section includes activities that address

- Communicating and reporting throughout an evaluation study
- Communicating and reporting strategies for various evaluation processes and findings

The following information is provided as a brief introduction to the topics covered in these activities.

Keeping evaluation stakeholders informed about an evaluation's progress is good professional practice. Reporting an evaluation's findings in ways that facilitate understanding and use is also important. There are several things to consider when communicating with and reporting to an evaluation's stakeholders before, during, and after an evaluation (Torres, 2001).

WHY COMMUNICATE AND REPORT?

- To convey information about the program to build awareness and support and to provide the basis for asking questions

- To describe how a program is working and to what effect
- To aid decision making about support for participation and involvement in the evaluation or program
- To demonstrate results and accountability
- To aid decision making about continued funding, prospective funding, and replication at other sites/organizations
- To learn, grow, and improve the program
- To inform decision making by program staff and management about changes that will improve the program

WHO ARE YOUR COMMUNICATING AND REPORTING STAKEHOLDERS?

Primary Stakeholders

- Usually request the evaluation
- Typically are major decision makers
- Can consist of program staff, supervisors, senior managers, and funders

Secondary Stakeholders

- Usually are involved but with little or no daily contact
- Can consist of program participants, their supervisors or managers, and others affected by the evaluation

Tertiary Stakeholders

- Usually are more distant but are possibly interested in findings
- Can consist of future program participants, the general public, and members of same profession

WHEN AND WHY ARE YOU COMMUNICATING AND REPORTING?

During the Evaluation

- To include stakeholders in decision making about evaluation design/ activities
- To inform different stakeholders about upcoming evaluation activities
- To keep stakeholders informed about the progress of the evaluation

After the Evaluation

- To convey information about the program and its evaluation
- To demonstrate results and accountability
- To learn, grow, and improve the program

Depending on what, when, and with whom you are communicating and reporting, the following formats might be used (Torres, Preskill, & Piontek, 2005):

- Comprehensive written reports
- Working sessions
- Executive summaries
- Personal discussions
- Newsletters, bulletins, briefs, and brochures
- News media communications
- Video presentations
- Memos and postcards
- Verbal presentations
- Posters
- E-mail

It is important to remember that, regardless of the format used to communicate and report an evaluation's progress and findings, the communication should be well written, well designed, and easy to use.

RESOURCES

Patton, M. Q. (1997). *Utilization-focused evaluation: The new century text* (3rd ed.). Thousand Oaks, CA: Sage.

Posavac, E. J., & Carey, R. G. (2003). *Program evaluation: Methods and case studies* (6th ed.). Upper Saddle River, NJ: Prentice Hall.

Russ-Eft, D., & Preskill, H. (2001). *Evaluation in organizations: A systematic approach for enhancing learning, performance, and change.* Boston: Perseus.

Sonnichsen, R. C. (2000). *High impact internal evaluation: A practitioner's guide to evaluating and consulting inside organizations.* Thousand Oaks, CA: Sage.

Torres, R. T. (2001). Communicating and reporting evaluation activities and findings. In D. Russ-Eft & H. Preskill, *Evaluation in organizations: A systematic approach to enhancing learning, performance, and change* (pp. 347-380). Boston: Perseus.

Torres, R. T., Preskill, H., & Piontek, M. (2005). *Evaluation strategies for communicating and reporting: Enhancing learning in organizations* (2nd ed.). Thousand Oaks, CA: Sage.

Worthen, B., R., Sanders, J. R., & Fitzpatrick, J. L. (1997). *Program evaluation: Alternative approaches and practical guidelines* (pp. 407-431). New York: Longman.

Activity 59

Communicating and Reporting Evaluation Formats

Overview

This activity introduces participants to several formats that can be used to communicate an evaluation's progress and activities as well report on an evaluation's findings.

Instructional Objectives

Participants will

- Understand the importance of communicating and reporting throughout an evaluation study
- Learn about several different communicating and reporting formats
- Consider when to use various communicating and reporting formats during an evaluation

Number of Participants

- Minimum number of participants: 9
- Maximum number of participants: 45

Time Estimate: 45 to 90 minutes

This activity requires approximately 45 to 90 minutes, depending on the number of participants (or groups) and the time available for discussion.

Materials Needed

- Pens/pencils
- Index cards (3 in. × 5 in.) with information from handout "Formats for Communicating and Reporting Evaluation Processes and Findings"
- Flipchart, markers, tape

Instructional Method

Small-group work

Procedures

Prior to Class

Facilitator's tasks:

- Copy the information on the handout "Formats for Communicating and Reporting Evaluation Processes and Findings" onto index cards.
- Divide the number of participants by 9 (there are 9 index card categories) and make the necessary number of cards (e.g., if there are 27 participants, make 3 copies of each index card category).

During Class

Facilitator's tasks:

- Shuffle the cards and give one to each participant.
- Ask participants to walk around the room and find others with matching card categories. (In your introductory remarks, you may wish to announce these categories in advance or let participants figure it out on their own.)
- Write on a flipchart (or overhead or PowerPoint slide) the following instructions:
  - Discuss the information on your card. Come to an understanding of what this strategy means for communicating and reporting.
  - Identify three to five situations or times when this communicating and reporting format would be effective.
  - Identify three to five situations or times when this format would not be an effective communicating and reporting format.
  - Write your responses on a piece of flipchart paper.
  - Be prepared to share your ideas with the larger group.
- Ask each group to introduce their communicating and reporting format and explain what they wrote on their flipchart page. (The participants' job is to ensure that the larger group understands the use of each group's format.)
- Provide additional information and feedback on participants' comments.

- Debrief the activity with the following questions:
  - What did you learn about communicating and reporting from this activity?
  - What formats might you consider using in the future that you had not thought about before?
  - Which of these formats do you think have the greatest likelihood of increasing the use of evaluation findings? Why? Under what circumstances?

Formats for Communicating and Reporting Evaluation Processes and Findings

Handout for Activity 59

The following are several formats that can be used to communicate about and report on an evaluation's progress and activities as well as its findings.

Index Card Category 1

Comprehensive Written Reports

Comprehensive written reports are the most traditional and frequently used format for communicating about an evaluation and its findings. In their most conventional form, comprehensive written reports are written in an academic style and adhere to the standards of social science research reporting. The objective is to give a full accounting of the evaluation purpose, design, methods, findings, and recommendations so that a reader otherwise uninformed about the program or the evaluation can judge the relevance of the design, the appropriateness of both the data collection and the analysis methods, and the validity of the conclusions and recommendations.

Index Card Category 2

Working Sessions

Working sessions are facilitated meetings with primary audiences that can be used for almost any aspect of the evaluation—to design an evaluation, to draft evaluation instruments, to present and interpret findings. Participants have the chance to reflect, share their perspectives, and engage in dialogue about various aspects of evaluation. Working sessions are an ideal format to work on the evaluation's overall design, instrument development, or any other aspects of the evaluation that require the input and perspectives of several individuals. In addition, working sessions can be effective at the beginning of the evaluation for building consensus and ownership. Finally, they are particularly well suited for presenting evaluation findings to audiences for developing action plans based on the recommendations.

SOURCE: Adapted from Torres, Preskill, and Piontek (2005).

Index Card Category 3

Executive Summaries

Typically, comprehensive written reports are accompanied by an executive summary that focuses primarily on the evaluation findings. It includes brief background and methodological information to orient the reader. Key audiences who are very busy frequently only read the executive summary. Being shorter, executive summaries have the advantage of being deliverable in numerous ways. They can be written in memo style and faxed or attached to an e-mail. They can be produced on eye-catching paper and formatted with bullets and boxes for easy assimilation of text.

Index Card Category 4

Newsletters, Bulletins, Briefs, and Brochures

Newsletters, bulletins, briefs, and brochures are existing communication channels that can be used to reinforce or introduce information about the evaluation and its findings. For many readers, these documents have the advantage of already being part of an information stream that they regularly receive and assimilate in their work or professional lives.

Index Card Category 5

Video Presentations

Video presentations are sometimes used to create stand-alone, widely distributable, visual communications about an evaluation, usually to report findings. The major determinant for use of this format is typically cost. These kinds of presentations can be particularly useful when you want to provide a visually engaging presentation to numerous audiences who are not in the same location. For local audiences, you can incorporate some interaction by including question-and-answer or discussion periods during or at the end of the presentation.

Index Card Category 6

Memos and Postcards

Memos are short communications that are delivered internally within organizations or sent (via fax or e-mail) to outside organizations. They are often used throughout an evaluation for keeping stakeholders abreast of evaluation activities, soliciting feedback, requesting participation in working sessions, and reporting interim or final findings in summary form. Postcard communications can be used to send reminders and updates. They are usually limited to a single message and can include a graphic design or a catchy typeface on bright paper to draw attention.

Index Card Category 7

Posters

Posters or other visual displays of information about the evaluation can be viewed by audiences at a single event, they can be reused at additional events, or they can be placed where they will be accessible to audiences over a period of time (e.g., in the hall or entry area of any organization). Posters are typically used in settings or as part of events that have a broader purpose than providing information about a particular evaluation. A poster display can include any amount or type of information about the evaluation, and it can be interactive or static. A representative for the evaluation can be present to orient audiences and answer specific questions.

Index Card Category 8

E-mail

E-mail can be used to schedule meetings, to keep audiences informed about evaluation activities, to answer questions, to carry on written conversations with a group of individuals, and to send drafts of written communications and reports and solicit feedback. Any evaluation communication or report can be part of a text file attached to an e-mail. In this way, e-mail is simply serving as a mode of delivery in the same way as postal mail, albeit faster.

Index Card Category 9

Verbal Presentations

Verbal presentations can be used for communicating and reporting on every aspect of an evaluation. They can be part of working sessions or other meetings where evaluation activities or findings need to be addressed. Verbal presentations can vary in the extent to which they are interactive with the audience. Even if verbal presentations allow for only minimal audience interaction, they need not be boring or static. PowerPoint or other overhead slides, flipcharts, and other props can make verbal presentations more accessible to audience members.

Reference

Torres, R. T., Preskill, H., & Piontek, M. (2005). *Evaluation strategies for communicating and reporting: Enhancing learning in organizations* (2nd ed.). Thousand Oaks, CA: Sage.

Activity 60

Challenges in Communicating and Reporting

Overview

This activity invites participants to consider a situation in which an evaluator faces both ethical and practical issues in writing and delivering a final evaluation report.

Instructional Objectives

Participants will

- Consider the pros and cons of inviting stakeholders to review a draft evaluation report as part of an evaluation's communicating and reporting strategy
- Consider the ethical implications of accepting a stakeholder's revisions to a draft evaluation report
- Determine alternative ways of communicating and reporting to minimize the manipulation of an evaluation report's content

Number of Participants

- Minimum number of participants: 3
- Maximum number of participants: unlimited when participants are in groups of 3 to 5

Time Estimate: 30 to 45 minutes

This activity requires approximately 30 to 45 minutes, depending on the number of participants (or groups) and the time available for discussion.

SOURCE: This activity was contributed by Andy Tibble, Evaluation Consultant, Albuquerque, New Mexico.

Materials Needed

- Pens/pencils
- Flipchart, markers, tape
- Handout "The Pocket Veto"

Instructional Method

Case scenario

Procedures

Facilitator's tasks:

- Ask participants to get into groups of three to five people.
- Distribute the handout "The Pocket Veto."
- Instruct participants to read the case scenario and then, in their groups, respond to the discussion questions.
- Ask groups to identify three "ah-ha's," opinions, or questions this case raises. Participants are to note these reactions on a flipchart page.
- Invite each group to share its three thoughts with the larger group.
- Debrief the activity with the following questions:
  - What was your overall impression of the evaluator's situation?
  - What would you have done in this situation?
  - What is one thing this case reminds you about regarding communicating about and reporting on an evaluation's process and findings with stakeholders?
  - What do you think the relationship is between communicating and reporting and the use of evaluation findings?

The Pocket Veto

Handout for Activity 60

A state-government leadership training program was interested in conducting a program evaluation. The training program was conducted as a joint effort between three state agencies and was based on facilitative leadership principles. The program's steering committee was concerned that without data to establish the efficacy of the training program, it might not survive the upcoming change in political administration. The steering committee consisted of three people: Two of these individuals were state government employees at the division director level, and the third was the program's facilitator, a consultant with a great deal of experience in the design and delivery of leadership training programs. A graduate student from a local university who had consulted with one of the state agencies agreed to develop an evaluation plan and conduct the evaluation as an independent study for his master's program.

The evaluation design was a case study, and data were collected using focus group interviews with training participants and the managers who supervise their work. In addition, the training participants and their managers were asked to complete a survey. The stated purpose of the evaluation was to determine the longer-term impacts of the training on participants and on the agencies within which they work.

At the initial contracting meeting with the evaluation steering committee, it was agreed committee members would provide material support for the evaluation effort, including office supplies, conference rooms, postage, and data collection assistance. They also agreed that the evaluation must be a collaborative effort in which there would be regular communication with the evaluator and meetings to interpret the evaluation findings prior to the evaluator's final written report. Data were to be collected in March and April, and the report was due by July 31.

The data collection phase of the evaluation went very well—a majority of the training program's participants and their managers attended the focus group interviews and completed the surveys. The findings pointed to an overall satisfaction with the program.

As agreed to during the evaluation's design, the steering committee attended an interpretation meeting in which the evaluator presented the analyzed data in a series of tables and charts (including quotations). The purpose of this meeting was to further interpret the data and to assign meaning to the findings as well as begin the process of developing recommendations. During this meeting, the committee members worked hard to define the legitimate claims and recommendations they could reasonably make for the program.

Following this meeting, the evaluator wrote a draft of the evaluation report, complete with an executive summary, and forwarded it to each of the three steering committee members, requesting their feedback on the report. After 3 weeks, and with the report's due date quickly approaching, the evaluator finally received corrected drafts from both division directors. He made their requested changes (they were minor and did not change the substance of the findings or recommendations). It was now early August and the third member, the consultant, had still not provided her feedback on the report. A day before the newly agreed-on deadline, the consultant finally sent the evaluator a revised executive summary. The summary had been cut from five pages to two and was full of grammatical and structural errors. In the evaluator's view, the revised executive summary was incomprehensible. Rather than attempt to correct this version, the evaluator sent to all three members of the steering committee an e-mail with an attachment of the final report and both versions of the executive summary. The evaluator added a note that suggested members might find both versions of the summary useful. Further, the evaluator advised them that the project deadline had passed and that the report was essentially complete. He also wrote that if the consultant made further revisions, the evaluator would remove his own name from the final document.

A few weeks later, the evaluator contacted one of the division directors to find out what had happened with the evaluation report. Both of the agency directors were uncomfortable communicating the report's findings without the support of the consultant—particularly because the fall session of the leadership training program had just begun. The evaluation report remained on the desk of the consultant for revisions. The report had, as the evaluator put it, "been effectively pocket vetoed." A few weeks later, the evaluator sent an e-mail to the steering committee, program participants, and agency managers thanking them for their participation in the evaluation and assuring them that a report had been written based on the data they had provided. The e-mail directed them to contact the steering committee for further information about the evaluation's findings and recommendations.

Discussion Questions

- What did the evaluator do well in this situation?
- What could the evaluator have done to ensure timely feedback on the report from all three steering committee members?
- What other communicating and reporting strategies could the evaluator have used?
- What are the ethical implications concerning communicating and reporting in this case scenario?
- What other factors might have influenced the steering committee's behavior in providing feedback on the report?

Activity 61

Developing a Communicating and Reporting Plan

Overview

This activity asks participants to develop an evaluation communicating and reporting plan.

Instructional Objectives

Participants will

- Understand the role of communicating and reporting throughout an evaluation study
- Understand the importance of developing a communicating and reporting plan at the beginning of the evaluation
- Begin designing a communicating and reporting plan that addresses several factors related to stakeholder characteristics and their information needs

Number of Participants

- Minimum number of participants: 2
- Maximum number of participants: unlimited

Time Estimate: 45 to 60 minutes

In addition to providing the necessary background information about communicating about and reporting on an evaluation's processes and findings, this activity requires approximately 45 to 60 minutes.

SOURCE: This activity was contributed by Rosalie T. Torres, Torres Consulting Group, Alameda, California.

Materials Needed

- Pens/pencils
- Handout "Evaluation Communicating and Reporting Plan: Worksheet 1"
- Handout "Evaluation Communicating and Reporting Plan: Worksheet 2"

Instructional Method

Individual work

Procedures

Facilitator's tasks:

- Distribute the handout "Evaluation Communicating and Reporting Plan: Worksheet 1" to all participants.
- Discuss the content of Steps 1–3 on Worksheet 1.
- Explain that participants will be designing an evaluation communicating and reporting plan that can be used for a current or forthcoming evaluation.
- Instruct participants to individually complete Steps 1–3 on Worksheet 1, while thinking about a particular evaluation study.
- Distribute "Evaluation Communicating and Reporting Plan: Worksheet 2" to all participants.
- Discuss the content of Steps 4–8 on Worksheet 2.
- Ask participants to individually complete Steps 4–8.
- Ask participants to pair up with one other person and to share their responses to both worksheets. (This should help them think through what they have written and obtain feedback from one other person.)
- Debrief the activity with the following questions:
  - What surprised you as you were putting this plan together?
  - How did thinking about stakeholder characteristics affect your decisions in the plan?
  - Did you select any formats that you have not used before? Which ones? Why?
  - What will you have to do to implement this plan?
  - What consequences do you think there are for not having a communicating and reporting plan at the beginning of an evaluation?
  - What benefits might there be from developing and implementing a communicating and reporting plan?

Evaluation Communicating and Reporting Plan: Worksheet 1

Handout for Activity 61

Step 1: List all of your evaluation's stakeholders.	*Step 2: Check the reasons for communicating with each stakeholder.*			*Step 3: Check the reasons for communicating with each stakeholder.*	
	During the Evaluation			*After the Evaluation*	
	Include in determining the evaluation's design and implementation	Inform about specific upcoming evaluation activities	Keep informed about progress of evaluation	Inform about the program and the evaluation (build awareness and support)	Convey evaluation's results for decision making and action

Evaluation Communicating and Reporting Plan: Worksheet 2

Handout for Activity 61

	Stakeholder Characteristics	*Format*	*Timing*	*Resources*
Step 4: Transfer each stakeholder from Worksheet 1 to the spaces below.	*Step 5: How would you describe each stakeholder or stakeholder group? Think about some key characteristics that might influence your decisions about communicating and reporting: how accessible the stakeholders are, their education level, their familiarity with the program and with evaluation, their role in decision making about the program.*	*Step 6: Given the reasons checked in Steps 2–3, and your description in Step 5, select and note appropriate format(s) for each stakeholder.*	*Step 7: Discuss & note timing for this communication/ report.*	*Step 8: Discuss and note resources needed for this communication/ report.*

10

Managing the Evaluation

BACKGROUND

This section includes activities that address

- Developing evaluation management plans
- Creating evaluation budgets
- Addressing challenges evaluators may face in implementing an evaluation

The following information is provided as a brief introduction to the topics covered in these activities.

Managing an evaluation project involves balancing three critical aspects of the project: time, costs, and desired outcome or result or scope (including the tasks and level of effort put into the project). A well-designed management plan can help the evaluator accomplish the following:

- Monitor the tasks and personnel
- Stay on schedule or negotiate schedule changes
- Monitor the costs or negotiate budget changes
- Keep the client and stakeholders informed of the evaluation's progress and any potential problems

DEVELOPING AN EVALUATION BUDGET

Most evaluations involve costs associated with the following items:

- Personnel/professional staff
- Materials, supplies, and equipment

- Communications (e.g., phone, postage)
- Printing and reproduction
- Travel
- Facilities
- Overhead and general administration
- Miscellaneous or contingency costs

ANTICIPATING AND HANDLING EVALUATION CHALLENGES

All evaluation projects involve unforeseen challenges, such as the following:

- The evaluation cannot be completed by the projected deadline.
- The evaluation experiences cost overruns.
- The client who commissioned the organization leaves.
- The organization undergoes a layoff, merger, or other significant change.
- There are political pressures to slant the evaluation findings in a certain direction.

It is important to take time to consider which challenges an evaluation may face, prior to implementation, and to identify strategies to avoid or overcome these potential problems.

RESOURCES

Forsberg, K., Mooz, H., & Cotterman, H. (2000). *Visualizing project management: A model for business and technical success* (2nd ed.). New York: Wiley.

Project Management Institute. (1996). *A guide to the project management body of knowledge.* Newtown Square, PA: Author.

Russ-Eft, D., & Preskill, H. (2001). *Evaluation in organizations: A systematic approach to enhancing learning, performance, and change.* Boston: Perseus.

Verzuh, E. (1999). *The fast forward MBA in project management.* New York: Wiley.

Wideman, R. M. (Ed.). (1992). *Project and program risk management.* Newtown Square, PA: Project Management Institute.

Worthen, B. R., Sanders, J. R., & Fitzpatrick, J. L. (1997). *Program evaluation: Alternative approaches and practice guidelines* (2nd ed.). New York: Longman.

Activity 62

Developing Evaluation Management Plans

Overview

This activity helps participants understand the reasons for, and the advantages of, creating various types of evaluation management plans.

Instructional Objectives

Participants will

- Understand the value of developing an evaluation management plan
- Compare various kinds of evaluation management plans

Number of Participants

- Minimum number of participants: 3
- Maximum number of participants: unlimited when participants are in groups of 3 to 5

Time Estimate: 45 to 60 minutes

This activity requires approximately 45 to 60 minutes, depending on the number of participants (or groups) and the time available for discussion.

Materials Needed

- Pens/pencils
- Handout "Analyzing Evaluation Management Plans"
- Handout "Sample Management Plans"

Instructional Method

Small-group work

Procedures

Facilitator's tasks:

- Ask participants to get into groups of three to five people.
- Distribute the handout "Analyzing Evaluation Management Plans."
- Distribute the handout "Sample Management Plans."
- Ask participants to review the plans and, in their groups, complete the handout "Analyzing Evaluation Management Plans."
- Invite groups to share their ideas with the larger group.
- Debrief the activity with the following questions:
  - What are the similarities and differences in these management plans?
  - Which management plans do you think are most important?
  - What are potential consequences of not developing evaluation management plans?
  - In your opinion, what is the most important reason to include one or more evaluation management plans?

Analyzing Evaluation Management Plans

Handout for Activity 62

Directions:

After reviewing the evaluation management plans, identify the advantages of each plan and the circumstances under which you might want to use this plan.

Evaluation Plan	*Advantages of This Plan: When Might You Use This Plan?*
Plan A	
Plan B	
Plan C	
Plan D	
Plan E	
Plan F	

Sample Management Plans

Handout for Activity 62

Sample Management Plan A

Task	*Responsibility*	*Start–End Dates*
Review initial plan/ proposal.	Evaluation team	10/1–10/5
Undertake literature review and document review.	Research associate	10/1–11/1
Meet with client.	Project director	10/15
Develop data collection plan and instruments.	Project director and research associate	10/1–11/1
Pilot-test instruments.	Research associate and data collection staff	11/1–11/15

Sample Management Plan B

Key Questions	*Supervisors*	*Employees*	*Records*
1. What organizational factors affect employees' morale?	Interviews	Survey	
2. How effective was the bonus plan in increasing employees' morale?	Survey	Survey	
3. How effective was the bonus plan in improving productivity?	Survey	Survey	X

Sample Management Plan C

Key Questions	*Data Collection Methods*	*Respondents*	*Responsibility*	*Dates*
1. What organizational factors affect employees' morale?	Interviews, surveys	Supervisors, employers	Evaluator team 3/1–5/1	3/1–3/5
2. How effective was the bonus plan in increasing employees' morale?	Surveys	Supervisors, employers	Team	3/1–5/1
3. How effective was the bonus plan in improving productivity?	Surveys, records	Supervisors, employers	Team	3/1–6/1

Sample Management Plan D

Methods	*Key Questions*	*Timing*	*Data Sources*	*Instruments*	*Personnel*
Document review	1, 2, 3, 4	January	Announce-ments, e-mails, phone logs	Document review form	Clerical staff
Focus group interviews	3, 4	February	Call center reps	Focus group guide	Evaluator, transcriber
Individual interviews	2, 3, 4	March	Vice president, managers	Interview guide	Evaluator, transcriber
Observations	3, 4	March, April	Call center reps	Observation check sheet	Evaluator, clerical staff

Sample Management Plan E

Key Questions	*Data Collection Methods*	*Respondents*	*Responsibility*	*Dates*
1. What organizational factors affect employees' morale?	Interviews, surveys	Supervisors, employers	Evaluator team	3/1–3/5 3/1–5/1
2. How effective was the bonus plan in increasing employees' morale?	Surveys	Supervisors, employers	Team	3/1–5/1
3. How effective was the bonus plan in improving productivity?	Surveys, records	Supervisors, employers	Team	3/1–6/1

Sample Management Plan F

Key Questions	*Proposed Data Collection Methods*	*Proposed Data Analyses*	*Potential Problems*
1. To what extent do trainees demonstrate cultural sensitivity?	Knowledge test	Percent correct on each item	Trainees may experience test anxiety
	Simulation	Percent correct	Observer may record inaccurately
			Data entry errors may occur
2. To what extent were those who received the training more successful in their assignment than those who did not receive the training?	Documents: training completion; assign.	Descriptive statistics (percentages)	Neither descriptive statistics nor regression analyses explain why the groups differ
	Demographic data	Multiple regression of completion data	Regression analysis will be difficult to explain to Executives.

Activity 63

Creating an Evaluation Budget

Overview

This activity engages participants in developing an evaluation budget for a data collection component of an evaluation plan.

Instructional Objectives

Participants will

- Understand various considerations in estimating evaluation project costs
- Recognize different approaches to developing an initial project budget
- Prepare a budget for the data collection component of an evaluation plan

Number of Participants

- Minimum number of participants: 4
- Maximum number of participants: unlimited when participants are in groups of 3 to 5

Time Estimate: 45 to 60 minutes

In addition to providing the necessary background information on the elements of an evaluation budget, this activity requires 45 to 60 minutes, depending on the number of participants (or groups) and the time available for discussion.

Materials Needed

- Pens/pencils
- Flipchart, markers, tape
- Handout "Data Collection: Plan A"
- Handout "Data Collection: Plan B"
- Handout "Worksheet for Creating an Initial Budget"

Instructional Method

Small-group work

Procedures

Facilitator's tasks:

- Ask participants to get into groups of three to five people.
- Distribute the handouts "Data Collection: Plan A" or "Data Collection: Plan B," and "Worksheet for Creating an Initial Budget."
- Explain that participants will be developing a budget for the data collection component of an evaluation plan.
- Instruct groups to decide on the hourly or daily rate they would charge if they were evaluation consultants.
- Ask groups to review the handouts "Data Collection: Plan A" or "Data Collection: Plan B," and complete the "Worksheet for Creating an Initial Budget."
- Request that participants write their budgets on a piece of flipchart paper and attach them to a wall.
- Ask groups to present their budget to the larger group.
- Debrief the activity with the following questions:
  - What differences do you see in these budgets? Why do you think these differences exist?
  - What similarities do you see in these budgets?
  - As you developed your budgets, what other information would have been helpful?
  - What, if anything, is missing from these budgets?
  - What might these differences tell us about the context of the evaluations?

Data Collection: Plan A

Handout for Activity 63

This evaluation involves 30-minute telephone interviews with 20 staff members located in various parts of the United States, as well as in Europe and Asia. All of the staff members speak English. The following table outlines the schedule for the data collection effort.

Task	*People Involved*	*Time*	*Notes*
Develop interview protocol.	Two evaluators	8 hrs.	
Review and revise protocol.	Project director Two evaluators	4 hrs.	
Select interviewees.	One evaluator	4 hrs.	
Train interviewers.	One evaluator Two interviewers	4 hrs.	
Schedule interviews.	Secretary	10 hrs.	
Conduct interviews.	One evaluator Two interviewers	10 hrs.	
Transcribe interviews.	Secretary	16 hrs.	
Analyze interviews.	Two evaluators	24 hrs.	
Write data collection report.	Project director Two evaluators	24 hrs.	
Review and revise data collection report.	Project director Two evaluators	8 hrs.	

Data Collection: Plan B

Handout for Activity 63

This evaluation involves an e-mail and Web-based survey of former students ($N = 500$) from one department within a community college. Because of previous experiences with low response rates from e-mail and Web-based surveys, the plan includes a follow-up of 10% of the nonrespondents using mail and telephone methods.

Task	*People Involved*	*Time*	*Notes*
Develop survey.	Two evaluators	16 hrs.	
Review and revise survey.	Project director Two evaluators	4 hrs.	
Post Web-based survey and send e-mail surveys and notices.	One research assistant	2 hrs.	
Send two e-mail reminders.	One evaluator assistant	1 hr.	
Randomly select 50 nonrespondents.	One evaluator	4 hrs.	
Prepare and send mail surveys.	One research assistant	8 hrs.	
Conduct telephone interviews.	Two evaluators	16 hrs.	
Write report.	Project director Two evaluators	24 hrs.	
Review and revise report.	Project director Two evaluators	8 hrs.	

Worksheet for Creating an Initial Budget

Handout for Activity 63

Budget Category	*Cost Estimates*
Personnel/professional staff	
Materials, supplies, and equipment	
Communications	
Printing and reproduction	
Travel	
Facilities	
Overhead and general administration	
Miscellaneous or contingency costs	
TOTAL	

Activity 64

Anticipating Evaluation Challenges

Overview

This activity increases participants' awareness of potential problems that may arise as they conduct an evaluation.

Instructional Objectives

Participants will

- Consider potential challenges that often affect an evaluation's design and implementation
- Discuss ways in which various challenges may impact an evaluation study
- Identify ways in which challenges to an evaluation can be minimized or avoided

Number of Participants

- Minimum number of participants: 3
- Maximum number of participants: unlimited when participants are in groups of 3 to 5

Time Estimate: 30 to 45 minutes

This activity requires approximately 30 to 45 minutes, depending on the number of participants (or groups) and the time available for discussion.

Materials Needed

- Pens/pencils
- Handout "Anticipating and Addressing Evaluation Challenges"

Instructional Method

Small-group work

Procedures

Facilitator's tasks:

- Ask participants to get into groups of three to five people.
- Distribute the handout "Anticipating and Addressing Evaluation Challenges."
- Ask groups to consider each of the evaluation challenges on the handout and discuss possible answers to the questions posed for each challenge.
- Debrief the activity with the following questions:
  - What similarities do you see in the kinds of challenges that have been identified as well as the strategies to overcome them?
  - What might these challenges tell us about the context of evaluation practice?
  - What are some general things evaluators can do to minimize the degree to which certain challenges impede or influence an evaluation study?

Anticipating and Addressing Evaluation Challenges

Handout for Activity 64

Evaluation Challenge	*What is the challenge? How might this challenge impact the evaluation?*	*What are possible strategies to avoid or overcome this challenge? Was there anything that could have been done to prevent this challenge?*
The client who commissioned the evaluation leaves the organization just as you are beginning to analyze the collected data.		
A primary stakeholder tells you that she needs the evaluation report 2 months earlier than indicated in the evaluation plan.		
Some of the people you need to interview refuse to return your phone calls, and many of those who have agreed to be interviewed do not show up at the scheduled interview times.		
Your evaluation requires you to visit five sites around the country. Airfares in the last 3 months have risen 15% (this was not planned for in the budget).		

11

Building and Sustaining Support for Evaluation

BACKGROUND

This section includes activities that address

- Recognizing and sharing evaluation successes
- Overcoming resistance to evaluation
- Building a supportive evaluation environment
- Critiquing an evaluation's effectiveness (metaevaluation)

The following information is provided as a brief introduction to the topics covered in these activities.

For organizations to benefit from evaluation, it is important that members not only understand what evaluation is and what it can offer but that they have an ongoing commitment to conducting evaluations and using the findings for decision making and action. The following strategies may help build a supportive evaluation environment:

- Stress the organizational benefits from evaluation.
- Tie evaluation to the organization's mission.
- Involve stakeholders throughout the evaluation process.
- Discuss and share evaluation successes throughout the organization.
- Emphasize the use of findings.
- Use evaluation to build individual, team, and organizational learning capacity.

- Start small; think big.
- Communicate the evaluation's findings to a broad audience using a variety of reporting formats.
- Link evaluation to knowledge management and development.

In addition, evaluations are most successful when (a) they are supported by the organization's leadership, (b) there are adequate financial and human resources, and (c) a culture of inquiry and learning exists.

Every evaluation should be planned to provide not only information about the program being evaluated but also information concerning the effectiveness of the evaluation's design and implementation. Evaluation that critiques its own practice is called metaevaluation (Scriven, 1991). Metaevaluation is an excellent means for judging the value and soundness of an evaluation process and system.

RESOURCES

Patton, M. Q. (1997). *Utilization-focused evaluation: The new century text* (3rd ed.). Thousand Oaks, CA: Sage.

Preskill, H., & Torres, R. T. (1999). *Evaluative inquiry for learning in organizations.* Thousand Oaks, CA: Sage.

Russ-Eft, D., & Preskill, H. (2001). *Evaluation in organizations: A systematic approach to enhancing learning, performance, and change.* Boston: Perseus.

Scriven, M. (1991). *Evaluation thesaurus* (4th ed.). Newbury Park, CA: Sage.

Activity 65

Reflecting on Evaluation Successes

Overview

This activity asks participants to identify their most effective and satisfying evaluation experiences as a means for envisioning and designing more positive evaluation experiences in their future work.

Instructional Objectives

Participants will

- Interview each other to elicit stories of their most positive evaluation experiences
- Look for themes that emerge from the participants' stories of excellent evaluations
- Consider the ways in which they may create more peak evaluation experiences in the evaluation work they do or will do in the future

Number of Participants

- Minimum number of participants: 6
- Maximum number of participants: unlimited when participants are in groups of 6

Time Estimate: 45 to 75 minutes

This activity requires approximately 45 to 75 minutes, depending on the number of participants (or groups) and the time available for discussion.

Materials Needed

- Pens/pencils
- Flipchart, markers, tape
- Handout "Peak Evaluation Experiences"

Instructional Method

Small-group work

Procedures

Facilitator's tasks:

- Ask participants to pair up with one other person.
- Distribute the handout "Peak Evaluation Experiences" and ask participants to interview each other for 7 to 10 minutes each using the questions on the handout. Explain that they should take notes on their partner's story.
- Ask pairs to join two other pairs (making groups of six people). Request that each pair tell the highlights of their partners' stories (2 to 3 minutes each).
- Instruct participants to identify the themes in their group's stories and to list those themes on a piece of flipchart paper.
- Ask groups to attach their flipchart paper to a wall.
- Invite groups to present the themes of their stories.
- Ask the larger group to identify common themes across groups.
- Debrief the activity with the following questions:
  - What surprised you the most about what you heard from each group's themes?
  - What did you learn about yourself? About someone else?
  - How might you create more of these positive experiences in the evaluation work you do?
  - What did this activity confirm for you?

Peak Evaluation Experiences

Handout for Activity 65

Directions:

Interview each other with the following questions for 7 to 10 minutes. Take notes as your partner speaks so that you may remember the essence or highlights of his or her story.

1. *Best Experience:* Reflect for a moment and remember an exceptional or best experience you have had conducting an evaluation or being involved with an evaluation. You remember feeling excited, proud, and extremely satisfied with the experience. Tell me a story about that time. (What made it the best? What role did you play? What role did others play? What were the key factors that helped make it an exceptional evaluation experience?)

2. *Values:* What do you value most about

- Yourself
- The work you do that is related to evaluation

3. *Three Wishes:* If you had three wishes that would ensure that every evaluation you are involved in would be as exceptional as the one you just described, what would they be?

Activity 66

Overcoming Resistance to Evaluation

Overview

This activity asks participants to identify ways in which organizations can become more supportive of evaluation practices.

Instructional Objectives

Participants will

- Brainstorm ways in which organizations may better understand and support evaluation activities
- Discuss the ways in which they can support developing a culture of evaluation in their own organizations

Number of Participants

- Minimum number of participants: 3
- Maximum number of participants: unlimited when participants are in groups of 3 to 5

Time Estimate: 20 to 45 minutes

This activity requires approximately 20 to 45 minutes, depending on the number of participants (or groups) and the time available for discussion.

Materials Needed

- Pens/pencils
- Flipchart, markers, tape

Instructional Method

Small-group work

Procedures

Facilitator's tasks:

- Ask participants to get into groups of three to five people
- Say, "Here's the problem: As you know, many organizations do not understand or appreciate the role evaluation can play in improving its processes and outcomes. As a result, organizations may not allocate sufficient personnel or financial resources to support evaluative kinds of studies and activities. And, in some cases, organization leaders do not encourage their employees to ask questions about how well things are going. So what can evaluators do?"
- Instruct participants to quickly write down possible solutions to this problem (5 minutes).
- Ask that each participant read one idea to his or her group and discuss the idea with the group for 3 to 5 minutes, without evaluating it. Explain that this open discussion may create a springboard to variations on the idea.
- Ask participants to write several of the ideas/solutions on a piece of flipchart paper.
- Instruct groups to attach their flipchart paper to a wall.
- Request that groups share their list of solutions with the larger group. Ask clarifying questions and invite other participants to comment.
- Debrief the activity with the following questions:
  - What solutions do you think were the most creative?
  - What solutions do you think might work in your organization?
  - What else might you need to do to "sell" evaluation in your organization?
  - What new insights did you gain from this activity?

Activity 67

Building a Supportive Evaluation Environment

Overview

This activity asks participants to consider the essential attributes of an organization where evaluation practice is supported and embedded in the organization's systems and structures.

Instructional Objectives

Participants will

- Consider various organizational characteristics that may influence the degree to which an evaluation is successful
- Discuss the organizational characteristics necessary for supporting ongoing evaluation practice

Number of Participants

- Minimum number of participants: 3
- Maximum number of participants: unlimited when participants are in groups of 3 to 5

Time Estimate: 45 to 75 minutes

This activity requires approximately 45 to 75 minutes, depending on the number of participants (or groups) and the time available for discussion.

Materials Needed

- Pair of dice for each group
- Flipcharts, markers, tape

SOURCE: This activity was adapted from the "Circle of Opportunity" exercise described in Michalko, M. (1991). *Thinkertoys*. Berkeley, CA: Ten Speed Press.

Instructional Method

Small-group work

Procedures

Facilitator's tasks:

- Ask participants to get into groups of three to five people.
- Explain that this activity will help participants identify various organizational characteristics that may support ongoing, embedded evaluation practices.
- Ask groups to draw a large circle on their flipchart paper and to number it like a clock (1 through 12).
- Ask groups to identify 12 characteristics of an organization that supports evaluation. For example, these characteristics may relate to the organization's structure, processes, systems, culture, climate, politics, and responsibilities.
- Ask groups to write one characteristic next to each number on their circle.
- Provide each group with a pair of dice.
- Instruct groups to throw one die to choose the first characteristic to focus on.
- Instruct groups to throw two dice to choose the second characteristic.
- Ask participants to consider the characteristics, both separately and combined. Instruct them to free associate about the individual characteristics and the combination of the two characteristics. (For example, if the first roll showed 6, and that characteristic was "leaders who use data for decision making," and the second roll showed 10, and that characteristic was "employees who are encouraged to ask questions," then participants would discuss each characteristic separately with regard to how it contributes to evaluation practice within an organization, and then they would discuss what it would mean for both characteristics to be combined.)
- Ask groups to write, on another piece of flipchart paper, 5 to 10 statements that are essential to developing and sustaining a supportive evaluation environment. (These should be based on their free-association discussions and the characteristics they have developed.)
- Invite groups to share their statements.
- Debrief the activity with the following questions:
  - Which characteristics do you think your organizations already have that will support evaluation work?
  - Which characteristics do you think are the most challenging to develop in an organization, and why?
  - What will you do to begin building a supportive evaluation environment in your organization?
  - What new insights did you gain from this activity? What had you not thought of before?

Activity 68

Evaluating the Evaluation (Metaevaluation)

Overview

This activity asks participants to evaluate a completed evaluation report or evaluation plan for its comprehensiveness and adherence to the evaluation standards and guiding principles.

Instructional Objectives

Participants will

- Understand the role of metaevaluation in ensuring high-quality evaluations
- Understand that conducting metaevaluations is one way to communicate the value of evaluation within organizations
- Practice evaluating an evaluation report or evaluation plan

Number of Participants

- Minimum number of participants: 3
- Maximum number of participants: unlimited when participants are in groups of 3 to 5

Time Estimate: 45 to 60 minutes

In addition to providing the necessary background information on metaevaluation, this activity requires approximately 45 to 60 minutes, depending on the number of participants (or groups) and the time available for discussion.

Materials Needed

- Pens/pencils
- Handout "Metaevaluation Worksheet"
- One or more completed evaluation reports or evaluation plans, which may be obtained from several sources:
  - Journals such as *American Journal of Evaluation, Evaluation and Program Planning,* or *Human Resource Development Quarterly*
  - Evaluation reports published on the Internet
  - Evaluation reports completed by the facilitator (if permission has been granted to make these available to others)
  - Evaluation reports developed by colleagues (if permission has been granted to make these available to others)
  - Evaluation plans developed by current or past participants (with names removed or with names included if permission has been obtained)

Instructional Method

Small-group work

Procedures

Facilitator's tasks:

- Ask participants to get into groups of three to five people.
- Provide each group with a completed evaluation study or evaluation plan.
- Distribute the handout "Metaevaluation Worksheet."
- Ask groups to review the evaluation report or plan and complete the worksheet.
- Ask groups to share their answers to the discussion questions.
- Debrief the activity with the following questions:
  - What similarities or differences are there in the metaevaluations provided by the different groups?
  - What might these differences tell us about the backgrounds, interests, and levels of expertise among the different metaevaluation evaluators?
  - In what ways does the conduct of metaevaluation help build organizational support for evaluation?
  - Under what circumstances should metaevaluations be conducted?

Metaevaluation Worksheet

Handout for Activity 68

You are part of an evaluation team that has been asked to conduct a metaevaluation of this completed (or proposed) evaluation. Each team member should take one or more of the following evaluation components to review. In some cases, the information needed to make suggestions is available in the report or plan. In other cases, the information may not be available. In the latter case, your team should develop one or two questions that you would ask the evaluators if you were to meet with them about this evaluation.

Evaluation Components	*What questions or comments would you have for the evaluators?*	*What suggestions would you make for improving the evaluation component?*
Rationale and purpose of the evaluation		
Identification of stakeholders		
Identification of key evaluation questions		
Evaluation design		
Sampling		
Validity		
Data collection methods and instruments		
Data analysis		
Recommendations		
Evaluation budget and expenditures		
Communication and reporting of findings		

12

Reflections on Learning

BACKGROUND

This section includes activities that involve participants reflecting on and synthesizing their learning from an evaluation course or workshop.

Activity 69

Headlining Learning

Overview

This activity provides participants an opportunity to reflect on what they have learned in the course (workshop) and to distill key concepts they want to remember.

Instructional Objectives

Participants will

- Reflect on and discuss with others what they have learned in the course (workshop)
- Develop a newspaper headline that represents their learning

Number of Participants

- Minimum number of participants: 3
- Maximum number of participants: unlimited when participants are in groups of 3 to 5

Time Estimate: 30 to 45 minutes

This activity requires approximately 30 to 45 minutes, depending on the number of participants (or groups) and the time available for discussion.

Materials Needed

- Poster board or newsprint paper
- Flipchart, markers, tape

Instructional Method

Visual representation

Procedures

Facilitator's tasks:

- Ask participants to get into groups of three to five people.
- Distribute poster board or newsprint to each participant.
- On a flipchart write the following list:
  - One thing you have learned from taking this course (workshop)
  - A key thought or piece of advice that will guide your future evaluation work
  - An action step you will take in the near future
  - A question to ponder
- Instruct participants to discuss these topics with each other, to brainstorm possibilities before they make up their minds about what will go into their headline.
- Invite participants to begin working on their own newspaper headlines.
- Ask participants to attach their headlines to a wall so that there will be a gallery of headlines.
- Invite participants to view the gallery of headlines (and to take their own when they leave).
- Debrief the activity with the following questions:
  - What did you hear in your small-group discussions that surprised you?
  - What are some of the action steps you will take when you get back to work?
  - How has your thinking about evaluation changed as a result of this course (workshop)?

Activity 70

Creating a Model of Learning

Overview

This activity asks participants to develop a visual representation of what they learned in the evaluation course (workshop).

Instructional Objectives

Participants will

- Discuss the three most important things they learned in the course (workshop)
- Collaboratively develop a visual representation that illustrates their collective learning about evaluation
- Present their visual representation to the rest of the group

Number of Participants

- Minimum number of participants: 3
- Maximum number of participants: unlimited when participants are in groups of 3 to 5

Time Estimate: 40 to 60 minutes

This activity requires approximately 40 to 60 minutes, depending on the number of participants (or groups), and the time available for discussion.

Materials Needed

- Arts and crafts supplies (e.g., glue, tape, scissors, pipe cleaners, Tinker Toys, magazines, fabric swatches, Styrofoam, pick-up sticks, Legos, poster board, rocks, marbles)
- Flipchart, markers, tape

Instructional Method

Visual representation

Procedures

Facilitator's tasks:

- Ask participants to get into groups of three to five people.
- Place a variety of arts and crafts supplies at each table.
- Explain that, as a group, participants are to develop a visual representation of the most important concepts or skills they learned in the course (workshop), using the arts and craft supplies at their table.
- Write the following question on a piece of flipchart paper: What are the three most important things you learned about evaluation? Instruct participants to reflect on their learning and then discuss the question.
- Invite participants, as a group, to develop their visual representation.
- Ask groups to present their visual representation and to explain how it depicts what they have learned.
- Debrief the activity with the following questions:
  - What were the learning themes that emerged from your group?
  - How did you decide to represent those themes in your visual representation?
  - What insights about evaluation practice did you gain from this activity?
  - What is your next step in applying what you learned from this course (workshop)?

Activity 71

Critical Incidents of Learning

Overview

This activity asks participants to reflect on specific experiences they have had with the evaluation course (workshop) and to share these experiences with others.

Instructional Objectives

Participants will

- Reflect on critical experiences they have had in the evaluation course (workshop).

Number of Participants

- Minimum number of participants: 3
- Maximum number of participants: unlimited when participants are in groups of 3 to 5

Time Estimate: 40 to 60 minutes

This activity requires approximately 40 to 60 minutes, depending on the number of participants (or groups) and the time available for discussion.

Materials Needed

- Pens/pencils
- Flipchart, markers, tape
- Handout "Critical Incidents of Learning"

Instructional Method

Small-group work

SOURCE: Adapted from Brookfield, S. D. (1995). *Becoming a critically reflective teacher.* San Francisco: Jossey-Bass.

Procedures

Facilitator's tasks:

- Ask participants to get into groups of three to five people.
- Distribute the handout "Critical Incidents of Learning."
- Instruct participants to individually respond to the questions on the handout.
- Instruct participants, in their groups, to discuss their responses to the handout's questions and write their responses on a piece of flipchart paper.
- Invite groups to share their responses with the larger group.
- Debrief the activity with the following questions:
  - What did this activity confirm for you?
  - What themes did you hear in the groups' responses?
  - What surprised you the most about what people had to say?
  - In what ways can your feedback be used to improve this course or workshop?
  - How will you apply your learning from this course or workshop?

Critical Incidents of Learning

Handout for Activity 71

1. When were you most engaged with what was happening in this course (workshop)?

2. At what point were you most bored or disengaged with what was happening in this course (workshop)?

3. What action did someone take in this course (workshop) that was most affirming and helpful?

4. What action did someone take in this course (workshop) that was most puzzling or confusing?

5. What surprised you the most during this course (workshop)?

Activity 72

The Elevator Speech

Overview

This activity facilitates individual and group reflection and enables participants to articulate what they have learned from the evaluation course (workshop).

Instructional Objectives

Participants will

- Discuss key concepts and skills they have learned during the evaluation course (workshop)
- Summarize their learning about evaluation into consecutively fewer words
- Present their summary statements to the larger group

Number of Participants

- Minimum number of participants: 2
- Maximum number of participants: unlimited when participants are in groups of 2 to 3

Time Estimate: 30 to 45 minutes

This activity requires approximately 30 to 45 minutes, depending on the number of participants (or groups) and the time available for discussion.

Materials Needed

- Pens/pencils
- Flipchart, markers, tape

SOURCE: Adapted from Thiagarajan, S. (n.d.). *Workshops by Thiagi*. Retrieved March 30, 2004, from www.thiagi.com.

Instructional Method

Small-group work

Procedures

Facilitator's tasks:

- Ask participants to get into pairs or triads.
- Instruct participants to discuss key concepts or skills they learned in the course (workshop).
- Explain that participants are to develop a 32-word statement that describes the most important concepts or skills they learned in the course (workshop). They should imagine that they are in an elevator and have only 15 seconds to explain what they learned about evaluation.
- Ask participants to write their statements on a piece of flipchart paper.
- Invite groups to read their 32-word statements.
- Ask groups to now reduce their statements to 16 words; they have only 10 seconds in an elevator.
- Ask groups to again pare down their statements, this time to eight words; they have only 5 seconds in an elevator.
- Instruct groups that finally they must reduce their statements to four words; they have 2 seconds in the elevator.
- Invite groups to share their four-word statements with the larger group.
- Debrief the activity with the following questions:
  - How difficult was it to summarize your learning?
  - What insights about your evaluation did you gain from doing this activity?
  - What did you find interesting about the evaluation statements from other groups?

About the Authors

Hallie Preskill, PhD, is Professor of Organizational Learning and Instructional Technologies at the University of New Mexico, Albuquerque. She teaches graduate-level courses in program evaluation (introductory and advanced); organizational learning; consulting; and training design, development, and delivery. She is coauthor of *Evaluation in Organizations: A Systematic Approach to Enhancing Learning, Performance, and Change* (with D. Russ-Eft); *Evaluative Inquiry for Learning in Organizations* (with R. T. Torres); and *Evaluation Strategies for Communication and Reporting* (with R. T. Torres & M. E. Piontek). She is coeditor of *Using Appreciative Inquiry in Evaluation* (New Directions for Evaluation, Vol. 100) and *Human Resource Development Review* (with D. Russ-Eft & C. Sleezer). She has served on the board of directors of the American Evaluation Association and the Academy of Human Resource Development and is the section editor of the *Teaching Evaluation* column in the *American Journal of Evaluation.* She received the American Evaluation Association's Alva and Gunnar Myrdal Award for Outstanding Professional Practice in 2002 and the University of Illinois Distinguished Alumni Award in 2004. For more than 20 years, she has provided consulting services in the areas of program evaluation, training, and organizational development. She has also written numerous articles and book chapters on evaluation methods and processes and has conducted program evaluations in schools and in health care, nonprofit, human service, and corporate organizations.

Darlene Russ-Eft, PhD, is Assistant Professor of Adult Education and Higher Education Leadership in the *new* School of Education at Oregon State University. She is also a principal in zmresearch, an evaluation and research group focused on human resource development in organizations, and she has served as a faculty member of the Evaluators' Institute. She is the former director of Research at AchieveGlobal, Inc. (one of the largest training and consulting firms) and the former director of Research Services at Zenger-Miller (a training firm focused on leadership). She is coauthor of *Evaluation in Organizations: A Systematic Approach to Enhancing Learning, Performance, and Change* (with H. Preskill) and *Everyone a Leader: A Grassroots Model for the New Workplace* (with H. Bergman & K. Hurson). She is coeditor of *What Works: Assessment, Development, and Measurement* and *What Works: Training and Development* (with L. J. Bassi) and *Human Resource Development Review* (with H. Preskill & C. Sleezer). She has served as the chair of the Research Committee of the American Society for Training and Development (ASTD) and as a member of the board of the American Evaluation Association. Dr. Russ-Eft is the current editor of *Human Resource Development Quarterly*, a refereed journal of the Academy of Human Resource Development (AHRD) and ASTD. She received the 1996 Times Mirror Editor of the Year Award for her research work and the AHRD Outstanding Scholar Award in 2000. For more than 20 years, she has consulted in the areas of program evaluation, research design, and training and development and has conducted evaluations in corporate, government, health care, nonprofit, educational, and community-based organizations. She has written numerous articles and book chapters on evaluation, training and development, and human resource development.